skinnytaste®

MEAL PREP

skinnytaste®
MEAL PREP

Healthy Make-Ahead Meals
and Freezer Recipes to
Simplify Your Life

Gina Homolka

with Heather K. Jones, R.D.

CLARKSON POTTER/PUBLISHERS
NEW YORK

To all my Skinnytaste fans, thank you for your loyalty and support. And to my mom and dad, who shared their passion for cooking and taught us the joys of being in the kitchen.

30
Breakfast

64
Hearty Salads

92
Warm Grain, Noodle & Vegetable Bowls

136
Smart Snacks

158
Freezer Favorites: Vegetarian

190
Freezer Favorites: Meat & Seafood

246
Big Batches & Planned-Overs

Hear that? That's the sound of your rumbling tummy—a reminder that dinnertime is right around the corner. Unfortunately, that dreaded end-of-day fatigue is settling in, and the thought of making a meal is just too much to bear. You do a quick mental check and the list of excuses for not cooking is suddenly longer than an average wait at the DMV: you didn't go food shopping, you got stuck at work, the kids' homework will take too much time, extracurricular activities will get you home too late, the family wants different things . . . and probably won't like what you make anyway. Still, you're hungry and you have to eat something. You want a meal that's healthy and filling, but quick and easy.

Sound familiar? It's a scenario most of us can relate to. I'm here to tell you it doesn't have to be this way—cooking doesn't have to be stressful. In fact, it can be something you look forward to, even something that helps you unwind. No need to chuckle, smirk, or eye-roll . . . I'm serious! If you view cooking as a ritual instead of a routine, you can actually shift your mindset and turn this daily to-do into a positive form of self-care.

That might seem like a far-fetched goal, but it's not all that difficult to achieve in an era where convenience is king. We're all looking to simplify and optimize our daily lives, and manufacturers are more than happy to assist. Shortcuts abound, from pre-cut fresh veggies and frozen produce to smart cooking gadgets (some even controlled remotely by your smart phone . . . brilliant!). You can tell Alexa to add ingredients to your shopping list and have them dropped off at your front door courtesy of grocery delivery services. There is certainly a movement to make cooking quick, simple, and healthy. I, personally, couldn't be more thrilled. In fact, I'm beyond excited to join in by writing this book, which is loaded with totally manageable and absolutely delicious recipes that are sure to please the entire family. When I was brainstorming topics for this cookbook, I polled my Facebook community and the top three requests on your list were meal prep ideas, easy freezer recipes, and make-ahead recipes. Easy is the name of the game, so I combined all three into one book.

Let's take a look at how these time-saving strategies fit into your busy life and make it possible to say farewell to frozen boxed lasagna, pass on the processed pizza, and ditch the drive-through for good!

Meal Prep:

These are meals that you prep in advance, pack up in the refrigerator, and enjoy for the next few days or even the whole week. Think Greek Chicken Pilaf Bowls (page 109), Chicken Larb Bowls (page 105), and Smashed Broccoli Pecorino Farro Bowls (page 133). Yum! You can also get parts of a meal ready in advance to streamline the cooking process. This might involve pre-chopping veggies for a stew or stir-fry, or boiling rice or quinoa ahead of time so it's ready for a meal during the week. You get the idea. It's preparing meal components when you have some downtime so they're ready to go when you're in a pinch.

Freezer Recipes:

These are meals you can make ahead of time and stash in your freezer. Soups, stews, and casseroles are ideal to prepare and pack away. Roasted Vegetable Lasagna (page 181), Freezer Chicken Black Bean Burritos (page 198), Turkey Cheeseburger Egg Rolls (page 229), and Turkey Taquitos (page 225) all fit the bill. You can prep two recipes at once—one to eat now, and one to freeze and eat another day—or make a bunch of recipes on a slow weekend to stock the freezer. And, of course, you can always freeze your leftovers if you're cooking for one or two people, or make a double batch of any recipe and freeze half for later. There is a lot of flexibility here!

Big Batches and Planned-Overs:

Not to be confused with leftovers, where you're simply reheating last night's dinner, *planned-overs* actually repurpose last night's leftovers in a completely new way! Imagine making a batch of Sheet Pan Herb Salmon with Broccolini and Tomatoes (page 264) for dinner on Sunday night and then whipping up some Salmon Fried Rice with Asparagus (page 267) on Tuesday! Or, rather than roasting one chicken for family dinner, why not cook two (it takes the same amount of time!) so you can enjoy a Paprika Roasted Whole Chicken for dinner one night (page 248) and have a Rotisserie Summer Chicken Bowl with Smoked Paprika Aioli (page 255) the next day. I have included plenty of planned-over recipes here, but you don't have to rely on me! Have fun coming up with your own ideas and take a photo to share with me on social media (tag #skinnytaste)! I love seeing what you create in the kitchen.

It's clear to see how these cooking strategies save you time and effort. If you're already preparing one recipe, it's easy to prep a second batch and store it for a future meal. Meal planning allows you to make use of your free time, so dinner rush hours are less frenzied. And just imagine opening your fridge to an already chopped salad (simply toss with your favorite dressing), precooked pasta, and a sauce that simply needs to be heated—a complete meal that you can get on the table in minutes!

Meal Planning Tools for Success

In addition to 120-plus mouthwatering recipes, I also provide dozens of tips and tricks to build your cooking confidence. Meal prepping is easy once you feel at ease in the kitchen. It's about spending a little extra time when you're a bit less busy, so you can fill your fridge with healthy make-ahead breakfasts like Sausage, Egg, and Cheese Breakfast Sandwiches (page 51), Piña Colada Yogurt Bowls (page 35), and Lemon Blueberry Buttermilk Sheet Pan Pancakes (page 45). You'll also learn how to meal prep some easy lunches like Vegan Hummus Kale Wraps (page 90), Slow Cooker Chicken Enchilada Rice Bowls (page 106), and Chili-Lime Chicken and Black Bean Cauli-Bowls (page 110) that you can simply grab from the fridge to eat when hunger strikes. Plus, there's nothing better than knowing there's a chicken soup, like Freezer-to-Instant-Pot Chicken and Dumpling Soup (page 195), prepped, frozen, and ready to whip up, or casseroles like Moussaka Makeover (page 233) or Sicilian Rice Ball (Arancini) Casserole (page 226), ready to bake. All you have to do is pop it in the oven when you get home. That's what this cookbook is all about. I get excited just talking about it—and I hope you get excited about the possibility of transforming mealtime in your house. Pre-planning takes all the angst out of cooking and it's super easy and doable with just a little bit of thought and foresight.

To give you an idea of just how easy it is, you don't even need to follow a formal recipe or meal plan! There's a mix-and-match section (page 97) featuring your favorite roasted in-season veggies, easy grain bases, pre-prepped proteins, and a wide variety of tasty toppings. No recipe required . . . just select and savor. There's a separate chapter for snackers (I heard you!). If you're craving something crunchy yet healthy, you can try the BBQ Roasted Green Peas (page 146), which are insanely addictive. If you're looking for a low-carb snack, whip up California Tuna Salad–Stuffed Cucumbers (page 142). I can't get enough of them.

You'll also find a meal plan (for those who like it all mapped out, page 26), meal prep tips, freezer basics, and useful nutritional info for every recipe as well as a recipe key. Trust me, you've got this! Cooking is now faster, less fussy, and more fun than you ever thought it could be. Who's ready to get cooking?

A NOTE ABOUT SALT

Different brands and different types of salt vary not only in sodium but also in taste. For consistency in my recipes—both for flavor and for nutrition information—I used Diamond Crystal Kosher. If you use another kind, just remember to taste as you go.

WEIGHT WATCHER POINTS

For those of you on Weight Watchers, all of the up-to-date Weight Watcher Points are conveniently located on my website under the cookbook tab: www.skinnytaste.com/cookbook.

RECIPE KEY
Look for these helpful icons throughout the book:

Q Quick
(ready in 30 minutes or less)

 V Vegetarian

 GF Gluten-Free

DF Dairy-Free

FF Freezer-Friendly

IP Instant Pot
(or any electric pressure cooker)

 **SC** Slow Cooker

AF Air Fryer

Meal Prep Basics

Getting dinner on the table night after night (especially on those pesky weeknights!) is no small feat. When you're juggling sports-practice carpools, work schedules, homework, studying, and more, sitting down to a home-cooked meal every weeknight can seem near impossible—and let's be honest, it might very well *be* impossible without a little bit of advance preparation. The key to making the magic happen in the kitchen lies in the pages of this book. Two simple words: meal prep. Prepping your meals in advance using time-saving tips and freezer-friendly recipes puts you on the fast track to healthy, tasty, family-friendly meals you can rely on all week long.

As a mother of two, I'm no stranger to the stress of getting everyone fed on time, let alone with a nutritious meal! Some days, quick-cooking dinners are my best friend, and other days, I need meals that can go straight from my freezer to my oven or Instant Pot (or any electric pressure cooker) and be ready in a matter of minutes. That's what you'll find here: Recipes that are *easy* to prep in advance, and *even easier* to finish up when it's time to eat.

Truth be told, meal prepping does take a little bit of advance planning, but don't let that discourage you! A few minutes of prep over the weekend can save you hours during a busy week. I'll be spilling all my secrets on how to make that weekend prep as simple and painless as can be. And no, that doesn't mean buying processed foods! I'm a big fan of healthy, whole, and wholesome ingredients, so I've jam-packed every recipe in this book with *real* food. You'll be meal prepping with fresh produce and ingredients you can pronounce (well, except maybe quinoa, but I can help you with that one—it's pronounced "keen-wah").

My tried-and-true strategies will help you master meal prep in no time. Here's how to get started:

STEP 1:

Choose Your Recipes

The first step is choosing your recipes, and in my opinion, this is the best part! You can select recipes from this cookbook, or pick from any of the limitless options online. For inspiration, take a look in your pantry to see what you may want to use up, so you can build a meal around that. I also like to get my husband and kids involved—we all come up with dinner ideas that we're excited about. You can also scan your grocery store circular to see what's on sale, choosing ingredients that are seasonal, so you score the best prices and quality. I jot down my ideas in *The Skinnytaste Meal Planner* (a notebook works just as well).

STEP 2:

Make a Shopping List

Heading to the store without a list is like hitting the bank without your ATM card. It's both futile and frustrating! Thanks to technology, making a shopping list is easier than ever: I simply say "Alexa, add milk to my shopping list" and it appears on my phone app. But an old-fashioned pen-and-paper list does the trick, too.

STEP 3:

Go Shopping

Step three is heading out to do your shopping. You might want to simplify by ordering online and having your groceries delivered (again, do what works for you). For recipes that use fresh seafood or vegetables that may spoil fast, I usually buy the day before or the day I plan to cook.

STEP 4:

Meal Prep!

Finally, find a day that works best for you to do all of your meal prepping. For many people, Sunday makes sense, but everyone's schedule is different. Then prepare some of the dishes that will hold up well in the fridge that you can reheat during the week. Recipes like soups, stews, chilis, and so on all reheat well. And don't be afraid of leftovers and planned-overs—those are the easiest lunches! Cook hard-boiled eggs, rice, quinoa, oatmeal, and more ahead of time and store them in airtight containers. As a general rule, they should last 4 to 5 days in the fridge.

Label everything with a name and date. You can use dry-erase markers on plastic containers or permanent markers on tape.

Don't stop at dinner.

As you strategize your meal prep for the days or week ahead, don't forget about breakfast, lunch, and snack time! What meals put the most pressure on your family? Maybe you don't mind throwing together a last-minute dinner, but packing lunches and getting breakfast ready every day has you stressed. No problem! Start by getting breakfast and lunch prep out of the way with recipes like Breakfast-on-the-Run Bowls (page 32) or Banh Mi Turkey Meatball Rice Bowls (page 118), and leave yourself some flexibility for dinners. Feel fine with packing lunches, but aren't sure what to snack on? I get it! Get a head start with some of my favorite snacks like Buffalo Chicken–Stuffed Celery Sticks (page 141) or Air-Popped Popcorn with Sea Salt (page 149).

Whether you're prepping one dinner a week or stocking your fridge with breakfasts, lunches, snacks, and dinners, you'll be saving tons of time, stress, and cash!

Prep as much as you can, but don't go all-or-nothing.

Just like eating healthfully, meal prepping is all about balance and moderation. Start small and be flexible with what you can get done each week. It's not all-or-nothing!

Set aside some time during the weekend to meal prep, but if you don't have a full day to dedicate to chopping, simmering, and roasting, there's no need to call the whole thing off! There are plenty of ways to get ahead of the week's menu. Here are some ideas, listed from the least effort to the most:

- **Prep some of your ingredients for recipes in advance to speed up cooking when the time comes.** This might be as simple as chopping some veggies, measuring spices, and whisking sauces—and then stopping there. Pack them

away until you're ready to use them. Some of my favorite freezer-dump recipes take advantage of this method! Check out Ribollita Soup (page 160) and Freezer-to-Instant-Pot Cream of Chicken and Wild Rice Soup (page 201).

- **Cook part of your recipe now and save the rest of the cooking for later.** You might make a homemade pasta sauce in advance to heat up later in the week along with the pasta and veggies to go with it.

- **Batch-cook your recipes.** Double a recipe and freeze half for the following week—this gets you even more ahead of the game!

- **Fully cook one or more recipes for the week ahead.** Then pull out what you want to eat each day and heat it up (if necessary). This method takes the most amount of prep time, but you get rewarded with the least amount of effort needed throughout the week.

Save a few things for the last minute.

While almost everything in this book can be made in advance, make sure to read the recipe directions all the way through before beginning. Some ingredients that turn brown, wilt, or get soggy should always be prepared at the last minute. Sliced avocados and fruits like apples and pears are notorious for browning if sliced too far in advance. You can toss these with lemon or lime juice to ward off browning, but still save the slicing for the last possible moment. Dressed greens will wilt if prepared too far in advance. When packing up a salad, keep the dressing in its own small container until just before you're ready to eat.

Sandwiches assembled more than a day in advance can lead to soggy bread. For instance, if you're planning to bring a sandwich with Tuna and White Bean Salad (page 77) for lunch, pack the salad in a lidded container and wrap up your bread or pita in beeswax wrap or another container of its own so it stays fresh and is delish when you're ready to eat.

Meal Prep and Freezer Containers

There's no point in prepping ahead if you don't have a place to store all that delicious food! Yes, that means clearing some space in your fridge and freezer. It also requires stocking up on storage containers. And for meals you plan to take to work, you'll want leakproof containers that are microwave- and dishwasher-safe. I keep my kitchen cabinets loaded with these meal prep and freezer essentials:

Meal Prep Containers

- **GLASS AND BAMBOO:** Glass are my favorite as they are the easiest to clean, but the downside is that they are heavier to carry around. You can buy glass meal prep containers in sets of four or five, with one, two, or three compartments. I have several shapes and sizes, and use both rectangular and round ones depending on what fits best. Pyrex sells a great eighteen-piece meal prep kit.

- **PLASTIC:** These are so much lighter and are microwave-, freezer-, and dishwasher-safe. They also come in different shapes and have compartments for sectioning foods. They usually stack, which takes up less space in your cabinets. Be sure to select BPA-free varieties, which are now easy to find.

Containers for Batch Storage and Freezing

- 8 × 8- and 9 × 12-inch freezable glass dishes for small and large casseroles. Keep in mind that baking from frozen is not advised. It's best to thaw in the refrigerator overnight before reheating.

- 8 × 8- and 9 × 12-inch foil pans for small and large casseroles you plan on baking from frozen.

- Large freezer- and microwave-safe lidded food containers (in 8- to 10-cup sizes) are ideal for items like pasta and full entrées. **NOTE:** Do not put food containers in the oven straight from the freezer. You will need to thaw your freezer meals in the refrigerator overnight if you plan to reheat in the oven.

- Medium lidded food containers (2 to 3 cups) are ideal for individually packed lunches, leftovers, or prepped veggies.

- Small lidded food containers (½ to 1 cup) are ideal for snacks, dressings, and dips.

- Gallon-size freezer-safe zip-top plastic bags are made of a thicker material that is less likely to be punctured and keeps freezer burn at bay; stick to these heavy-duty bags if you'll be storing prep in the freezer!

- Mason jars in quart and pint sizes are ideal for layering salads, storing oats, and so on.

Food Wrap

- Foil, paper, or plastic, there are lots of wraps to help you protect food from the frost of the freezer. Have you tried beeswax food wrap? This is a great natural alternative to plastic wrap for food storage. For fridge storage, it's perfect for wrapping extra cheese or half a lemon or covering a bowl when all your lidded food containers are in use.

Freezer Cooking & Storage 101

Making recipes on the weekend to enjoy during the week isn't the only way to meal prep! Your freezer is one of the most useful tools in your kitchen for make-ahead meals. This book is loaded with recipes you can freeze well in advance, and you can easily locate them by looking for recipes that are labeled "FF" (Freezer Friendly).

Freezing food not only lets you make meals far in advance, but if you freeze your leftovers, it's also a great way to cut back on food waste—good news for the environment and your wallet. Freezing food also allows you to stock up on ingredients when they're on sale, which is a great cash-saving strategy!

Ready to get freezing? Here are some of my best tips for make-ahead meals, leftovers, and extra or prepped ingredients.

Cool completely before freezing.

No matter what you're freezing, make sure it doesn't head to the freezer when it's still hot. Hot food produces steam, and when steam gets trapped in a sealed container in the freezer, you end up with ice crystals that can result in soggy food once it's thawed. You want to let hot foods cool completely before freezing. However, don't let foods sit out at room temperature all day to get primed for the freezer! Transfer hot foods to the fridge first to cool quickly and avoid harmful bacteria that thrives at room temperature. Then transfer items from the fridge to the freezer.

Leave a little extra room for liquids.

Ever forget a bottle of water in the freezer and come back to find an exploded icicle? I know I'm guilty! You don't need to worry about most foods exploding in the freezer—frozen fruits and veggies won't pop open a freezer bag, for example—but water does expand when it freezes. The same goes for watery liquids like chicken or veggie stock. For that reason, you'll want to fill freezer bags and containers only three-quarters of the way full when you're packing up liquid-y things like soups and stocks for the freezer to avoid popped-off tops and burst bags.

Signed, sealed, and delivered (to the freezer).

I'll take a hint from the famous song and let you know that signing and sealing are two of the most important steps in freezing your make-ahead food!

Jot down the item name and date on every meal-prep item you freeze. Depending on what's inside, I like to scribble other details as well, to help me out when I pull meals from the freezer. You might want to make a note of:

- Number of servings or portions

- Reheating/cooking directions

- If you're making freezer meal kits (page 25), label the container with the remaining ingredients you will need to complete the dish. A permanent marker is all you'll need to label freezer bags, but I also like to keep a roll of masking tape (Scotch Freezer Tape works great) or a sheet of address labels on hand for tagging plastic or glass containers. You'll find freezing and reheating instructions at the end of every recipe that can be stored in the freezer.

Keep in mind that labeling isn't limited to the freezer! Sticking a label with a date on fridge items can help eliminate those times when you dig to the back of the fridge and ask yourself, "Hmm . . . how old are these leftovers, anyway?"

If you're still following along with the song, you might have guessed that "sealing" is the next step to keeping frozen food fresh. If you've ever reached into your freezer to find an open bag of freezer-burned green beans, then you're probably well aware that air is a frozen food's worst enemy. It's a simple formula: Freezer air + food = freezer burn. It's not pretty.

Tightly sealing food that's headed to the freezer is your strongest defense against freezer burn. Freezer-safe zip-top bags are a great way to seal food in and keep air out, as are airtight lidded containers. If you plan to freeze meats and breads, which are particularly prone to freezer burn, learn to love layers: wrap your meat or bread first in plastic wrap, then foil, then a freezer bag.

Shop in-season (and on sale!) and freeze as you go.

Cooking with produce that's grown locally and in-season is your best bet for flavorful, nutritious meals. When fruits and vegetables are perfectly ripe and picked just before you eat them, you get the highest-quality—and best-tasting—produce, and that's always the ideal place to start. But what happens when you want to make Lemon Blueberry Buttermilk Sheet Pan Pancakes (page 45) in the dead of winter? That's when frozen fruit takes center stage!

Buying frozen fruits and veggies is always a smart option: the produce is picked when it's ripe, then frozen, and conveniently available year-round without sacrificing any nutrition. I also freeze my favorite fresh options whenever I can. When sweet, ripe berries or gorgeous asparagus hit my farmers' market, I like to stash them in my freezer so I have them on hand for meals throughout the year.

The same logic applies to stocking up on sale items at the store. When chicken breasts are on sale, I buy a bunch and freeze them raw or cook and shred them to keep in the freezer. Whether you're freezing fruits, veggies, meat, or leftovers, here are my go-to freezing tips:

How to freeze meat and fish:

- Wrap in several layers, squeezing extra air out as you go. Start with plastic wrap, then a layer of foil or a zip-top freezer bag. Wrap pieces individually if you'll want to take just one chicken breast, pork chop, etc. out to thaw at a time.

- Store for up to three months for most fish, four months for ground meats, and up to a year for whole cuts of meat.

How to freeze fruits and vegetables:

- You can freeze just about any fruit or vegetable except for celery, watercress, endive, lettuces, cabbages, cucumbers, and radishes. These foods have a high water content and become mushy when thawed. Some vegetables can be frozen raw, but most benefit from a quick blanch before freezing.

- Make sure fruits and vegetables are dry before freezing; otherwise, they'll freeze into a solid clump.

- If you want to prevent pieces from freezing together (and for freezing delicate fruits like berries), spread the pieces out in a single layer on a plastic wrap–lined sheet pan. Once they are fully frozen, transfer the pieces to your container and place it immediately in the freezer. With this method, any ice films form around each individual piece, rather than freezing all the pieces together in a big chunk.

- Pack fruits and veggies in zip-top freezer bags or airtight containers with as little air as possible.

- Store most fruits and veggies for up to a year.

- Freezing also works well for fresh herbs like basil, chives, oregano, mint, and tarragon. Wrap them in small bunches in plastic wrap or freezer-safe baggies, then use them when a recipe calls for fresh herbs. For recipes that call for minced or blended herbs (i.e., sauces and dressings), you can puree herbs at peak freshness and store in individual portions in your freezer. Some brands also make great ready-to-use frozen packs available in the freezer section of most supermarkets.

How to freeze cooked grains:

- **Step 1.** Cook larger batches of grains and let them cool completely on a large tray or sheet pan. You want them to dry so the extra moisture doesn't cause them to clump in the freezer. Use a fork to fluff the grains after a few minutes of cooling to vent the steam.

- **Step 2.** Measure out portions and store them in smaller freezer-safe plastic or eco-safe bags, laying them flat and stacking them on top of one another inside the freezer.

- **Step 3.** Label the bag with the name, date, and portion size so you know exactly how much to thaw when you need to whip up a lunch bowl or dinner.

- **Step 4.** To heat, microwave for about 3 minutes or cook over low heat in a heavy-bottom saucepan for 4 to 5 minutes, until heated through, adding a little liquid as necessary. You can also thaw them overnight in the refrigerator.

GRAINS THAT FREEZE WELL:

- Barley
- Black rice (aka forbidden rice)
- Brown rice
- Bulgur wheat
- Farro
- Jasmine rice
- Quinoa
- Wheat berries
- White rice

Store most cooked grains for up to a year.

How to freeze soups and sauces:

- Let soups and sauces cool completely before freezing.

- In zip-top freezer bags: Fill bags three-quarters of the way full, then force out as much air as possible and seal. Freeze flat and then stack bags to maximize space in your freezer.

- In airtight containers: Fill containers three-quarters of the way full and seal.

- Souper Cubes, available on Amazon, are also great. These are silicone freezing trays that come with a lid (like a giant ice cube tray) and the extra-large size lets you freeze perfect 1-cup portions.

- Store most soups for up to 6 months.

- Keep in mind that soups that contain milk or cream don't hold up well in the freezer. They usually take on a grainy texture and separate when thawed and rewarmed. For best results, hold back the dairy and add it in when you're reheating the soup.

How to freeze casseroles:

- Freeze assembled uncooked or partially cooked casseroles, as opposed to freezing precooked casseroles. Recipes like Indian-Inspired Shepherd's Pie (page 230) and Baked Spinach Stuffed Shells (page 170) make delicious freezer-to-oven casseroles.

- Assemble casseroles in freezer-safe and ovenproof dishes (glass and ceramic dishes tend to work best) and seal with several layers of plastic wrap and foil or with an airtight lid to keep out as much air as possible.

- Most frozen casseroles work best if you thaw them in the refrigerator overnight, then cook in the oven. Of course, if you forget to thaw and you want to bake from frozen, make sure you freeze your casseroles in freezer-to-ovenproof baking dishes (such as foil, as most glass or ceramic dishes will crack).

- Don't forget to remove any plastic wrap on your casseroles before baking (yes, I've done that!). I write a note to myself with a Sharpie on the foil to remind me.

Make Your Own Freezer Meal Kits

Many of the recipes in the freezer section of the book can be partially made ahead and frozen to create your own meal kit. Prep your ingredients and season your protein. If the recipe calls for ground meat or onions that need to be sautéed, do that first, then freeze in small containers or bags, leaving out the pantry staples like beans, tomatoes, etc., that take up too much space in your freezer or can't be frozen, or garnishes and citrus that add that pop of freshness at the end, and dairy. Label the kits with the recipe name, date, ingredients, and directions of what to add later. When you are ready to cook, throw your freezer kit into a pot or Instant Pot, right from the freezer, for a quick home-cooked meal. If your recipe calls for cooking in the slow cooker or oven, transfer the kit to the refrigerator overnight to thaw. You'll also want to ensure that your frozen block of food fits in your pot so you don't have to thaw or chip away at it when it's time to cook.

Skinnytaste Meal Plans

These four weeks of meals add up to around 1,500 calories per day.
Feel free to adjust these menus to fit your goals.

WEEK 1

	Sunday	Monday	Tuesday
Breakfast	**Instant Pot Egg White Steel-Cut Oats** (page 59)	**Instant Pot Egg White Steel-Cut Oats** (page 59)	**Sausage, Egg, and Cheese Breakfast Sandwiches** (page 51) (freeze leftovers) with 1 orange
Lunch	**Ramen Salad Bowls with Grilled Chicken** (page 66)	**Roasted Veggie and Barley Buddha Bowls** (page 126)	LEFTOVER **Ramen Salad Bowls with Grilled Chicken** (page 66)
Snack	1 ounce cheese and 1 pear	**"Everything" Nuts** (page 150) and 1 orange	**"Everything" Nuts** (page 150) and 1 apple
Dinner	**Roasted Vegetable Lasagna** (page 181) (roast extra veggies for Wednesday and Thursday lunch)	LEFTOVER **Roasted Vegetable Lasagna** (page 181)	**Slow Cooker Italian Pulled Pork** (page 272) over 1 cup whole wheat spaghetti and 4 ounces roasted asparagus

WEEK 2

	Sunday	Monday	Tuesday
Breakfast	LEFTOVER **Lemon Blueberry Buttermilk Sheet Pan Pancakes** (page 45) with 1 tablespoon maple syrup and 1 orange	2 scrambled eggs, 1 slice whole grain toast, and 1 pear	2 scrambled eggs, 1 slice whole grain toast, and 1 pear
Lunch	**Fiesta Quinoa Salad** (page 89) (make extra quinoa for Monday and Tuesday lunch)	**Roasted Winter Veggie Quinoa Bowls** (page 134)	**Roasted Winter Veggie Quinoa Bowls** (page 134)
Snack	6 Triscuits with 1 ounce cheese and 1 cup grapes	6 Triscuits with 1 ounce cheese and 1 cup grapes	**BBQ Roasted Green Peas** (page 146) and 1 apple
Dinner	**Paprika Roasted Whole Chicken** (page 248) with 3/4 cup brown rice and 1 cup mixed roasted veggies (make 2 chickens; use the extra for Wednesday and Thursday lunch)	**Black Bean and Butternut Enchilada Bake** (page 185) with 1/2 cup corn	**Chicken Souvlaki Pitas** (page 256) with 1/2 cup baked French fries

Wednesday	Thursday	Friday	Saturday
Sausage, Egg, and Cheese Breakfast Sandwiches (page 51) with 1 banana	6 ounces nonfat plain Greek yogurt with 1 cup berries and ¼ cup low-fat granola	6 ounces nonfat plain Greek yogurt with 1 cup berries and ¼ cup low-fat granola	**Lemon Blueberry Buttermilk Sheet Pan Pancakes** (page 45) with 1 tablespoon maple syrup
LEFTOVER **Roasted Veggie Buddha Bowls** (page 126)	LEFTOVER **Roasted Veggie Buddha Bowls** (page 126)	LEFTOVER **Instant Pot Chicken and Shrimp Gumbo** (page 206) with ¾ cup brown rice	LEFTOVER **Turkey Taquitos** (page 225) with ½ cup refried beans
California Tuna Salad–Stuffed Cucumbers (page 142)	**California Tuna Salad–Stuffed Cucumbers** (page 142)	1 ounce cheese and 1 pear	**PB+J Healthy Oatmeal Cookies** (page 153)
Pork Shoulder Ragu with Cauliflower Polenta (page 275) and a green salad with light vinaigrette	**Instant Pot Chicken and Shrimp Gumbo** (page 206) with ¾ cup brown rice (make extra rice for Friday lunch)	**Turkey Taquitos** (page 225) with ½ cup refried beans	Dinner Out!

Wednesday	Thursday	Friday	Saturday
Piña Colada Yogurt Bowls (page 35)	**Piña Colada Yogurt Bowls** (page 35)	**Piña Colada Yogurt Bowls** (page 35)	**Breakfast Fried Rice** (page 39) and 1 orange
Rotisserie Summer Chicken Bowls with Smoked Paprika Aioli (page 255)	**Rotisserie Summer Chicken Bowls with Smoked Paprika Aioli** (page 255)	LEFTOVER **Winter Brisket and Barley Soup** (page 238) with 2 ounces multigrain baguette	LEFTOVER **Moussaka Makeover** (page 233)
BBQ Roasted Green Peas (page 146) and 1 apple	1 ounce mixed nuts and 1 cup sliced strawberries	1 ounce mixed nuts and 1 cup sliced strawberries	**Pumpkin Hummus** (page 157) with 10 carrot sticks
Winter Brisket and Barley Soup (page 238) with 2 ounces multigrain baguette	**Frozen Fish Sticks with Dill Tartar Sauce** (page 242) (double the batch to freeze for later), 1 cup roasted potatoes, and 1 cup steamed broccoli	**Moussaka Makeover** (page 233) with a green salad and 1 tablespoon light vinaigrette	Dinner Out!

WEEK 3		Sunday	Monday	Tuesday
	Breakfast	**Greek Yogurt Raspberry Loaf** (page 63) with 1 apple	LEFTOVER **Greek Yogurt Raspberry Loaf** (page 63) and 1 banana	LEFTOVER **Greek Yogurt Raspberry Loaf** (page 63) and 1 banana
	Lunch	**Torta Pasqualina** (page 178) with 1 orange	LEFTOVER **Torta Pasqualina** (page 178) with 1 orange	**Chicken and Broccoli Rabe Wraps** (page 252) and 1 cup mixed berries
	Snack	1 ounce cheese and 1 cup grapes	LEFTOVER **Pumpkin Hummus** (page 157) with 10 carrot sticks	LEFTOVER **Pumpkin Hummus** (page 157) with 10 carrot sticks
	Dinner	**Pollo Asado** (page 251) with **Instant Pot Colombian Beans** (page 276), 2 ounces avocado, and 1 cup cauliflower "rice" (make 2 chickens; use the extra for Tuesday and Wednesday lunches)	**Chickpea Spinach Tomato Curry** (page 173) with ¾ cup basmati rice	**Sheet Pan Mediterranean Chicken and Veggies** (page 113)

WEEK 4		Sunday	Monday	Tuesday
	Breakfast	**Stuffed Bagel Balls** (page 42) and 1 cup mixed berries	**Breakfast-on-the-Run Bowls** (page 32)	**Breakfast-on-the-Run Bowls** (page 32)
	Lunch	**Greek Chickpea Salad** (page 78)	**Smashed Broccoli Pecorino Farro Bowls** (page 133)	**Smashed Broccoli Pecorino Farro Bowls** (page 133)
	Snack	**Buffalo Chicken–Stuffed Celery Sticks** (page 141) with 1 ounce raw almonds	**Buffalo Chicken–Stuffed Celery Sticks** (page 141) with 1 ounce raw almonds	1 medium banana and 1 tablespoon peanut butter
	Dinner	**Eggplant Parmesan** (page 174) with 1 cup whole wheat pasta and roasted broccoli (roast extra broccoli for Monday and Tuesday lunches)	LEFTOVER **Eggplant Parmesan** (page 174) with 1 cup whole wheat pasta and a green salad	**Sheet Pan Herb Salmon with Broccolini and Tomatoes** (page 264) and ¾ cup brown rice

Wednesday	Thursday	Friday	Saturday
LEFTOVER **Sausage, Egg, and Cheese Breakfast Sandwiches** (page 51) and 1 apple (cook from frozen [leftover from week 2])	LEFTOVER **Sausage, Egg, and Cheese Breakfast Sandwiches** (page 51) and 1 orange (cook from frozen [leftover from week 2])	6 ounces nonfat Greek yogurt with 1 teaspoon honey, 1 cup berries, and 2 tablespoons pecans	**Italian Sausage and Ricotta Frittata** (page 55) and 1 orange
Chicken and Broccoli Rabe Wraps (page 252) and 1 cup mixed berries	LEFTOVER **Lentil Soup with Bacon** (page 241) and 2 ounces multigrain baguette	LEFTOVER **Lentil Soup with Bacon** (page 241) and 2 ounces multigrain baguette	LEFTOVER **Slow Cooker White Bean Chicken Chili** (page 213) with 1 tablespoon sour cream, 2 tablespoons pepper Jack cheese, 1 ounce avocado, and 1 ounce baked tortilla chips
Air-Popped Popcorn with Sea Salt (page 149) and 1 ounce mixed nuts	**Air-Popped Popcorn with Sea Salt** (page 149) and 1 ounce mixed nuts	6 Triscuits with 1 ounce cheese and 1 cup grapes	**Deviled Eggs with Lox** (page 138)
Lentil Soup with Bacon (page 241) and 2 ounces multigrain baguette	**Italian Stuffed Jalapeño Peppers** (page 218) with 2 cups romaine, 1 tablespoon freshly grated Parmesan, and 1 tablespoon light Caesar dressing	**Slow Cooker White Bean Chicken Chili** (page 213) with 1 tablespoon sour cream, 2 tablespoons pepper Jack cheese, 1 ounce avocado, and 1 ounce baked tortilla chips	Dinner Out!

Wednesday	Thursday	Friday	Saturday
2 scrambled eggs, 1 slice whole grain toast, and 1 pear	2 scrambled eggs, 1 slice whole grain toast, and 1 pear	6 ounces nonfat Greek yogurt with 1 cup berries and ¼ cup low-fat granola	**Breakfast Quesadillas** (page 52)
Spicy Salmon Poke Bowls (page 268)	**Spicy Salmon Poke Bowls** (page 268)	LEFTOVER **Indian-Inspired Shepherd's Pie** (page 230) with ½ cup wilted spinach	LEFTOVER **Frozen Fish Sticks with Dill Tartar Sauce** (page 242) and 10 carrot sticks (cook from frozen; leftover from week 2)
1 ounce raw almonds and 1 cup grapes	1 medium banana and 1 tablespoon peanut butter	1 ounce raw almonds and 1 cup grapes	**PB&J Healthy Oatmeal Cookies** (page 153)
DIY Chicken Taco Kits (page 217) with 1 ounce avocado	**Indian-Inspired Shepherd's Pie** (page 230) with ½ cup wilted spinach (make 2 pies; freeze one for later)	**Stuffed Chicken Parmesan and Asparagus** (page 114) with ¾ cup whole wheat orzo	Dinner Out!

Breakfast

Breakfast-on-the-Run Bowls

(Q) (V) (GF) (DF) (AF)

SERVES 2

4 large hard-boiled eggs (see below for air fryer directions)

1 cup halved cherry tomatoes

1 small Hass avocado

½ lemon

1 teaspoon extra-virgin olive oil

⅛ teaspoon kosher salt

Freshly ground black pepper

Pinch of crushed red pepper flakes (optional)

You know those days when you wake up feeling like your best self? Eyes wide open, fully you, and just ready for the day? I always try to pick apart the pattern so I can choose to make those days happen more often. Usually my feel-awesome day starts with exercise, maybe an inspiring podcast, and always a solid breakfast. But your morning meal doesn't have to be time-consuming or complicated: This simple breakfast bowl is my go-to on most weekday mornings.

Cut the hard-boiled eggs in half and place in 2 bowls. Top each bowl with ½ cup tomatoes and half of the avocado. Squeeze lemon juice over the avocado and drizzle with the olive oil, then season with salt, black pepper to taste, and red pepper flakes (if using).

Air-Frying Eggs: There are so many ways to boil an egg, from making them on the stove or in an Instant Pot, to using an air fryer. Most mornings, I turn to my air fryer to make them because they practically cook themselves unattended. No water, and no need to stand near the stove while they cook. Place cold eggs in the air fryer and cook at 250°F for about 17 minutes. If you like your yolk a little soft, run the eggs under cold water and peel them right away to stop the eggs from cooking. If you like the yolk firm, wait about 5 minutes before peeling.

Variations:

· Add leftover veggies from the night before.
· Add cucumbers and olives for a Mediterranean twist.
· Add leftover grains like quinoa or farro.

Per Serving (1 bowl) ● Calories 285 ● Fat 21.5 g ● Saturated Fat 5 g
Cholesterol 422 mg ● Carbohydrate 10 g ● Fiber 5 g ● Protein 14 g
Sugars 4 g ● Sodium 356 mg

Piña Colada Yogurt Bowls

Q V GF DF

SERVES 4

½ cup unsweetened shredded coconut

¼ cup slivered almonds

3 cups nonfat plain, Greek, or dairy-free yogurt

2 cups finely diced fresh or canned pineapple in juice

FRIDGE: UP TO 4 DAYS

Yogurt bowls are my favorite quick-and-easy breakfast when I'm not in the mood for eggs. You can use any plain yogurt as the blank-canvas base, then top it with your favorite fruit, nuts, granola, etc. This sweet and crunchy piña colada version is topped with pineapple, toasted almonds, and coconut. You don't need to add sugar or sweeteners, because the pineapple is sweet enough. To make these ahead, toast the almonds and coconut and pack them separately. Keep the fruit packed in separate containers, then combine everything just before eating.

Preheat the oven to 325°F.

On a small sheet pan, spread the coconut and almonds in an even layer. Toast for 3 to 5 minutes, until the coconut is golden brown.

SERVE NOW: For each serving, spoon ¾ cup yogurt into a small bowl. Add ½ cup pineapple with some of its juice and 3 tablespoons of the almond/coconut mixture and stir well. Eat immediately.

MEAL PREP: Pack the fruit, almond/coconut mixture, and yogurt in separate containers, or use a 3-compartment meal prep container for each serving and place ¾ cup yogurt into the large part of the dish. In the smaller compartments, place 3 tablespoons almond/coconut mixture on one side and the pineapple on the other. When ready to eat, combine and stir well.

Per Serving (1 bowl) ● Calories 289 ● Fat 14 g ● Saturated Fat 9 g Cholesterol 4 mg ● Carbohydrate 30 g ● Fiber 4.5 g ● Protein 14 g Sugars 24 g ● Sodium 149 mg

Avena (Oatmeal Smoothie)

(Q) (GF) (DF)

SERVES 4

1 cup quick-cooking oats*

1½ cups fat-free milk or dairy-free milk of your choice

4 tablespoons raw sugar

2 teaspoons ground cinnamon

4 servings collagen peptides (optional)

2 cups crushed ice

*Read the label to be sure this product is gluten-free.

> FRIDGE: UP TO 4 DAYS
> (COOKED OATMEAL,
> WITHOUT THE MILK)

An easy breakfast on-the-go and an inspired way to add whole grains and fiber to your morning! Oat milk is the latest dairy-free milk trend, and I'm not surprised. I've been drinking oatmeal smoothies (aka *avena*) all my life! Served over ice with lots of cinnamon, it's a popular and refreshing beverage in Colombia and South America. Karina, my oldest daughter, would request it for breakfast at least three times a week when she was younger. Cooking the oats in water first is key since it gives your smoothie the creamiest texture. I also love including collagen peptides in my smoothies (my nails, skin, and hair have never looked better!), but that's totally optional.

Cook the oats in 2 cups water in a small pot over medium heat. When it boils, cook for about 1 minute, stirring often until it becomes thick and starts bubbling. Remove from heat and let it cool for 5 minutes.

Pour the milk, sugar, and cinnamon into a high-powered blender. Add the cooled oats, collagen peptides (if using), and ice. Blend on high until very smooth.

SERVE NOW: Serve chilled in a glass over ice.

MEAL PREP: After cooking the oats, you can refrigerate the oatmeal for up to 4 days. When ready to eat, for each serving blend one-fourth of the cold oatmeal with 6 tablespoons milk, 1 tablespoon raw sugar, ½ teaspoon ground cinnamon, 1 serving collagen peptides, and ½ cup ice.

Per Serving (1½ cups) ● Calories 158 ● Fat 1.5 g ● Saturated Fat 0.5 g
Cholesterol 2 mg ● Carbohydrate 32 g ● Fiber 2.5 g ● Protein 6 g
Sugars 17 g ● Sodium 43 mg

Breakfast Fried Rice

SERVES 4

6 large eggs

⅛ teaspoon kosher salt

Cooking spray

4 slices center-cut bacon, chopped

8 scallions, white parts minced, green parts thinly sliced

2 cups riced cauliflower (raw or frozen)

2 cups leftover cooked short-grain brown rice, cold

3 tablespoons reduced-sodium soy sauce* or gluten-free tamari

1 teaspoon toasted sesame oil

2 teaspoons Sriracha sauce

*Read the label to be sure this product is gluten-free.

FRIDGE: UP TO 4 DAYS

FREEZER: UP TO 3 MONTHS

Bacon and eggs meet Chinese-American takeout! Fried rice is one of my favorite foods (in fact, I would often eat it for breakfast during my college days!), so loading it up with bacon and extra eggs just makes good food-sense to me. I use brown rice (it's a complex carb that takes longer to break down, which means you'll stay fuller longer) and riced cauliflower, which helps bulk up the portions and adds a healthy dose of nutrients (bonus!).

In a medium bowl, whisk the eggs and season with the salt.

Heat a large nonstick skillet over high. When hot, coat with the cooking spray, add the eggs, and quickly scramble for 1 to 2 minutes. When the eggs are cooked through, remove them from the pan and set aside.

Add the bacon and cook until browned, 4 to 5 minutes, then use a slotted spoon to transfer the bacon onto a paper towel. Leave 1 teaspoon of bacon fat in the pan, then add the scallion whites and cook for 30 to 60 seconds. Add the riced cauliflower and cook until soft, about 5 minutes.

Add the rice and soy sauce and cook for 2 to 3 minutes, stirring frequently, until heated through. Return the egg and bacon to the pan and toss with the sesame oil, Sriracha, and scallion greens.

MEAL PREP: Divide the rice among 4 airtight containers, about 1¼ cups each. To reheat from the fridge, microwave the rice in 30-second intervals until heated through. To reheat from frozen, transfer the rice to the refrigerator to thaw, or reheat in the microwave from frozen in 30-second intervals until heated through.

SKINNY SCOOP Not a fan of cauliflower? No worries, you can swap any riced veggie you wish—try it with riced broccoli, carrots, etc. You can also use ham instead of bacon, or make it meatless, easy-peasy!

Per Serving (1¼ cups) ● Calories 285 ● Fat 11.5 g ● Saturated Fat 3.5 g
Cholesterol 282 mg ● Carbohydrate 29 g ● Fiber 3.5 g ● Protein 16 g
Sugars 3 g ● Sodium 717 mg

Baked Oatmeal Cups, Four Ways

SERVES 6

BASE

Cooking spray

2½ cups old-fashioned or quick-cooking oats*

1½ cups unsweetened vanilla almond milk

½ teaspoon vanilla extract

¼ cup lightly packed light brown sugar

¼ teaspoon kosher salt

½ teaspoon baking powder

½ teaspoon ground cinnamon

½ cup unsweetened applesauce

MIX-IN OPTIONS

(See opposite)

* Read the label to be sure this product is gluten-free.

FRIDGE: UP TO 4 DAYS

FREEZER: UP TO 3 MONTHS

The best way to avoid the free donuts in the office break room is to pack your own heart-healthy breakfast that's loaded with fiber, keeping you full until lunch. These portable oatmeal cups are a cross between baked oatmeal and a muffin. They are perfect to make ahead for the week or to pop in the freezer to have them handy throughout the month. You can eat them cold right out of the refrigerator or warm them up for a satisfying and filling start to your day.

Preheat the oven to 350°F. Generously spray a standard 12-cup muffin tin with cooking spray.

Make the oatmeal: In a food processor, pulse the oats about 15 times until fine (they should be a similar consistency to instant oats, with a few bigger pieces). Transfer to a large bowl and add the milk and vanilla. Set aside to allow the oats to absorb the milk, about 5 minutes.

In a small bowl, combine the brown sugar, salt, baking powder, and cinnamon. Add to the bowl of soaked oats along with the applesauce and mix-in options (see opposite page). Gently fold until thoroughly combined. With a heaping ⅓ measuring cup, scoop the oatmeal mixture into the prepared muffin tin.

Bake, rotating halfway through, until set, about 25 minutes. Let cool in the pan for 10 minutes. Carefully remove with an offset spatula or paring knife, then transfer to a wire rack to cool completely. Once cooled, store in an airtight container or zip-top plastic bag.

To reheat, microwave for about 30 seconds (or 1 minute if frozen) or until heated through.

Mix-in options

Apple Cinnamon

GF DF FF

1 tablespoon unsalted butter
2 large apples, peeled and diced into ½-inch pieces
1 teaspoon light brown sugar
½ teaspoon ground cinnamon

In a small skillet, melt the butter over medium heat. Add the apple, brown sugar, and cinnamon and sauté, stirring to evenly coat the apple, until softened, about 3 minutes. Transfer to the bowl with the soaked oats and continue with the recipe.

Per Serving (2 oatmeal cups) ● Calories 238
Fat 5 g ● Saturated Fat 1.5 g ● Cholesterol 5 mg
Carbohydrate 45 g ● Fiber 6 g ● Protein 5 g
Sugars 19 g ● Sodium 136 mg

Peaches and Cream

GF FF

1 tablespoon unsalted butter
2 medium peaches, peeled and diced into ½-inch pieces
⅛ teaspoon ground nutmeg
⅛ teaspoon ground ginger
½ cup nonfat Greek yogurt

In a small skillet, melt the butter over medium heat. Add the peaches, nutmeg, and ginger and gently sauté, just until the peaches are evenly coated, about 1 minute. Transfer the peaches and the yogurt to the bowl of soaked oats and continue with the recipe.

Per Serving (2 oatmeal cups) ● Calories 227
Fat 5 g ● Saturated Fat 1.5 g ● Cholesterol 5 mg
Carbohydrate 40 g ● Fiber 5 g ● Protein 7 g
Sugars 16 g ● Sodium 142 mg

Blueberry Banana

GF DF FF

1 large ripe banana, mashed
1 cup wild blueberries

Transfer the mashed banana and whole blueberries to the bowl of soaked oats and continue with the recipe.

Per Serving (2 oatmeal cups) ● Calories 213
Fat 3 g ● Saturated Fat 0.5 g ● Cholesterol 0 mg
Carbohydrate 43 g ● Fiber 5.5 g ● Protein 5 g
Sugars 14 g ● Sodium 136 mg

Mixed Berry

GF DF FF

2 cups mixed berries (I like chopped strawberries, whole blackberries, and whole raspberries)
1 teaspoon granulated sugar

In a small saucepan, combine the berries, sugar, and ¼ cup water over medium heat. Bring to a gentle boil, then reduce the heat to medium-low. Simmer the berries, stirring often and mashing them gently with a wooden spoon. Cook until thickened, 8 to 10 minutes. Remove from the heat and let cool for 3 minutes before transferring to the bowl of soaked oats. Continue with the recipe.

Per Serving (2 oatmeal cups) ● Calories 202
Fat 3 g ● Saturated Fat 0.5 g ● Cholesterol 0 mg
Carbohydrate 40 g ● Fiber 6 g ● Protein 5 g
Sugars 14 g ● Sodium 135 mg

Stuffed Bagel Balls

V **GF** **FF** **AF**

SERVES 8

1 (8-ounce) package ⅓-less-fat cream cheese

2 cups (10 ounces) unbleached all-purpose or white whole wheat flour, plus more for dusting*

4 teaspoons baking powder

1½ teaspoons kosher salt (use less if using table salt)

2 cups nonfat Greek yogurt (I like Stonyfield)

1 egg white, beaten

Olive oil spray

OPTIONAL TOPPINGS

Everything bagel seasoning, sesame seeds, poppy seeds, dried garlic flakes, dried onion flakes

*For gluten-free bagel balls, swap the flour with Cup4Cup gluten-free mix. Add 5 minutes to the bake time.

> FREEZER: UP TO 3 MONTHS

Tommy is obsessed with Bantam Bagel balls stuffed with cream cheese! But since they're often sold out when we try to buy them at our neighborhood Starbucks or in the frozen aisle of the supermarket, I was determined to make them at home for him. We usually eat half on a Sunday morning or for a special occasion, like his birthday, and freeze the rest—they reheat well and taste like they're fresh out of the oven. Just pop them in the microwave for a few seconds until they are heated through and soft.

Place the cream cheese block on a small cutting board and cut into 16 cubes of equal size. Transfer to the freezer while you make the dough so it stays cold and firm.

In a medium bowl combine the flour, baking powder, and salt and whisk well.

Add the yogurt and mix with a fork or spatula until well combined. It will look like small crumbles.

Place the dough onto a lightly floured work surface. Knead the dough a few times until it is tacky, but not sticky (the dough should not stick to your hands), and no longer lumpy. You may have to add more flour to your hands and work surface.

Divide the dough into 16 balls of equal size. Working one at a time, flatten each ball, then place 1 cube of cream cheese in the center of each. Cover the cream cheese with the dough, seal well so no cream cheese leaks out while baking, and roll into a ball.

Brush the dough with egg white and sprinkle with toppings of your choice (if using).

(recipe continues)

Per Serving (2 balls) ● Calories 215 ● Fat 5.5 g ● Saturated Fat 3 g
Cholesterol 17 mg ● Carbohydrate 29 g ● Fiber 1 g ● Protein 12 g
Sugars 2 g ● Sodium 568 mg

Oven Method:

Preheat the oven to 375°F. Adjust an oven rack to the top position, about 6 inches from the heating element. Place parchment paper or a silicone baking mat on a baking sheet. If using parchment paper, spray with oil to avoid sticking.

Bake the dough balls for 22 to 25 minutes, until golden. Let cool at least 10 minutes before eating.

Air Fryer Method:

Spray the basket to avoid sticking.

Preheat the air fryer to 330°F. Add just enough dough balls to the air fryer basket to make a single layer without overcrowding. Cook for 11 to 12 minutes, turning halfway, until golden. Remove from the air fryer and place on a wire rack to cool for at least 10 minutes before eating. Repeat with the remaining batches of dough balls.

MEAL PREP: Bake as directed. Once the bagel balls are cool, transfer to zip-top plastic bags and freeze for up to 3 months. Reheat in batches in the microwave in 30-second intervals until heated through in the center, about 1 minute. Let them cool for 2 to 3 minutes before serving, as the centers will be very hot.

SKINNY SCOOP You can get super creative with the cream cheese filling and toppings! Try adding chopped scallions to the cream cheese and top with dried onion, or add chopped lox to the cream cheese and top with sesame seeds. For a sweeter option, add chopped raisins and cinnamon to the cream cheese and top with cinnamon and sugar.

Lemon Blueberry Buttermilk Sheet Pan Pancakes

(Q) (FF)

SERVES 8

Cooking spray

1½ cups unbleached all-purpose flour

½ cup white whole wheat flour

2 tablespoons granulated sugar

2 teaspoons baking powder

1 teaspoon baking soda

1 teaspoon kosher salt

2 tablespoons unsalted butter, melted and cooled slightly

2 cups low-fat (1%) buttermilk

2 large eggs

Juice and grated zest from 1 medium lemon

2 teaspoons vanilla extract

1½ cups blueberries

OPTIONAL TOPPINGS

Confectioners' sugar, pure maple syrup, honey, or light whipped cream

FRIDGE: UP TO 4 DAYS

FREEZER: UP TO 2 MONTHS

Sheet pan pancakes—essentially, a giant pancake baked in the oven—is the most genius way to whip up pancakes. Make them once, and you'll never make them any other way again! No more waiting, flipping, and eating in shifts. All you need is a good-quality rimmed sheet pan and some parchment paper so they don't stick. They come out golden and fluffy, speckled with blueberries throughout.

Preheat the oven to 425°F. Spray a rimmed 13 × 18-inch sheet pan with cooking spray (this will keep the parchment in place). Cut a piece of parchment paper to cover the bottom completely. Place on the sheet pan and spray more oil on the parchment and around the sides of the sheet pan.

In a medium bowl, whisk together the flours, sugar, baking powder, baking soda, and salt. In another medium bowl, whisk together the butter, buttermilk, eggs, lemon juice and zest, vanilla, and ¼ cup water until thoroughly combined.

Add the wet ingredients to the dry ingredients and whisk until just combined. Do not overmix (or worry if there are some lumps).

Gently fold in the blueberries with a spatula.

Pour the batter into the prepared sheet pan. Spread evenly with a spatula, then tap the sheet pan on the counter a few times to settle the batter. Bake, rotating the pan halfway through, until golden and set, about 15 minutes.

Let cool for 5 minutes in the pan. Place a large cutting board over the top of the pan and flip the pancake onto the cutting board. Cut into 16 squares. Add toppings as desired and serve.

MEAL PREP: Cool completely before transferring to an airtight container. To reheat from the fridge, microwave for 40 seconds, flipping halfway through. To reheat from frozen, microwave for 45 seconds. Flip and cook for an additional 45 seconds, or until heated through.

Per Serving (2 squares) ● Calories 214 ● Fat 5 g ● Saturated Fat 2.5 g Cholesterol 57 mg ● Carbohydrate 35 g ● Fiber 2.5 g ● Protein 7 g Sugars 9 g ● Sodium 503 mg

Strawberry and Cottage Cheese Jars

Q GF

SERVES 4

2½ cups (13.5 ounces) fresh strawberries, hulled and diced into ¼-inch pieces

2½ tablespoons raw sugar

¾ teaspoon cornstarch

½ teaspoon fresh lemon juice

3 cups 1%-fat unsalted small curd cottage cheese

FRIDGE: UP TO 5 DAYS

I'm crazy for cottage cheese, especially the type that comes with fruit on the side. But many brands sold in the dairy aisle don't contain much actual fruit! Plus, they can be highly processed; some even contain high fructose corn syrup. That's what inspired me to start making them from scratch. Believe it or not, these are so easy—they take just about 20 minutes, start to finish. Strawberries are my favorite, but any fruit will work, so feel free to swap in others, like peaches or raspberries.

In a medium saucepan, combine the strawberries, sugar, cornstarch, and lemon juice over medium heat. Bring to a boil, stirring occasionally. The strawberries will release juice without any mashing required.

Reduce the heat and simmer, stirring occasionally, until the sauce is thickened, 12 to 15 minutes. Remove from the heat and let cool to room temperature. It will thicken slightly as it cools. Serve with the cottage cheese.

MEAL PREP: Divide the cottage cheese and the strawberry sauce among meal prep containers, keeping the sauce separate from the cottage cheese until ready to eat. (Use a meal prep container with compartments or use separate containers for the cottage cheese and sauce.)

SKINNY SCOOP Cottage cheese is available in different curd sizes—usually small, medium, or large. It's an excellent source of protein for relatively few calories. It is also packed with many nutrients, including B vitamins, calcium, phosphorus, and selenium.

Per Serving (¾ cup cottage cheese + scant ⅓ cup strawberry sauce) • Calories 183
Fat 2 g • Saturated Fat 1 g • Cholesterol 7 mg • Carbohydrate 20 g • Fiber 2 g
Protein 22 g • Sugars 17 g • Sodium 691 mg

Sausage, Egg, and Cheese Breakfast Sandwiches

SERVES 4

Olive oil spray

4 small chicken or turkey breakfast sausage links* (3¼ ounces total), casings removed

¼ cup diced yellow onion

½ medium red bell pepper, diced

1 garlic clove, minced

⅛ teaspoon kosher salt

Freshly ground black pepper

4 large eggs

1 tablespoon fat-free milk

4 light whole grain or gluten-free English muffins, split

4 slices (2 ounces) cheddar cheese

*Read the label to be sure this product is gluten-free.

FRIDGE: UP TO 4 DAYS

FREEZER: UP TO 3 MONTHS

Skip the drive-through during the morning rush and make your own breakfast sandwiches ahead of time to reheat and eat during the week. Double the recipe and you'll have enough for the month. For a delicious variation, swap out the sausage for ham, or make them vegetarian by omitting the meat. Rise and dine!

Preheat the oven to 350°F. Spray an 8 × 8-inch nonstick, silicone, or glass baking dish with olive oil spray.

Spray a medium nonstick skillet with oil and heat over medium heat. Add the sausage and cook, breaking it up with a wooden spoon or spatula, until just cooked through, 3 to 4 minutes. Transfer to a plate and set aside.

In the same skillet, add the onion, bell pepper, garlic, salt, and black pepper to taste. Sauté until softened, stirring often so the garlic doesn't burn, about 3 minutes. Transfer the veggies to the same plate with the sausage and let cool for 5 minutes.

In a large bowl, beat the eggs just until uniform. Add the milk, sausage, and veggies and mix to combine. Transfer the mixture to the prepared pan and bake until set, 18 to 20 minutes.

Let the mixture cool in the pan for 5 minutes, then slice into 4 equal squares. Alternatively, you can cut the eggs into 4 rounds using a 3¾-inch cookie cutter.

SERVE NOW: Toast the English muffins to desired doneness, divide the egg squares among the bottoms of the English muffins, top each with a slice of cheese, and add the muffin tops.

MEAL PREP: Do not toast your English muffins before assembling the sandwiches. Tightly wrap each sandwich individually in plastic wrap or foil. Store the sandwiches in the refrigerator or freezer. To reheat from the fridge, unwrap the sandwich and microwave until heated through, 45 to 60 seconds, or reheat in the toaster oven. If reheating from frozen, microwave for 2 minutes, flipping halfway through, until heated through.

Per Serving (1 sandwich) ● Calories 283 ● Fat 13.5 g ● Saturated Fat 5.5 g Cholesterol 216 mg ● Carbohydrate 28 g ● Fiber 8.5 g ● Protein 19 g Sugars 3 g ● Sodium 510 mg

Breakfast Quesadillas

SERVES 4

6 large eggs, beaten

1 (4-ounce) can diced green chiles, drained

¼ teaspoon kosher salt

Olive oil spray

4 large (8-inch) low-carb whole wheat or gluten-free tortillas

1⅓ cups shredded reduced-fat cheddar or Mexican blend cheese*

¼ cup chopped fresh cilantro

¼ cup chopped red onion

1 cup jarred or homemade salsa, for serving

1 small (4-ounce) avocado, cut into 4 wedges, for serving

*Read the label to be sure this product is gluten-free.

FRIDGE: UP TO 5 DAYS

Combining two of my favorite things—quesadillas and eggs—this dish totally speaks my food love language! Fluffy scrambled eggs, green chiles, avocado, fresh herbs, and of course, cheese—I really can't think of a better way to start your morning.

In a medium bowl, whisk the eggs, chiles, and salt.

Heat a large nonstick skillet over medium heat, spray with olive oil, and add the eggs. Let the eggs set on the bottom, then stir a few times until scrambled and cooked through, about 3 minutes. Transfer to a plate and set aside. Wipe the skillet clean.

Reheat the skillet over medium-high heat and spray with oil once it is really hot. Place a tortilla in the skillet and mound ⅓ cup cheese on the lower half, leaving about 1 inch around the edge. Top with one-fourth of the eggs, cilantro, and red onion, then fold in half. Cook until the cheese is melted through and the tortilla is golden on the bottom, 2 to 3 minutes. Set aside and repeat with the remaining 3 tortillas. Cut each into wedges. Serve hot with salsa and avocado.

MEAL PREP: Place the quesadillas and salsa into separate airtight containers and store in the fridge. When ready to eat, serve at room temperature or reheat (see Skinny Scoop). Add the avocado the morning you plan on eating the quesadillas to avoid browning.

SKINNY SCOOP Quesadillas are some of my favorite things to meal prep, but I don't recommend reheating them in the microwave, or they'll get soggy. Instead, I eat them at room temperature if I've packed them to take with me, or if I'm home I reheat them on a skillet or in my air fryer.

For recipes with avocado for meal prep, it's best to cut the avocado the morning you are going to eat it and wrap the rest tightly with plastic wrap. A squeeze of lime juice on the avocado will help prevent it from browning.

Per Serving (1 quesadilla + ¼ cup salsa + 1 ounce avocado) • Calories 337 • Fat 21 g Saturated Fat 7.5 g • Cholesterol 299 mg • Carbohydrate 26 g • Protein 25 g Fiber 14.5 g • Sugars 4 g • Sodium 1,148 mg

Italian Sausage and Ricotta Frittata

SERVES 4

Cooking spray

8 large eggs

½ cup freshly grated Pecorino Romano cheese

¼ cup chopped fresh parsley

¾ teaspoon kosher salt

Freshly ground black pepper

2 links Italian chicken sausage,* casings removed

½ cup part-skim ricotta cheese (I like Polly-O)

Whole wheat Italian bread, for serving (optional)

*Read the label to be sure this product is gluten-free.

> FRIDGE: UP TO 4 DAYS

My husband Tommy's dad is a Brooklyn-born Italian, and this is the only frittata his family prepares for parties, holidays, or even simple family lunches or dinners. I've had it on many a Sunday while visiting his family, and I've always loved the flavorful simplicity of this dish. I lightened mine up using less ricotta and Italian chicken sausage, and Tommy never even knew! Serve this with a salad, olives, and some good Italian bread.

Adjust an oven rack to the second highest position. Preheat the oven to 350°F. Lightly spray a 10-inch ovenproof skillet with cooking spray.

In a medium bowl, whisk the eggs, Pecorino, parsley, salt, and pepper to taste. Set aside.

In the ovenproof skillet over medium heat, add the sausages and use a wooden spoon to break them up into small pieces. Cook until browned and cooked through, about 4 minutes.

Add the egg mixture to the skillet, and use a tablespoon to dollop it with the ricotta. Bake until the top is set, 16 to 18 minutes.

Switch the oven to broil (high) and cook the frittata an additional 3 to 4 minutes, until the top is browned.

With a spatula, carefully slide the frittata out of the skillet onto a cutting board and cut into 4 even wedges.

MEAL PREP: Divide among 4 airtight containers and store in the fridge. When ready to eat, reheat and serve with Italian bread (if using).

Per Serving (1 wedge) ● Calories 296 ● Fat 18.5 g ● Saturated Fat 7.5 g
Cholesterol 420 mg ● Carbohydrate 4 g ● Fiber 0 g ● Protein 27 g
Sugars 0.5 g ● Sodium 834 mg

Classic
Egg Salad

Q GF DF

SERVES 4

6 large hard-boiled eggs, peeled
   and roughly chopped

3 tablespoons mayonnaise

1 teaspoon finely chopped
   red onion

¼ teaspoon kosher salt

Freshly ground black pepper

⅛ teaspoon sweet paprika,
   for garnish

Chopped fresh chives, for garnish

FRIDGE: UP TO 4 DAYS

You can always find at least one batch of egg salad in my refrigerator. It's the perfect, simple make-ahead dish for breakfast or lunch, and sometimes I even eat it right out of the bowl with a spoon! I also love it over whole grain toast or in a wrap.

Combine all the ingredients in a medium bowl and refrigerate until ready to eat.

SKINNY SCOOP For variations, add pickle juice or diced pickles, capers, or Dijon mustard. You can also add veggies like chopped celery or carrots, or swap the chives for fresh dill.

Per Serving (½ cup) ● Calories 191 ● Fat 16 g ● Saturated Fat 3.5 g
Carbohydrate 1 g ● Cholesterol 320 mg ● Fiber 0 g ● Protein 10 g
Sugars 1 g ● Sodium 337 mg

Instant Pot Egg White Steel-Cut Oats

GF DF IP

SERVES 5

1 cup steel-cut oats*

3 cups water

½ cup unsweetened nut milk or milk of your choice

1 tablespoon honey

1 teaspoon vanilla extract

½ cup egg whites (from 3 large eggs)

1¼ cups fresh fruit (sliced strawberries and banana is my favorite combo)

5 tablespoons smooth peanut butter

2½ teaspoons hemp seed hearts

* Read the label to be sure this product is gluten-free.

> FRIDGE: UP TO 6 DAYS

Steel-cut oatmeal is the ultimate wholesome comfort breakfast food, especially when you pile on good-for-you toppings and add-ins. For instance, mixing in egg whites is a total game-changer! It makes the oatmeal so fluffy and contributes extra protein. And you can't even taste it (a bonus for picky eaters). Fresh fruit and peanut butter are my favorite oatmeal toppings. Keep in mind that the base of this recipe is basically a blank canvas, so you can play around with different nut butters and dried fruit options, in addition to other toppings, like maple syrup, walnuts, and cinnamon. I make a big batch once on the weekend (thanks to the Instant Pot, it's so easy!) and have breakfast ready for the week. Transfer them to individual mason jars and refrigerate, then pop them in the microwave for breakfast on-the-run.

Combine the oats and water in your Instant Pot (or any electric pressure cooker) and stir. Cover and cook for 6 minutes on high pressure. Allow the pressure to naturally release.

In a medium bowl, whisk the milk, honey, vanilla, and egg whites. Add to the oats, stirring constantly to mix in without making scrambled egg whites. Divide among 5 bowls. Top each bowl with ¼ cup fresh fruit. In a small microwave-safe bowl, melt the peanut butter in the microwave for 30 seconds or less. Whisk and drizzle 1 tablespoon over each bowl. Top each with ½ teaspoon hemp seeds.

MEAL PREP: Divide the oats among 5 glass jars or microwave-safe containers and let cool before storing. When ready to serve, microwave for 2 to 3 minutes, until warmed through. Top as directed.

SKINNY SCOOP To make this on the stove, in a large pot bring 4 cups water to a boil. Stir in the oats and cook until they begin to thicken, about 5 minutes. Reduce the heat to low and simmer, uncovered, stirring frequently, until thickened and cooked, about 30 minutes. Remove from the heat, let cool slightly for 5 minutes, then add the remaining ingredients.

Per Serving (generous ¾ cup oats + toppings) ● Calories 295 ● Fat 12.5 g Saturated Fat 2.5 g ● Cholesterol 0 mg ● Carbohydrate 35 g ● Fiber 5.5 g Protein 12 g ● Sugars 9 g ● Sodium 131 mg

Almond Flour Banana Crumb Muffins

SERVES 12

1 cup almond flour

⅓ cup coconut flour

2 teaspoons baking powder

½ teaspoon baking soda

¼ teaspoon kosher salt

2 tablespoons unsalted butter, at room temperature

⅓ cup unpacked light brown sugar

2 large eggs

3 medium very ripe bananas, mashed (1⅔ cups)

½ teaspoon vanilla extract

CRUMB TOPPING

¼ cup finely chopped almonds

¼ cup packed light brown sugar

ROOM TEMPERATURE: UP TO 2 DAYS

FRIDGE: UP TO 5 DAYS

FREEZER: UP TO 3 MONTHS (TO REHEAT, MICROWAVE FOR A FEW SECONDS UNTIL WARM OR THAW IN THE FRIDGE)

In our house, the bananas seem to get ripe faster than we can eat them . . . sound familiar? But that's never a problem, because my family loves when I bake banana muffins, so the riper the better! These muffins are loaded with bananas, and instead of using wheat flour, I make them gluten- and grain-free with almond and coconut flours. For the crumb topping, I simply chop up the almonds and mix them with brown sugar. They come out so incredibly moist!

Preheat the oven to 325°F. Line a standard 12-cup muffin tin with liners.

In a medium bowl, whisk together the flours, baking powder, baking soda, and salt. Set aside.

In a large bowl, combine the butter and sugar and cream together with an electric mixer. Add the eggs, bananas, and vanilla. Beat at medium speed until thick. Scrape down the sides of the bowl. Add the flour mixture, then blend at low speed until just combined.

Make the almond-crumb topping: In a small bowl, combine the almonds and sugar.

Scoop the batter into the muffin tin, then evenly divide the crumb mixture over the top. Bake until a toothpick inserted in the center comes out clean, 35 to 40 minutes. Let cool and serve.

MEAL PREP: Once completely cool, wrap the muffins individually in plastic wrap and store.

Per Serving (1 muffin) ● Calories 175 ● Fat 8.5 g ● Saturated Fat 2 g
Cholesterol 36 mg ● Carbohydrate 21 g ● Fiber 3 g ● Protein 5 g
Sugars 13.5 g ● Sodium 185 mg

Greek Yogurt Raspberry Loaf

(FF)

SERVES 12

Olive oil spray

1½ cups fresh raspberries

1¾ cups all-purpose flour

1½ teaspoons baking powder

½ teaspoon baking soda

½ teaspoon kosher salt

¾ cup turbinado sugar

3 tablespoons unsalted butter, at room temperature

2 large eggs

3 large egg whites

1 teaspoon vanilla extract

Grated zest from 1 lemon

1 cup nonfat plain Greek yogurt

FRIDGE: UP TO 4 DAYS

FREEZER: UP TO 3 MONTHS (TO REHEAT, MICROWAVE FOR A FEW SECONDS UNTIL WARM OR THAW IN THE FRIDGE)

As much as I love to bake, I don't have the time for it each day—there's just too much going on during the week. Instead, I bake on the weekends with my kids and freeze whatever we don't eat (quick breads like this freeze really well). Having a small stash of home-baked goodness, like this moist Greek yogurt loaf, in your freezer will bring much-appreciated comfort on busy mornings.

Preheat the oven to 350°F.

Spray a 5 × 9-inch loaf pan with oil.

In a medium bowl, toss the berries with 1 tablespoon flour and set aside.

In a large bowl, mix the remaining flour with the baking powder, baking soda, and salt.

Reserve 1 tablespoon sugar and set aside. In another medium bowl, use an electric mixer on medium speed to beat the butter and remaining sugar until fluffy, about 2 minutes.

In a small bowl, use a whisk to beat the eggs, egg whites, and vanilla until smooth. Add to the butter-sugar mixture and mix with an electric mixer on medium-high speed until combined, about 30 seconds. Add the lemon zest and briefly mix until combined, about 10 seconds. Add the flour mixture and mix on low speed until combined, about 30 seconds. Fold in the yogurt with a spatula, then fold in the raspberries. Pour into the prepared pan and sprinkle with the reserved 1 tablespoon sugar.

Bake until the top is golden and a toothpick inserted in the center comes out clean, 50 to 55 minutes. Let cool for 1 to 2 hours before eating.

MEAL PREP: Let the loaf cool, then cut into slices and wrap the slices individually in plastic wrap. Transfer the wrapped slices to a large zip-top storage bag and store.

Per Serving (1 slice) • Calories 174 • Fat 4 g • Saturated Fat 2 g
Cholesterol 39 mg • Carbohydrate 29 g • Fiber 1.5 g • Protein 6 g
Sugars 13 g • Sodium 197 mg

Hearty Salads

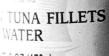

CALLIPO
SINCE 1913

PRODUCED IN ITALY
FROM SELECTED
YELLOWFIN TUNA
HAND PACKED

TUNA FILLETS
WATER

T. 6 OZ (170g)

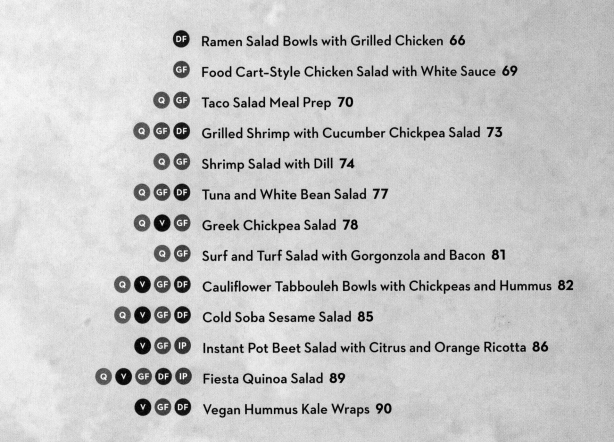

Ramen Salad Bowls with Grilled Chicken

DF

SERVES 5

MARINADE AND DRESSING

¼ cup reduced-sodium soy sauce

⅔ cup freshly squeezed orange juice (from 2 large oranges)

¼ cup canola oil

2 tablespoons toasted sesame oil

2 tablespoons unseasoned rice vinegar

4 teaspoons raw honey

1¼ pounds boneless, skinless chicken breast

Olive oil spray

SALAD

1 (3-ounce) package instant ramen noodles

⅓ cup slivered almonds

7 cups coleslaw mix

½ medium red bell pepper, halved horizontally and sliced into thin strips

3 scallions, thinly sliced

FRIDGE: UP TO 4 DAYS

The toasted ramen noodles in this Asian-inspired dish give the salad an amazing crunch! Plus it's packed with healthy goodies like shredded cabbage, slivered almonds, bell pepper, and grilled chicken. Here, I used part of the dressing to marinate the chicken, but if you happen to have leftover chicken or a rotisserie chicken on hand, that would work great, too.

Marinate the chicken: In a medium bowl, combine the soy sauce, orange juice, canola oil, sesame oil, rice vinegar, and honey. Whisk to combine and set half (¾ cup) aside for the dressing. Working one at a time, place a chicken breast in a zip-top plastic bag and pound with a mallet or rolling pin to about ½ inch thick, being careful not to puncture the bag. Place all the pounded chicken breasts in one bag and add the remaining ¾ cup marinade. Let marinate in the refrigerator for at least 30 minutes or up to overnight.

When ready to cook, preheat a grill pan over medium-high heat (or preheat a grill to medium-high). Spray the pan with oil (or rub the grates with oil).

Remove the chicken from the marinade (discard the marinade) and grill until the chicken is cooked through, about 5 minutes per side. Set aside to cool and then slice into strips.

For the salad: Preheat the oven to 350°F.

With the package still sealed, break the ramen into small pieces (about ½ inch) with a mallet or rolling pin. Open the package, discard the seasoning packet, and spread the ramen pieces and almonds on a medium sheet pan in an even layer. Toast, stirring halfway through, until golden brown, 6 to 10 minutes.

In a large bowl, combine the slaw mix, bell pepper, and scallions. Toss well.

SERVE NOW: Divide the salad evenly among 5 plates or bowls, about 1½ cups each. Add the ramen-almond mix and grilled chicken, and top with the dressing.

MEAL PREP: Combine the salad ingredients, except the ramen-almond mix, in a large bowl. Divide the salad evenly among 5 airtight containers. Pack the dressing (2 tablespoons each) and the ramen mix (¼ cup each) in separate containers.

Per Serving (2 cups salad + 3 ounces chicken + 2 tablespoons dressing)
Calories 425 • Fat 25 g • Saturated Fat 3 g • Cholesterol 73 mg
Carbohydrate 22 g • Fiber 3.5 g • Protein 29 g • Sugars 11 g • Sodium 597 mg

Food Cart–Style Chicken Salad with White Sauce

GF

SERVES 4

CHICKEN

1½ pounds (about 4 large) boneless, skinless chicken thighs, fat trimmed

Juice of ½ lemon

2 garlic cloves, minced

1¼ teaspoons ground cumin

1 teaspoon olive oil

1 teaspoon kosher salt

1 teaspoon dried oregano

¾ teaspoon sweet paprika

½ teaspoon ground turmeric

Olive oil spray (I like my Misto or Bertolli)

WHITE SAUCE

1 cup whole-milk yogurt

2 tablespoons light mayonnaise

1 tablespoon apple cider vinegar

1 teaspoon fresh lemon juice

½ teaspoon kosher salt

½ teaspoon sugar

⅛ teaspoon freshly ground black pepper

SALAD

6 cups chopped iceberg or romaine lettuce

2 medium tomatoes, quartered

½ small red onion, sliced

Prepared mild harissa, for drizzling (optional)

FRIDGE: UP TO 4 DAYS

My family is obsessed with street-cart halal chicken, and since all of the best chicken trucks are in New York City (which is over an hour commute from our house), I knew I had to figure out a way to prepare this at home. When I worked in the city full-time, I would often hit up the halal chicken trucks for lunch—the smell of the sizzling chicken always lured me in! I usually swapped out the rice for a salad with tomatoes, red onions, and romaine. Tommy has been asking me to re-create the halal white sauce (a mayo-based sauce with vinegar, sugar, and lemon) for years, so here I lightened it up using yogurt, and guess what? He loved it! The yogurt sauce acts as a creamy dressing for the salad, and finishing this dish with a drizzle of prepared harissa takes it from awesome to over-the-top.

Prepare the chicken: In a large bowl, combine the chicken with the other ingredients, mixing to coat thoroughly. Let marinate in the refrigerator for at least 15 minutes or up to overnight.

Prepare the white sauce: In a small bowl, combine the yogurt with the other ingredients. Refrigerate until ready to use.

When ready to cook, heat a large nonstick griddle or skillet over medium-high heat. Spritz the pan with olive oil. When hot, add the chicken and cook, undisturbed, until the bottom is completely browned, about 5 minutes. Flip the chicken and cook the second side until browned, 4 to 5 minutes more.

Reduce the heat to low and let the chicken continue cooking until just about cooked through in the thickest parts (no worries if it's not completely cooked at this point), about 10 minutes.

Transfer the chicken to a cutting board and slice it into thin strips. Return the chicken to the skillet over medium heat. Cook until browned all over and cooked through, 8 to 10 minutes.

SERVE NOW: Divide the lettuce, tomato, and red onion among 4 serving bowls. Top with the chicken and drizzle with the white sauce and harissa (if using).

MEAL PREP: Divide the chicken among 4 separate airtight containers, the salad ingredients among 4 containers, and the white sauce and harissa (if using) in small containers. To serve, reheat the meat in the microwave or on the stovetop, then assemble the salad.

Per Serving (1 bowl) ● Calories 322 ● Fat 13.5 g ● Saturated Fat 4 g Cholesterol 173 mg ● Carbohydrate 13 g ● Fiber 2.5 g ● Protein 37 g Sugars 8 g ● Sodium 668 mg

Taco Salad Meal Prep

Q GF

SERVES 4

MEAT

Olive oil spray

1 pound 93% lean ground turkey

1 teaspoon garlic powder

1 teaspoon ground cumin

1 teaspoon kosher salt

½ teaspoon chili powder*

½ teaspoon sweet paprika

½ teaspoon dried oregano

½ small onion, minced

2 tablespoons minced red bell pepper

4 ounces canned tomato sauce

DRESSING

½ cup jarred mild salsa

4 teaspoons extra-virgin olive oil

Juice of ½ lime

SALAD

6 cups chopped romaine lettuce

1 cup pico de gallo (see page 101)

Greek yogurt or sour cream, for serving (optional)

½ cup shredded cheddar cheese*

4 lime wedges, for serving

*Read the label to be sure this product is gluten-free.

FRIDGE: UP TO 4 DAYS

I'm not surprised this taco salad is a fan favorite on my blog—it's easy and versatile, and literally everyone in our house loves it. The dressing is just jarred salsa mixed with olive oil and lime, making it super simple to assemble, but extra delish! This salad is fabulous for dinner or lunch, and if you're packing it as a grab-and-go meal in the morning, just be sure to keep the greens and other salad components separate from the meat. That way, you can heat up the turkey before adding it to the salad.

Spray a large nonstick skillet with oil and set it over medium-high heat. Brown the turkey using a wooden spoon to break it into smaller pieces as it cooks. When no longer pink, add the garlic powder, cumin, salt, chili powder, paprika, and oregano and mix well. Stir in the onion, bell pepper, tomato sauce, and ½ cup water. Cover and reduce the heat to low. Simmer until the flavors meld and the sauce thickens, about 20 minutes.

While the meat is cooking, make the dressing: In a small bowl, combine the salsa, olive oil, and lime juice.

SERVE NOW: Divide the lettuce among 4 plates. Top with the meat, then the pico de gallo, yogurt (if using), and cheese. Drizzle with the dressing and serve with the lime wedges alongside.

MEAL PREP: Divide the meat equally among 4 meal prep containers; the dressing among 4 small containers; the lettuce in 4 zip-top plastic bags; and the pico de gallo, yogurt (if using), and cheese in small containers. To serve, reheat the meat in the microwave or on the stovetop, then assemble the salad.

SKINNY SCOOP For more protein and nutrition, add black or pinto beans to the turkey meat during cooking. You can also add crushed tortilla chips on top for texture, or swap the cheese for avocado to make it dairy-free.

Per Serving (1 salad) ● Calories 322 ● Fat 19.5 g ● Saturated Fat 6 g Cholesterol 99 mg ● Carbohydrate 12 g ● Fiber 3.5 g ● Protein 27 g Sugars 5 g ● Sodium 907 mg

Grilled Shrimp with Cucumber Chickpea Salad

(Q) (GF) (DF)

SERVES 2

SALAD

1 (15-ounce) can low-sodium chickpeas,* drained and rinsed

3 Persian cucumbers, diced

½ cup quartered grape tomatoes

2 tablespoons diced red onion

Juice and grated zest from ½ large lemon

¼ teaspoon kosher salt

Freshly ground black pepper

1 teaspoon extra-virgin olive oil

1 teaspoon red wine vinegar

SHRIMP

½ tablespoon extra-virgin olive oil

½ tablespoon fresh oregano

½ tablespoon chopped fresh parsley

1 garlic clove, minced

¼ teaspoon crushed red pepper flakes

⅛ teaspoon kosher salt

Freshly ground black pepper

¾ pound peeled and deveined extra jumbo shrimp (12 total), tails removed

*Read the label to be sure this product is gluten-free.

FRIDGE: UP TO 4 DAYS

You've probably noticed by the number of chickpea recipes I have in this book just how much I love them! This yummy salad with tomatoes, red onions, cucumbers, and (of course!) chickpeas, topped with spicy grilled shrimp, can be served warm or eaten chilled straight out of the refrigerator. Tommy doesn't share my passion for chickpeas, but he loves beans, and in this recipe any canned white bean can be swapped in their place. I typically don't meal prep seafood more than two days in advance, but I tested this on the fourth day and it was just as good as the first.

Prepare the chickpea salad: Combine the chickpeas, cucumbers, tomatoes, and red onion in a bowl with half of the lemon juice and half of the lemon zest, the salt, and pepper to taste. Drizzle with the oil and vinegar and toss to evenly coat.

Prepare the shrimp: Combine the oil, the remaining lemon juice and zest from preparing the salad, the oregano, parsley, garlic, pepper flakes, salt, and black pepper to taste in a small bowl and mix well. Add the shrimp and toss to coat.

Preheat a grill pan over high heat (or preheat a grill to high). When hot, oil the pan or the grates and add the shrimp; cook for 2 to 3 minutes on each side, until charred and opaque.

SERVE NOW: Top the salad with the grilled shrimp and serve.

MEAL PREP: Divide the chickpea salad between 2 meal prep containers, about 1½ cups each. Place the shrimp in a separate container in the refrigerator. Reheat the shrimp and serve on top of the salad, or the shrimp can be served chilled.

Per Serving (1½ cups salad + 6 shrimp) ● Calories 438 ● Fat 10 g
Saturated Fat 1 g ● Cholesterol 203 mg ● Carbohydrate 44 g
Fiber 12 g ● Protein 43 g ● Sugars 6 g ● Sodium 810 mg

Shrimp Salad with Dill

Q GF

SERVES 4

1 lemon, halved

1¼ pounds peeled and deveined jumbo shrimp

¼ cup light mayonnaise

¼ cup nonfat Greek yogurt

½ cup chopped celery

¼ cup loosely packed chopped fresh dill

2 tablespoons chopped red onion

Pinch of kosher salt

FRIDGE: UP TO 4 DAYS

This creamy shrimp salad is one of my favorite dishes to keep on hand for the week. It's so delicious, the biggest problem is that it takes all my willpower not to stand in front of the fridge and graze on it all day long! It's even easier to make than egg salad; just be sure to cook the shrimp yourself with lemon—it only takes 2 to 3 minutes and is worth it for the best flavor. To keep it creamy yet light, I do a combo of mayo and yogurt mixed with celery for crunch and lots of fresh dill for flavor. In the summer I like to serve this lobster roll–style on top of a toasted split-top bun, or if I'm watching carbs, in lettuce wraps. You can even double the recipe to bring this to a potluck—trust me, everyone will thank you!

Bring a large pot of water to a boil with ½ of the lemon. When boiling, add the shrimp and cook for 2 to 3 minutes, until just opaque and cooked through. Don't overcook or they will become rubbery. Transfer to an ice bath to stop the shrimp from cooking.

Chop the shrimp and transfer to a medium bowl. Add the mayo, yogurt, celery, dill, onion, 2 teaspoons lemon juice, 1 teaspoon lemon zest, and salt and mix well. Divide among 4 airtight containers and chill in the refrigerator until ready to eat.

SKINNY SCOOP To turn this salad into shrimp rolls, place 4 hot dog buns on a platter, top each with ¼ cup shredded lettuce and some sliced tomato, and top with the shrimp salad.

Per Serving (scant 1 cup) ● Calories 193 ● Fat 5.5 g ● Saturated Fat 1 g
Cholesterol 175 mg ● Carbohydrate 6 g ● Fiber 1 g ● Protein 27 g
Sugars 2 g ● Sodium 486 mg

Tuna and White Bean Salad

Q GF DF

SERVES 2

2 tablespoons extra-virgin olive oil

2 tablespoons red wine vinegar

2 tablespoons finely chopped fresh parsley

1 tablespoon fresh lemon juice

¼ cup chopped red onion

2 tablespoons capers, drained (reserve 1 tablespoon brine)

2 (5-ounce) cans albacore tuna in water, drained and flaked

1 (15-ounce) can small no-salt-added white beans, such as navy,* rinsed and drained

*Read the label to be sure this product is gluten-free.

FRIDGE: UP TO 3 DAYS

I always have albacore tuna and a variety of canned beans in the pantry, which makes this easy no-mayo tuna salad a great fix whenever hunger strikes. It's made with just a few simple ingredients, so you can whip it up anytime. For variety, you can swap the white beans for chickpeas, or you can use olives instead of capers. If you want to add some fresh leafy greens, stir in some baby arugula, spinach, or torn radicchio.

In a large bowl combine the oil, vinegar, parsley, and lemon juice. Add the red onion and capers, plus the reserved brine. Toss in the tuna and beans and mix well. Serve or divide between 2 airtight containers to store.

SKINNY SCOOP For eco-friendly tuna brands that protect marine life, look for packages labeled as "pole-and-line caught," "troll caught," or "FAD-free."

Per Serving (1¾ cups) • Calories 466 • Fat 18 g • Saturated Fat 3.5 g
Cholesterol 33 mg • Carbohydrate 36 g • Fiber 10.5 g • Protein 45 g
Sugars 1 g • Sodium 617 mg

Greek Chickpea Salad

SERVES 4

SALAD

1 (15-ounce) can chickpeas,* rinsed and drained

2 cups diced Persian cucumber

1 green bell pepper, sliced

1⅓ cups halved grape tomatoes

20 pitted Kalamata or Gaeta olives

¼ cup sliced red onion (sliced lengthwise)

4 ounces fresh feta cheese, cut into 4 thick slices

DRESSING

Juice of 2 fresh lemons

2 tablespoons extra-virgin olive oil

2 teaspoons minced fresh oregano leaves

¼ teaspoon kosher salt

Freshly ground black pepper

*Read the label to be sure this product is gluten-free.

FRIDGE: UP TO 5 DAYS

I'm obsessed with chickpeas and with Greek salad, so this combo is one that I could eat every day! When I visited Greece, I ate traditional Greek salad every chance I got. Since they never use lettuce in the salad—just cucumbers, olives, red onion, bell pepper, and feta cheese—it's perfect for meal prep because you don't have to worry about the greens wilting. Fiber- and protein-packed canned chickpeas keep you feeling satiated longer, and it can't get easier because there's nothing to cook!

Prepare the salad: In each of four 4-cup containers or bowls, arrange ⅓ cup chickpeas, ½ cup cucumber, ¼ bell pepper, ⅓ cup tomatoes, 5 olives, and 1 tablespoon red onion. Top each with 1 ounce feta.

Prepare the dressing: In a small bowl, whisk together the lemon juice, oil, oregano, salt, and pepper to taste.

Serve about 1½ tablespoons dressing on the side with each salad.

Per Serving (1 salad) ● Calories 335 ● Fat 17.5 g ● Saturated Fat 5.5 g
Cholesterol 25 mg ● Carbohydrate 35 g ● Fiber 7 g ● Protein 13 g
Sugars 5 g ● Sodium 793 mg

Surf and Turf Salad with Gorgonzola and Bacon

Q GF

SERVES 2

6 ounces sirloin, trimmed

Kosher salt

Freshly ground black pepper

3 slices center-cut bacon, chopped

6 jumbo shrimp, peeled and deveined

3 cups chopped butter lettuce

¾ cup cooked corn (from 1 small ear)

½ cup halved cherry tomatoes

1 ounce Gorgonzola cheese, crumbled

2 teaspoons extra-virgin olive oil

Chopped fresh chives, for garnish

> FRIDGE: UP TO 3 DAYS

When I worked full-time in NYC I usually packed my own lunch. On nights that we had steak for dinner, I always made a steak salad with the leftovers. Here, I created a quick surf and turf salad (similar to a Cobb), made with lean sirloin and shrimp. When you mix it all together with the bacon, corn, and Gorgonzola, it's heavenly. It's also really filling, so instead of a heavy dressing, I just finish the whole thing with a drizzle of olive oil.

Season the steak with ½ teaspoon salt and black pepper to taste. Let rest for 15 minutes before cooking.

Heat a skillet over medium heat and add the bacon. Cook until crisp and the fat is rendered. Transfer the bacon to a paper towel using a slotted spoon. Remove and discard all but 1 teaspoon of the bacon fat.

Increase the heat to high. Brush half the reserved bacon fat on both sides of the steak. When the skillet is hot, add the steak and cook for 2 to 3 minutes on each side for medium-rare if the steaks are thin, or longer if thicker or to cook to your desired doneness. Rest on a plate, tented with foil, for about 5 minutes. Reduce the heat to medium-high and add the remaining reserved bacon fat. Add the shrimp and cook for about 3 minutes, or until opaque and cooked through.

Chop or slice the steak and chop the shrimp.

SERVE NOW: Divide the lettuce between 2 plates, then top with the steak, shrimp, corn, tomatoes, bacon, and Gorgonzola. Drizzle each with 1 teaspoon olive oil, the chives, a pinch of salt (optional), and black pepper to taste. Serve immediately.

MEAL PREP: Pack the steak and shrimp separately from the rest of the salad in 2 meal prep containers. Eat cold, topped with olive oil, salt, and pepper.

Per Serving (1 salad) ● Calories 370 ● Fat 16.5 g ● Saturated Fat 5.5 g Cholesterol 175 mg ● Carbohydrate 11 g ● Fiber 2.5 g ● Protein 44 g Sugars 3 g ● Sodium 935 mg

Cauliflower Tabbouleh Bowls with Chickpeas and Hummus

SERVES 4

1 pound cauliflower florets

1 cup peeled, seeded, and diced cucumber

2 tablespoons finely diced red onion

1/4 cup finely chopped fresh parsley

1 1/2 tablespoons chopped fresh mint leaves

1/2 cup diced tomato

1/2 tablespoon extra-virgin olive oil

2 tablespoons fresh lemon juice

4 teaspoons red wine vinegar

1/2 teaspoon kosher salt

2 (15-ounce) cans chickpeas,* rinsed and drained

1/2 cup store-bought hummus

*Read the label to be sure this product is gluten-free.

> FRIDGE: UP TO 4 DAYS

Tabbouleh is a flavorful Middle Eastern salad typically made with bulgur (a whole grain), lots of fresh herbs, cucumbers, and tomatoes. Replacing bulgur with raw, riced cauliflower turns it into a fabulous low-carb, gluten-free salad that's still easy to make. The raw cauliflower adds crunch and freshness, which is perfect paired with the chickpeas and creamy hummus. The best part: There's absolutely nothing to cook.

Place half of the cauliflower in a food processor and pulse until it has the texture of rice. Don't overprocess or it will get mushy. Set aside and repeat with the remaining cauliflower. (Makes 4 cups.)

Place the riced cauliflower in a large bowl and add the cucumber, onion, parsley, mint, tomato, olive oil, lemon juice, vinegar, and salt. Toss well and refrigerate until chilled.

Make the bowls: Divide the cauliflower tabbouleh, chickpeas, and hummus among 4 bowls or airtight containers. You can assemble them separately and combine on the fly or use meal prep containers with 3 compartments.

SKINNY SCOOP For the best taste and quality, it's better to make the cauliflower rice from scratch rather than using packaged since you're eating this raw. Packaged cauliflower can sit for a while before being purchased and isn't as fresh and crisp.

Per Serving (1 1/4 cups cauliflower tabbouleh + 3/4 cup chickpeas + 2 tablespoons hummus) • Calories 406 • Fat 10 g • Saturated Fat 1 g Cholesterol 0 mg • Carbohydrate 64 g • Fiber 14.5 g • Protein 19 g Sugars 4 g • Sodium 704 mg

Cold Soba Sesame Salad

Q V GF DF

SERVES 4

SALAD

8 ounces dry soba noodles
(use pure buckwheat soba or
rice noodles for gluten-free)

1 cup bite-size broccoli florets

½ cup sugar snap peas,
cut into thirds

1 small red bell pepper, thinly sliced

1 cup grated or shredded carrots

3 scallions, green parts only,
thinly sliced

¼ cup chopped cilantro, plus more
for garnish

Crushed roasted peanuts, for serving
(optional)

DRESSING

¼ cup reduced-sodium soy sauce*
or tamari

2 tablespoons unseasoned rice
vinegar

2 tablespoons mirin

1 tablespoon toasted sesame oil

1 teaspoon grated fresh ginger

1 garlic clove, crushed

1 teaspoon Sriracha sauce, plus more
for serving (optional)

2 teaspoons toasted sesame seeds,
plus 1 teaspoon for garnish

*Read the label to be sure this
product is gluten-free.

FRIDGE: UP TO 4 DAYS

When it's hot outside and you want a refreshing meal, you can't beat this noodle salad. It's an ideal light dinner or lunch and it's also perfect to eat al fresco on summer evenings. You can play around with this recipe and use whatever veggies you have on hand—try it using cucumbers or zucchini. For more protein you can add edamame or crushed roasted peanuts, or throw in some leftover shredded chicken. If you like it spicy, add more Sriracha to the mix.

Bring a large pot of water to a boil (do not add salt). Add the noodles and cook according to the package directions. Add the broccoli and peas about 1 minute before the noodles are ready, then drain together in a large colander and rinse with cold water for about 30 seconds, agitating with your hands.

Make the dressing: In a small glass measuring cup, whisk together the soy sauce, rice vinegar, mirin, sesame oil, ginger, garlic, Sriracha, and sesame seeds.

SERVE NOW: Divide the noodles, broccoli, and peas among 4 shallow bowls, about 1½ cups each, and top with the bell pepper, carrots, scallions, and cilantro. Top each with 2½ tablespoons dressing, a sprinkle of sesame seeds, and peanuts (if using), and serve right away.

MEAL PREP: Divide the noodles, broccoli, and peas among 4 meal prep bowls, about 1½ cups each, and top with the bell pepper, carrots, scallions, cilantro, and sesame seeds. Divide the dressing equally (about 2½ tablespoons each) and the peanuts (if using), each in their own separate smaller containers. Serve cold.

Per Serving (2 cups) • Calories 297 • Fat 5 g • Saturated Fat 0.5 g
Cholesterol 0 mg • Carbohydrate 56 g • Fiber 3 g • Protein 11 g
Sugars 7 g • Sodium 984 mg

Instant Pot Beet Salad with Citrus and Orange Ricotta

SERVES 4

10 small uncooked red and golden beets (3 ounces each)

1 large pink grapefruit, peeled

2 large sweet oranges, zested and peeled

1 cup part-skim ricotta cheese

2 teaspoons honey

¼ cup chopped raw pistachios

Chopped fresh mint, for garnish

CHAMPAGNE VINAIGRETTE

1 tablespoon champagne vinegar

2 tablespoons chopped shallots

1 teaspoon honey

2 tablespoons extra-virgin olive oil

⅛ teaspoon kosher salt

Freshly ground black pepper

FRIDGE: UP TO 4 DAYS

Beets and citrus pair so well together in this gorgeous winter salad. Typically in most restaurants you see beet salads paired with goat cheese, but I love them with ricotta mixed with a little orange zest and honey. Unlike goat cheese, ricotta is lighter and more delicate in flavor, which really allows the flavor of the beets and fresh citrus to shine. Cooking the beets in an Instant Pot is quicker than roasting them, and the skins peel off so easily. Here I combined red and golden beets because I love the colors together, but you can use whatever you find.

Wash and trim the beets. Transfer to an Instant Pot (or any electric pressure cooker) on the steaming rack. Pour 1½ cups water into the bottom of the Instant Pot. Cover and cook on high pressure for 25 minutes, then quick release.

Using a sharp knife, poke the beets. If the knife pierces the flesh without too much resistance, they're done. If the beets still seem a little too hard, cook them under high pressure for an additional 2 to 3 minutes.

Allow the beets to cool for 10 minutes, then remove the skin. Cut the beets into 1½-inch chunks.

Meanwhile, remove the white membranes off the grapefruit and orange and separate the pieces. Into a small bowl, squeeze the juice from 3 grapefruit slices and set aside for the vinaigrette. Cut up the remaining grapefruit and orange slices into 1½-inch chunks.

Combine 1 teaspoon of the orange zest with the ricotta and 2 teaspoons honey and mix well.

Make the vinaigrette: Add the reserved grapefruit juice, champagne vinegar, shallots, and honey to a small bowl and whisk to combine. Add the olive oil and season with the salt and pepper to taste.

Toss the beets with the vinaigrette. Beets can be cooked and stored in the refrigerator for up to 5 days.

SERVE NOW: Divide the beets with the vinaigrette among 4 bowls or place on a large serving platter. Add a dollop of ricotta to the grapefruit and orange, sprinkle with pistachios and mint, and serve right away.

MEAL PREP: Divide the beets with the vinaigrette and citrus among 4 meal prep containers. Pack ricotta, mint, and pistachios separately; add them just before eating.

Per Serving (1 salad) • Calories 379 • Fat 16 g • Saturated Fat 4.5 g
Cholesterol 19 mg • Carbohydrate 50 g • Fiber 11.5 g • Protein 14 g
Sugars 26 g • Sodium 305 mg

Fiesta Quinoa Salad

Q V GF DF IP

SERVES 4

1 cup red or tri-color quinoa, rinsed well

1²/₃ cups reduced-sodium vegetable or chicken broth*

5 tablespoons fresh lime juice

1 tablespoon extra-virgin olive oil

¼ teaspoon kosher salt

Freshly ground black pepper

½ medium red onion, chopped

1 fresh jalapeño pepper, seeds and membranes removed, chopped

1 cup cooked corn, from fresh or frozen

¾ cup canned black beans,* rinsed and drained

2 small vine tomatoes, seeded and diced

¼ cup chopped fresh cilantro

*Read the label to be sure this product is gluten-free.

FRIDGE: UP TO 5 DAYS

When the weather warms up I love making cold salads like this that keep well in the fridge for a quick lunch or as a dinner side dish with grilled chicken or shrimp. The trick to making fluffy and flavorful quinoa every time is twofold: (1) use broth instead of water, and (2) use less liquid than the package directions suggest. Trust me, too much water will leave your quinoa mushy and overdone! I've provided both stovetop and Instant Pot directions here for perfectly cooked quinoa.

To make the quinoa on the stove: In a medium pot over high heat, combine the quinoa and broth and bring to a boil. Reduce the heat to medium-low, cover, and cook until the broth is completely absorbed, 20 to 24 minutes. When done, fluff with a fork. Set aside to cool.

To make the quinoa in an Instant Pot: Place the quinoa and 1½ cups broth into an Instant Pot (or any electric pressure cooker). Seal and cook on high for 2 minutes. Natural release, then open when the pressure subsides, about 10 minutes. Fluff with a fork, then set aside to cool.

In a large mixing bowl, combine the lime juice, oil, salt, and black pepper to taste. Mix in the cooked quinoa, onion, jalapeño, corn, black beans, tomatoes, and cilantro. Divide among 4 airtight containers or jars.

SKINNY SCOOP I make several variations of this salad—you can add in a diced avocado just before serving for a dose of healthy fats, or toss in some diced mango, which adds a slight sweetness.

Per Serving (scant 1²/₃ cups) ● Calories 291 ● Fat 6.5 g ● Saturated Fat 1 g
Cholesterol 0 mg ● Carbohydrate 49 g ● Fiber 8.5 g ● Protein 11 g
Sugars 4 g ● Sodium 417 mg

Vegan Hummus Kale Wraps

(V) (GF) (DF)

SERVES 2

2 large, firm lacinato kale leaves

3 ounces (from ½ large) Hass avocado, thinly sliced

¼ medium lemon, halved

⅔ cup store-bought hummus (I use Sabra Supremely Spicy)

½ small red bell pepper, thinly sliced

½ cup shredded carrots

8 slices red onion

FRIDGE: UP TO 3 DAYS

These vegan kale wraps are a perfect way to add more plant-based foods to your diet. They're basically a handheld salad, rolled and filled with hummus, veggies, and avocado. Kale is a hearty leafy green that holds up well as a healthy edible wrap. Just be sure to look for large leaves of lacinato kale (often called dinosaur kale), rather than the curly variety. You can also play around with different hummus flavors; here I used Sabra Supremely Spicy because I love the heat, but roasted pepper hummus, garlic hummus, or even plain is also delish in these wraps. You can pair this light wrap with pita chips or fruit.

Cut the stem out of each kale leaf. Using a potato peeler, shave the protruding stem so it will be pliable and easily fold when making your wrap.

Lay the avocado slices out on your surface. Squeeze lemon juice from one wedge over the slices, then carefully flip each slice and squeeze lemon juice from the remaining wedge on the other side (this keeps the avocado from browning).

Spread ⅓ cup hummus over each leaf. Divide the bell pepper, avocado, carrots, and onion between the leaves. Starting at the bottom, carefully roll each leaf around the filling, then roll it like a burrito, creating a cylindrical wrap with the ends open. Eat immediately or store for meal prep.

MEAL PREP: Wrap each kale wrap in parchment paper and then wrap in plastic wrap or store in a reusable baggie in the fridge.

Per Serving (1 wrap) ● Calories 253 ● Fat 13.5 g ● Saturated Fat 2 g
Cholesterol 0 mg ● Carbohydrate 29 g ● Fiber 8.5 g ● Protein 6 g
Sugars 5 g ● Sodium 227 mg

Warm Grain, Noodle & Vegetable Bowls

Mix-and-Match: Design Your Own Grain, Noodle, or Veggie Bowls

Bowls are my most-used piece of dishware. Unlike plates, which discourage you from mixing a meal's different components, bowls are vessels that empower you to combine multiple flavors and top everything off with a grand finale of dressing. Enter: the grain bowl.

Meal prepping doesn't always have to involve using a recipe—it can be as simple as roasting some veggies ahead of time, cooking a few grains along with some protein, and preparing your favorite sauce or dressing. The best part? As long as you use fresh, in-season ingredients, they're hard to mess up!

Use the shopping list on the next page to inspire your grocery haul. Throw a few ingredients from each section into your shopping cart and you'll have lots of ingredient options to mix-and-match throughout the week. You can prep beforehand as much as you're able—cutting vegetables ahead of time, making vinaigrettes, freezing a pesto, etc. Then put them together later—it's very flexible and easy to swap in different vegetables or meats you have on hand. Think of the lists that follow as starting points; the sky is the limit for your favorite ingredients!

Stock Your Kitchen, *choose some items from this list*

Protein/Dairy

- Cheese
- Chicken (boneless, skinless thighs or breasts)
- Eggs
- Extra-firm tofu
- Fish (salmon, etc.)
- Frozen shrimp
- Greek yogurt
- Ground meat (turkey, chicken, pork, or beef)
- Steaks (flank or sirloin)

Vegetables and Fruit

FRESH

- Apples
- Asparagus
- Avocados
- Beets
- Bell peppers
- Broccoli
- Broccolini
- Brussels sprouts
- Carrots
- Cauliflower
- Celery
- Cucumbers
- Ginger
- Green beans
- Herbs
- Kale
- Lemons
- Limes
- Pears
- Scallions
- Sweet potatoes
- Tomatoes
- Zoodles

FROZEN

- Broccoli
- Cauliflower rice or broccoli rice
- Diced butternut squash
- Edamame
- Peas, mixed veggies, corn
- Spinach

Pantry

- Barley
- BBQ sauce
- Broth or stock
- Canned beans
- Canned fish (salmon, tuna, anchovies)
- Canned tomatoes
- Coconut milk
- Couscous
- Dijon mustard
- Farro
- Hot sauce
- Ketchup
- Nuts and seeds
- Olive oil
- Pasta, gluten-free or whole wheat
- Polenta
- Quinoa (also available frozen)
- Reduced-sodium soy sauce or gluten-free tamari
- Rice and soba noodles
- Rice, brown or forbidden (also available frozen)
- Salsa
- Sriracha
- Taco shells
- Tahini
- Tomato sauce
- Tortellini
- Tortillas, corn and flour

Make Your Bowls

Start with your base

I start with about ¾ cup cooked grains, but you can also go low-carb and use a veggie rice such as cauliflower rice, carrot rice, shredded Brussels sprouts, or broccoli rice. For extra flavor, I like to cook my grains in chicken or vegetable broth. Here are some of my favorite bowl bases:

- Barley
- Cauliflower, carrot, or broccoli rice
- Couscous
- Farro
- Oatmeal (for breakfast bowls)
- Orzo
- Quinoa
- Sautéed shredded Brussels sprouts
- Soba, buckwheat, or rice noodles
- Spiralized zucchini
- White, brown, or black rice
- Wild rice

Pick a protein

Protein is usually the star of the bowl, so use top-quality ingredients. For cooked protein, a good rule of thumb is 4 to 6 ounces per serving. Choose one of the following:

- Canned chickpeas
- Cooked chicken or turkey sausage
- Cooked salmon
- Flaked fish
- Grilled chicken breast
- Grilled halloumi or feta cheese
- Hard-boiled, soft-boiled, or fried eggs
- Leftover chicken from a rotisserie chicken
- Lox or smoked salmon
- Marinated tofu
- Sautéed ground beef, turkey, or chicken
- Seared steak
- Shredded cooked pork
- Steamed shrimp

Add your vegetables

Add just enough vegetables to your bowl to cover roughly half to three-quarters of the grains, leaving enough room for your protein. Use whatever's in season or comes in your CSA. Here are some of my favorites:

- Blanched green beans
- Charred eggplant
- Chopped cucumbers
- Diced red onions
- Grilled corn
- Grilled or roasted asparagus, zucchini, or bell peppers
- Halved cherry tomatoes
- Pickled onions
- Pico de gallo
- Roasted cauliflower, Brussels sprouts, or broccoli
- Roasted root vegetables
- Roasted winter squashes
- Sautéed spinach, kale, or bok choy
- Shredded cabbage, carrots, or broccoli
- Shredded lettuce or baby greens
- Sliced avocado

Next, add a dressing or sauce

The sauce usually inspires the theme for the bowl and adds a blast of flavor to tie all the ingredients together. Want to go Greek? Tzatziki is a must. Mexican? Add some pico de gallo. Choose one of the following, or create your own sauce!

- Chimichurri (see page 101)
- Fresh lemon or lime wedges, for squeezing
- Store-bought or homemade hummus (see page 157)
- Store-bought or homemade pesto (see Spinach Arugula Pesto, page 101)
- Jarred harissa
- Jarred salsa or homemade pico de gallo (see page 101)
- Olive tapenade
- Sour cream
- Spicy Peanut-Hoisin Sauce (see page 101)
- Sriracha
- Tahini
- Tzatziki (see page 256)
- White sauce (see page 69)

Finally, add some crunchy bits or fresh herbs

Texture is optional but keeps it interesting. Raw or toasted seeds or nuts are delish, or add some roasted chickpeas or legumes. Fresh herbs bring in a little brightness at the end and tie the whole dish together.

Here are a few ideas to get you started:

Brown rice +
sautéed pepper
and onions +
leftover roasted
chicken +
black beans +
guacamole +
pico de gallo

Farro +
chickpeas +
avocado +
cucumbers +
cherry tomatoes +
tzatziki +
feta cheese +
dill

Quinoa +
roasted sliced
portobello
mushrooms +
air-fried tofu +
tahini dressing

Couscous +
grilled chicken +
grilled zucchini
and bell
peppers +
pesto

Sauces

Spinach Arugula Pesto

SERVES 4

½ cup packed fresh basil leaves

½ cup packed baby spinach and arugula mix

1 garlic clove

¼ cup grated Parmesan cheese

¼ teaspoon kosher salt

Freshly ground black pepper

3 tablespoons extra-virgin olive oil

In a food processor, pulse the basil, spinach and arugula mix, garlic, Parmesan, salt, and pepper to taste until smooth. Slowly add the olive oil while pulsing. Refrigerate for up to 4 days.

Per Serving (2 tablespoons) • Calories 119
Fat 12 g • Saturated Fat 2.5 g • Cholesterol 6 mg
Carbohydrate 0.5 g • Fiber 0 g • Protein 3 g
Sugars 0 g • Sodium 169 mg

Spicy Peanut-Hoisin Sauce

SERVES 4

2½ tablespoons smooth peanut butter or nut or seed butter of your choice

1 tablespoon reduced-sodium soy sauce* or gluten-free tamari

1 tablespoon hoisin sauce*

1 tablespoon Sriracha sauce

1 teaspoon toasted sesame oil

½ teaspoon grated fresh ginger

2 tablespoons warm water

*Read the label to be sure this product is gluten-free.

Mix all the ingredients in a small bowl and refrigerate until ready to use. Refrigerate for up to 4 days.

Per Serving (2 tablespoons) • Calories 85
Fat 6.5 g • Saturated Fat 1 g • Cholesterol 0 mg
Carbohydrate 5 g • Fiber 1 g • Protein 3 g
Sugars 3 g • Sodium 312 mg

Chimichurri

SERVES 4

2 tablespoons finely chopped red onion

2 tablespoons apple cider vinegar

¼ teaspoon kosher salt

2 tablespoons extra-virgin olive oil

3 tablespoons finely chopped fresh cilantro

2 tablespoons finely chopped fresh parsley

1 garlic clove, minced

1 tablespoon water

⅛ teaspoon freshly ground black pepper

⅛ teaspoon crushed red pepper flakes, or more to taste

Combine the onion, vinegar, salt, and olive oil in a small bowl and let it sit for about 5 minutes. Add the remaining ingredients and mix. Refrigerate for up to 4 days.

Per Serving (2 tablespoons) • Calories 65
Fat 7 g • Saturated Fat 1 g • Cholesterol 0 mg
Carbohydrate 1 g • Fiber 0 g • Protein 0 g
Sugars 0 g • Sodium 72 mg

Pico de Gallo

SERVES 4

1 cup chopped tomatoes

⅓ cup chopped onion

¼ cup chopped fresh cilantro

Juice of ½ lime

Pinch of kosher salt

Freshly ground black pepper

Combine all the ingredients in a small bowl. Refrigerate for up to 4 days.

Per Serving (⅓ cup) • Calories 16 • Fat 0 g
Saturated Fat 0 g • Cholesterol 0 mg
Carbohydrate 4 g • Fiber 1 g • Protein 0.5 g
Sugars 2 g • Sodium 21 mg

Juicy Italian Chicken Meatballs

SERVES 4

MEATBALLS

Olive oil spray

1 pound ground chicken

2/3 cup freshly grated Pecorino Romano cheese

1/2 cup (3.5 ounces) packed frozen riced cauliflower, thawed

1/4 cup chopped fresh parsley

1 large egg

1 tablespoon tomato paste

2 garlic cloves, minced

1/2 teaspoon kosher salt

2 medium zucchini, for serving

Fresh basil, for garnish

SAUCE

1 teaspoon olive oil

3 garlic cloves, crushed with the side of a knife

1 (28-ounce) can crushed tomatoes with basil (I like Tuttorosso)

1/4 teaspoon kosher salt

1 bay leaf

Crushed red pepper flakes (optional)

FRIDGE: UP TO 5 DAYS

FREEZER: UP TO 3 MONTHS

Turkey's in timeout! I like to use ground chicken for lean, juicy meatballs. I also skip the bread crumbs to go grain-free. Instead, I add lots of frozen riced cauliflower and Pecorino Romano cheese to the mix, which makes them so tender. Trust me, you won't miss the bread crumbs.

Make the meatballs: Adjust an oven rack to the second highest position and preheat the broiler to high. Spray a large baking sheet with oil.

In a medium bowl, combine the ground chicken, Pecorino, cauliflower, parsley, egg, tomato paste, garlic, and salt. Mix with wet hands, then gently form into 12 meatballs, a scant 1/4 cup each, and transfer to the baking sheet. Broil the meatballs until the tops are golden, 8 to 10 minutes.

Make the sauce: In a large pot, heat the oil over medium heat. Add the garlic and cook until golden. Add the crushed tomatoes, salt, bay leaf, and pepper flakes (if using) and bring to a boil. Lower the heat and simmer, covered, until the flavors begin to meld, about 5 minutes.

When the meatballs are done, gently place them into the sauce and cover. Reduce the heat to low and cook until the meatballs are tender and cooked through, about 10 minutes more. Discard the bay leaf.

SERVE NOW: Spiralize the zucchini and place in a medium bowl. Microwave for 2 to 3 minutes, until tender. Serve with the meatballs and sauce, topped with fresh basil.

MEAL PREP: Spiralize the zucchini and divide the raw zucchini among 4 airtight containers. Top each with 3 meatballs, sauce, and fresh basil. To serve, heat in the microwave for 2 to 3 minutes (the zucchini will cook).

SKINNY SCOOP Avoid using ground chicken made from all breast meat, which would make the meatballs too dry. Also, you can make a double batch and freeze the rest!

Per Serving (3 meatballs + 3/4 cup sauce) ● Calories 345 ● Fat 16.5 g
Saturated Fat 6 g ● Cholesterol 159 mg ● Carbohydrate 21 g
Fiber 5.5 g ● Protein 34 g ● Sugars 11 g ● Sodium 993 mg

Chicken Larb Bowls

Q GF DF

SERVES 4

Olive oil spray

1 pound 93% lean ground chicken

1 small shallot, chopped

3 tablespoons soy sauce* or
gluten-free tamari

3 tablespoons fresh lime juice

1 tablespoon *sambal oelek*, plus
more for serving

¼ cup chopped fresh cilantro

¼ cup minced fresh mint leaves

2 scallions, thinly sliced

3 cups cooked brown rice, for serving

1 large English cucumber, peeled and
sliced, for serving

1 lime, cut into wedges, for serving

*Read the label to be sure this
product is gluten-free.

FRIDGE: UP TO 5 DAYS

Larb is a spicy minced meat salad that's popular throughout Laos and Thailand. The first time I tried this dish it was a wonderful flavor explosion—citrusy, herby, and a little spicy! Larb is typically served in lettuce wraps, but to make this dish more substantial, I serve it over brown rice. You can make this with any protein, such as ground pork, shrimp, or even lamb. Top it with a drizzle of *sambal oelek* (a Southeast Asian hot chile paste) for extra kick.

Heat a large skillet over high heat. When hot, spray with the oil. Brown the ground chicken, using a wooden spoon to break it into small pieces, until no longer pink, 5 to 6 minutes. Add the shallot and cook until softened, 2 to 3 minutes.

Add the soy sauce, lime juice, and *sambal oelek* and cook for about 1 minute to meld the flavors. Remove from the heat, stir in the cilantro and mint, and top with the scallions.

Divide the rice among 4 bowls or airtight containers and top each with the larb, cucumber, and a lime wedge.

Per Serving (1 bowl) ● Calories 358 ● Fat 10.5 g ● Saturated Fat 3 g
Cholesterol 98 mg ● Carbohydrate 42 g ● Fiber 4.5 g ● Protein 25 g
Sugars 2 g ● Sodium 826 mg

Slow Cooker Chicken Enchilada Rice Bowls

SERVES 4

CHICKEN

1½ pounds boneless, skinless chicken breasts

1 teaspoon kosher salt

1 teaspoon ground cumin

1 (8-ounce) can tomato sauce

1 garlic clove, minced

½ tablespoon canned chipotle peppers in adobo sauce

⅛ teaspoon chipotle chile powder

¾ cup shredded pepper Jack or cheddar cheese*

BOWLS

3 cups cooked brown rice, heated

1 medium (5-ounce) avocado, sliced

OPTIONAL TOPPINGS

Chopped fresh cilantro, sliced fresh jalapeño peppers, chopped scallions, sour cream or Greek yogurt

* Read the label to be sure this product is gluten-free.

FRIDGE: UP TO 4 DAYS

FREEZER: UP TO 3 MONTHS

Meal prepping is best when it doesn't require *too* much effort because, really, who wants to spend the whole weekend cooking? Even as someone who loves to cook, I could easily come up with a list of other ways to waste my time (cute puppy or hilarious baby videos, anyone?). That's where these easy enchilada bowls come in. They're kind of like burrito bowls, only with enchilada sauce and melted cheese on top. Yum! Throwing everything into the slow cooker frees up your whole day.

Prepare the chicken: Season the chicken with ½ teaspoon salt and ½ teaspoon cumin. Place in the slow cooker. In a medium bowl, combine the tomato sauce with the remaining salt and cumin, the garlic, chipotle peppers, and chile powder and mix well. Pour over the chicken. Cover and cook on low for about 4 hours.

When cooked, remove the chicken, shred with two forks, and return to the slow cooker. If eating right away, add the cheese, cover, and cook on high until the sauce is hot and the cheese melts, about 20 minutes.

SERVE NOW: Divide the rice among 4 bowls, and top each one with 1 cup chicken and cheese, one-fourth of the avocado, and other toppings, if using.

MEAL PREP: Skip adding the cheese to the chicken in the slow cooker. Divide the chicken and rice among 4 airtight containers, add the cheese on top (it will melt once you reheat), and store. Place the avocado and optional toppings in a separate container. To reheat, microwave in 30-second increments until hot. Add the avocado and toppings and serve.

SKINNY SCOOP For variations, add 1 cup rinsed and drained canned black beans* or 1 cup frozen corn with the chicken.

Per Serving (1 bowl) ● Calories 520 ● Fat 18.5 g ● Saturated Fat 6.5 g
Cholesterol 131 mg ● Carbohydrate 41 g ● Fiber 6 g ● Protein 46 g
Sugars 3 g ● Sodium 921 mg

Greek Chicken Pilaf Bowls

GF

SERVES 4

Greek Lemon Marinade (page 194)

1½ pounds boneless, skinless chicken breasts, diced into ¾-inch pieces

Olive oil spray

1 pint cherry or grape tomatoes, halved

1 medium zucchini, cut into bite-size pieces

1 small orange bell pepper, cut into 1-inch pieces

1 small red onion, diced

1 tablespoon extra-virgin olive oil

1 teaspoon dried oregano

½ teaspoon kosher salt

½ teaspoon sweet paprika

Freshly ground black pepper

½ cup crumbled feta cheese

2 teaspoons unsalted butter

¼ cup (¾ ounce) whole wheat angel hair spaghetti, broken into small pieces*

1 cup uncooked instant brown rice (such as Uncle Ben's)

2 cups low-sodium chicken broth

1 medium lemon, quartered (optional)

*Use brown rice pasta to make this gluten-free.

> FRIDGE: UP TO 4 DAYS

In my family home growing up, the only foods we ate in bowls were soup, cereal, and ice cream. Today, however, I really love to eat everything in a big bowl! These Greek-inspired bowls start with a healthy brown rice pilaf, layered with roasted colorful vegetables and marinated chicken. Feta cheese crumbled on top really makes the dish over-the-top delicious, but if you're dairy-free, you can skip the cheese.

In a small bowl, prepare the marinade according to the recipe instructions on page 194.

Place the chicken in a zip-top plastic bag and add the marinade to the bag. Allow to marinate for at least 30 minutes or up to overnight in the refrigerator.

Preheat the oven to 450°F. Spray a large sheet pan with oil.

Place the marinated chicken on one side of the pan and the tomatoes, zucchini, bell pepper, and onion on the other side. Discard any remaining marinade. Drizzle the vegetables with the olive oil and season with the oregano, salt, paprika, and black pepper to taste, and toss to combine.

Roast for 18 to 20 minutes, until the veggies are charred and the chicken is cooked through. Add the feta on top. Set aside.

Prepare the rice: Melt the butter in a deep skillet with a fitted lid over medium heat. When the butter is melted, add the broken spaghetti and the rice. Cook, stirring constantly, for 2 to 3 minutes, until slightly toasted. Add the chicken broth and bring to a boil. Reduce the heat to a simmer. Cover and cook for 10 to 12 minutes, until the rice is tender and the broth is absorbed. Remove from the heat and let sit for 5 minutes, then fluff with a fork.

SERVE NOW: Divide the rice pilaf among 4 bowls (¾ cup each) and top with the roasted veggies, chicken, and feta cheese. Serve with lemon (if using).

MEAL PREP: Divide the rice pilaf among 4 meal prep containers (¾ cup each), top with the roasted veggies, chicken, and feta cheese, then add a lemon wedge (if using) to each container (for serving later) and refrigerate.

Per Serving (1 bowl) ● Calories 551 ● Fat 16.5 g ● Saturated Fat 5.5 g
Cholesterol 131 mg ● Carbohydrate 54 g ● Fiber 5.5 g ● Protein 47 g
Sugars 6 g ● Sodium 662 mg

Chili-Lime Chicken and Black Bean Cauli-Bowls

(Q) (GF) (DF) (FF)

SERVES 4

CHICKEN

1½ pounds boneless, skinless chicken thighs (about 4 large thighs), fat trimmed

1½ teaspoons chili-lime seasoning salt (I like Tajín Clásico)

½ teaspoon garlic powder

¼ teaspoon smoked paprika

½ teaspoon ground cumin

1 teaspoon olive oil

½ teaspoon kosher salt

½ teaspoon dried oregano

Olive oil spray

BEANS

1 teaspoon olive oil

½ cup minced poblano pepper

⅓ cup minced onion

¼ cup chopped fresh cilantro

2 garlic cloves, minced

1 (15-ounce) can low-sodium black beans,* undrained

¼ cup canned tomato sauce

½ teaspoon kosher salt

BOWLS

3 cups frozen cauliflower rice, prepared as directed

2 teaspoons fresh lime juice

¼ teaspoon kosher salt

¼ cup chopped fresh cilantro

Lime wedges, for serving

1 cup halved cherry tomatoes, for serving

4 ounces (from 1 small) Hass avocado, for serving

*Read the label to be sure this product is gluten-free.

While testing this recipe I devoured it in minutes—it was THAT good! The chicken is seasoned with a chili-lime spice blend that gives it so much flavor. And the quick black beans, cooked with poblano peppers, onions, and cilantro, are sure to be my new favorite way to whip up beans. I initially debated using cauliflower rice in this recipe, but after tossing it with the lime juice, cilantro, and beans, I almost forgot it was cauliflower! I like to use chicken thighs for this, which are much juicier than chicken breasts, but if you prefer breasts those can be used instead.

Prepare the chicken: Season the chicken with the chili-lime seasoning, garlic powder, paprika, cumin, oil, salt, and oregano. Set aside.

Prepare the beans: Heat the oil in a medium skillet over medium heat. Add the poblano pepper, onion, cilantro, and garlic and cook until soft, about 3 minutes. Add the beans (including the liquid), tomato sauce, 2 tablespoons water, and salt. Cover and cook over medium-low heat to let the flavors meld, about 5 minutes. Set aside.

Heat a large nonstick griddle or skillet over medium-high heat and spray with oil. When hot, add the chicken and cook until the bottom is completely browned before flipping, about 5 minutes. Cook on the other side until browned, 4 to 5 minutes. Reduce the heat to low and let the chicken continue cooking, 12 to 14 minutes, until cooked through in the thickest parts. Set aside on a cutting board and tent with foil for 5 to 10 minutes, then slice the chicken into thin strips.

Combine the cauliflower with the lime juice, salt, and cilantro.

SERVE NOW: Divide the cauliflower rice among 4 bowls (¾ cup each) and add ½ cup black beans and chicken. Serve with the lime wedges, tomatoes, and sliced avocado. Squeeze lime over everything before eating.

MEAL PREP: Divide the cauliflower rice among 4 meal prep containers (¾ cup each) and add ½ cup black beans and one-fourth of the chicken. Keep the lime wedges, tomatoes, and avocado separate from the items to be reheated. Squeeze lime juice over everything before eating.

SKINNY SCOOP Tajín is a chili-lime seasoning salt available in most supermarkets. It's also great sprinkled over fresh grilled corn, guacamole, mango, edamame, or anywhere you want a little zing. It's a must-have for your spice cabinet!

Per Serving (1 bowl) ● Calories 414 ● Fat 13.5 g ● Saturated Fat 2.5 g Cholesterol 162 mg ● Carbohydrate 30 g ● Fiber 12.5 g ● Protein 42 g Sugars 5 g ● Sodium 1,001 mg

Sheet Pan Mediterranean Chicken and Veggies

GF

SERVES 4

Olive oil spray

8 boneless, skinless chicken thighs (about 2 pounds total), fat trimmed

4 cups cauliflower florets

1 large (10-ounce) zucchini, diced

1 large red onion, cut into 8 wedges

1 (14-ounce) can artichoke hearts, drained

1 lemon with 1 tablespoon grated lemon zest

2 tablespoons extra-virgin olive oil

1½ teaspoons kosher salt

1 teaspoon garlic powder

1½ tablespoons fresh oregano

Freshly ground black pepper

½ teaspoon sweet paprika

1 cup halved grape tomatoes

¼ cup pitted and halved Kalamata olives

2 ounces feta cheese, crumbled, for serving

FRIDGE: UP TO 4 DAYS

There's nothing easier than throwing ingredients onto a pan and letting the oven do the work. Here, chicken and vegetables are infused with lemon, olives, and herbs, then topped with feta cheese—so simple and so, so good! Plus, you'll have a complete meal ready in less than an hour.

Position two oven racks in the center and bottom third of your oven. Preheat the oven to 450°F. Spray two large rimmed baking sheets generously with olive oil.

In a large bowl, combine the chicken, cauliflower, zucchini, red onion, artichoke hearts, juice from ½ lemon, olive oil, 1¼ teaspoons salt, garlic powder, oregano, and black pepper to taste and toss well, using your hands to evenly coat.

Spread out in a single layer onto the prepared baking sheets. Sprinkle the paprika over both sides of the chicken. Roast until the bottom of the vegetables are golden, about 20 minutes.

Remove the pans from the oven, turn the vegetables and chicken over, and add the tomatoes and olives. Rotate the pans top and bottom and cook for about 10 minutes more, or until the vegetables are tender and the chicken is cooked through in the center. Squeeze the remaining ½ lemon over everything and add the remaining ¼ teaspoon salt.

Slice the chicken. Divide among 4 bowls or meal prep containers with the vegetables and top with the feta cheese and lemon zest.

Per Serving (2 thighs + 1½ cups veggies) • Calories 568 • Fat 29 g Saturated Fat 7 g • Cholesterol 228 mg • Carbohydrate 28 g Fiber 13.5 g • Protein 53 g • Sugars 9 g • Sodium 937 mg

Stuffed Chicken Parmesan and Asparagus

(Q) (GF) (FF)

SERVES 4

Olive oil spray

4 boneless, skinless chicken breasts (8 ounces each)

1 teaspoon kosher salt

Freshly ground black pepper

1½ cups (6 ounces) shredded whole-milk mozzarella cheese*

1 large egg

½ cup Italian seasoned bread crumbs, whole wheat or gluten-free

2 tablespoons grated Parmesan cheese

1 bunch (about 1 pound) thin asparagus, ends trimmed, halved lengthwise

1 cup Basil Pomodoro Sauce (page 294) or store-bought marinara sauce

Chopped fresh basil, for garnish

*Read the label to be sure this product is gluten-free.

FRIDGE: UP TO 4 DAYS

FREEZER: UP TO 3 MONTHS. THAW OVERNIGHT IN THE REFRIGERATOR BEFORE REHEATING.

What's better than chicken Parmesan? Chicken Parmesan stuffed with cheese! This dish is seriously decadent—the chicken comes out so juicy, and oozing with cheese in the center. Baking the chicken takes away the stress, mess, and extra fat and calories from frying. Roast some asparagus while you cook the chicken, and the whole meal will be ready at the same time.

Preheat the oven to 400°F. Line 1 large sheet pan with foil and spray with olive oil.

Season the chicken with ½ teaspoon salt and pepper to taste. Pound the thicker end of the chicken slightly to make both sides even. Cut a pocket into the side of each breast while leaving the ends intact. Fill each piece with ¼ cup mozzarella. Use 1 to 2 toothpicks on each breast to keep the pockets closed.

In a small bowl, beat the egg. In a larger shallow bowl, combine the bread crumbs and Parmesan. Working piece by piece, dip the chicken in the egg, then in the bread crumb mixture, then place to one side of the prepared sheet pan. When finished, spray both sides of the chicken with oil.

Place the asparagus on the other side of the sheet pan. Spritz with olive oil and season with the remaining ½ teaspoon salt and black pepper to taste.

Bake for about 20 minutes, tossing the vegetables and flipping the chicken halfway through, until the chicken is golden and cooked through in the center.

SERVE NOW: Remove the chicken from the oven and top each piece with ¼ cup marinara sauce and 2 tablespoons of the remaining mozzarella. Return to the oven and bake until the mozzarella is melted, 2 to 3 minutes. Remove the toothpicks and top the chicken with basil. Serve with the asparagus on the side.

MEAL PREP: Bake the chicken and asparagus as directed without the sauce and mozzarella topping. Transfer the cooked asparagus and chicken to 4 meal prep containers and let cool. Top with ¼ cup marinara and 2 tablespoons mozzarella and store. Reheat in the microwave for 2 to 3 minutes.

Per Serving (1 piece chicken + 4 ounces asparagus) ● Calories 501
Fat 18.5 g ● Saturated Fat 8 g ● Cholesterol 227 mg ● Carbohydrate 18 g
Fiber 4.5 g ● Protein 66 g ● Sugars 6 g ● Sodium 1,234 mg

Pesto Chicken and Roasted Veggie Farro Bowls

SERVES 4

1 pound (2) boneless, skinless chicken breasts, cut in half lengthwise

Italian Marinade (page 194)

½ cup Spinach Arugula Pesto (page 101)

Olive oil spray

4 cups broccoli florets

2 red bell peppers, cut into 1-inch pieces

1 large medium onion, quartered and separated

½ teaspoon kosher salt

3 cups cooked farro, heated

FRIDGE: UP TO 4 DAYS

These hearty chicken grain bowls make perfect packable lunches (or ready-to-eat dinners) for several days—just grab a container on your way out the door in the morning. The chicken is so flavorful, marinated in my go-to homemade Italian marinade (see page 194). I usually cook it right in my air fryer, but you can also make it in a skillet or grill pan. The pesto sauce is packed with healthy ingredients like spinach, arugula, and basil, making a flavor-packed sauce that ties everything together.

Marinate the chicken in the marinade for at least 4 hours or up to overnight. Cook in the air fryer or grill pan according to the directions on page 193, then slice.

Prepare the pesto according to the directions on page 101.

Preheat the oven to 400°F. Spray a large sheet pan with oil.

Place the broccoli, bell peppers, and onion on the prepared pan. Generously spray with olive oil and season with salt. Roast for about 20 minutes, turning halfway through.

SERVE NOW: Toss the farro with half of the pesto sauce and transfer to 4 bowls (¾ cup farro each). Top each bowl with ¾ cup veggies, 1 piece of chicken, and 1 tablespoon of the remaining pesto.

MEAL PREP: Toss the farro with half of the pesto sauce and transfer to 4 meal prep containers (¾ cup farro each). Top each with ¾ cup veggies and 1 piece of chicken. Pack the remaining pesto in 4 small containers (1 tablespoon pesto each). Reheat in the microwave without the pesto, then add on top just before eating.

Per Serving (1 bowl) ● Calories 496 ● Fat 18 g ● Saturated Fat 3.5 g Cholesterol 77 mg ● Carbohydrate 49 g ● Fiber 9 g ● Protein 38 g Sugars 5 g ● Sodium 544 mg

Banh Mi Turkey Meatball Rice Bowls

GF DF FF

SERVES 4

PICKLED VEGETABLES

1 cup shredded carrots

2 radishes, cut into matchsticks

6 tablespoons distilled white vinegar

3 tablespoons sugar

¼ teaspoon kosher salt

MEATBALLS

Olive oil spray

1 pound 93% lean ground turkey

3 garlic cloves, finely minced

1 teaspoon minced fresh ginger

2 tablespoons reduced-sodium soy sauce* or gluten-free tamari

¼ cup panko bread crumbs, regular or gluten-free

1 large egg, lightly beaten

3 scallions, chopped, white and green parts separated

SAUCE

2½ tablespoons reduced-sodium soy sauce* or gluten-free tamari

1½ tablespoons seasoned rice vinegar

1 tablespoon hoisin sauce

½ tablespoon brown sugar

1 teaspoon toasted sesame oil

1 teaspoon minced fresh ginger

1 small garlic clove, minced

BOWLS

3 cups cooked brown rice

1 cup shredded red cabbage

1 cup thinly sliced English cucumbers

1 jalapeño pepper, sliced

¼ cup fresh cilantro leaves

Sriracha sauce, for serving (optional)

*Read the label to be sure this product is gluten-free.

A banh mi is a Vietnamese sandwich made with a baguette, vegetables, and various types of protein, but I think it's even better turned into a bowl! While these banh mi meatball bowls are not made in a traditional preparation, my family devours them. The pickled veggies and herbs make these bowls super fresh and colorful, and (meal-prep bonus!) all the ingredients can be prepared in advance without a lot of effort.

Prepare the pickled vegetables: In a small bowl, toss the carrots and radishes with the vinegar, sugar, and salt and place in the refrigerator.

Prepare the meatballs: Position an oven rack in the center of the oven and preheat to 400°F. Spray a large sheet pan with oil.

In a large bowl, combine the ground turkey, garlic, ginger, soy sauce, bread crumbs, egg, and the white parts of the scallions. Mix thoroughly. Using your hands, form into 16 meatballs, about 1.25 ounces each. Place the meatballs evenly spaced on the prepared sheet pan. Bake for about 18 minutes, or until cooked through.

Prepare the sauce: In a medium pot, combine all the sauce ingredients, then add the cooked meatballs, tossing to coat. Bring to a boil over medium heat and cook for about 1 minute, to thicken the sauce slightly.

Drain the pickled veggies.

SERVE NOW: To assemble the bowls, place ¾ cup rice in each bowl and top with 4 meatballs and sauce. Add ¼ cup shredded cabbage, one-fourth of the pickled veggies, and ¼ cup cucumber, and top with the sliced jalapeños, cilantro, and green parts of the scallions. Drizzle with Sriracha (if using).

MEAL PREP: Divide the rice and meatballs among 4 meal prep containers, keeping the pickled veggies, sliced jalapeños, and cilantro in separate small containers or storage bags. To serve, reheat the rice and meatballs in the microwave for 2 to 3 minutes, then assemble the bowls.

Per Serving (1 bowl) ● Calories 435 ● Fat 13.5 g ● Saturated Fat 3.5 g ● Cholesterol 131 mg ● Carbohydrate 51 g ● Fiber 5 g ● Protein 29 g ● Sugars 8 g ● Sodium 894 mg

Thai Shrimp Cakes with Cucumber Salad

(Q) (GF) (DF)

SERVES 4

SHRIMP CAKES

1 pound peeled and deveined shrimp

2 teaspoons Thai red curry paste

Juice of ½ lime

1 garlic clove, minced

2 tablespoons chopped scallion

¾ teaspoon grated fresh ginger

1 teaspoon reduced-sodium soy sauce* or gluten-free tamari

Cooking spray

CUCUMBER SALAD

2 large cucumbers, peeled, halved lengthwise, seeded, and sliced crosswise ¼ inch thick

⅓ cup thinly sliced red onion

2 tablespoons fresh lime juice

½ tablespoon toasted sesame oil

¼ teaspoon kosher salt

Chopped fresh cilantro

¼ cup chopped roasted peanuts

3 cups cooked brown basmati rice, for serving

*Read the label to be sure this product is gluten-free.

FRIDGE: UP TO 4 DAYS

Thai red curry paste adds so much flavor to these easy-to-make shrimp cakes. They come out crispy on the outside and so juicy on the inside. If you're going the lower-carb route, you can swap the brown rice for cauliflower (or broccoli) rice.

Make the shrimp cakes: Pat the shrimp well with paper towels to dry. In the bowl of a food processor, combine the shrimp, curry paste, lime juice, garlic, scallion, ginger, and soy sauce. Pulse 10 to 12 times, until the shrimp is minced and the mixture is evenly combined.

Using wet hands to prevent the shrimp mixture from sticking to them, create 4 patties, about 4 ounces each, flattened so they cook evenly.

Heat a large skillet or griddle over medium heat. Spray with oil and cook the shrimp patties until cooked through in the center, 4 to 5 minutes on each side.

Make the salad: In a medium bowl, combine the cucumbers, onion, lime juice, sesame oil, and salt. Top with cilantro and peanuts.

SERVE NOW: Divide the rice, shrimp cakes, and salad among 4 plates.

MEAL PREP: Transfer the shrimp and rice to 4 meal prep containers, with the salad in 4 separate containers. To serve, reheat the shrimp and rice, and top with the salad.

Per Serving (1 cake + ¾ cup rice + ¾ cup salad) ● Calories 364
Fat 8.5 g ● Saturated Fat 1.5 g ● Cholesterol 136 mg ● Carbohydrate 43 g
Fiber 5 g ● Protein 28 g ● Sugars 4 g ● Sodium 493 mg

Kofta Meatball Couscous Bowls

Q FF

SERVES 4

MEATBALLS

Cooking spray

1 pound ground chicken

3 tablespoons grated red onion

3 garlic cloves, minced

2 tablespoons chopped fresh parsley

2 tablespoons chopped fresh mint

2 teaspoons ground coriander

1 teaspoon kosher salt

3/4 teaspoon ground cumin

1/4 teaspoon ground cinnamon

1/8 teaspoon cayenne pepper

1/8 teaspoon ground ginger

1/8 teaspoon freshly ground black pepper

COUSCOUS

1 1/2 cups reduced-sodium chicken broth

1 cup uncooked couscous

SALAD

1 medium tomato, finely diced

1 cucumber, peeled, seeded, and diced

1/4 cup diced red onion

2 tablespoons chopped fresh parsley

2 tablespoons chopped mint

1 tablespoon olive oil

Juice of 1/2 lemon

1/4 teaspoon kosher salt

FRIDGE: UP TO 4 DAYS

FREEZER: FREEZE MEATBALLS AND COUSCOUS UP TO 3 MONTHS

Koftas are really flavorful balls of ground meat—usually beef, chicken, lamb, or pork—mixed with spices and/or onions. My neighbor, who's from Armenia, makes them (on skewers) all summer on the grill. Here, I use ground chicken mixed with fresh mint and parsley and turn them into bowls served over couscous alongside a cucumber-tomato salad. I recommend using fattier ground chicken that has a blend of both breast and dark meat for the juiciest meatballs.

Adjust an oven rack to the second highest position. Preheat the oven to 425°F. Spray a large sheet pan with oil.

Make the meatballs: In a large bowl, combine the chicken with the other meatball ingredients and mix until well blended. Form into 12 balls, about 1 1/2 ounces each.

Bake until cooked through, 6 to 7 minutes. Switch the oven to broil and cook until browned, 2 to 3 minutes more.

Make the couscous: In a medium saucepan, bring the broth to a boil. Add the couscous, then cover and remove from the heat. Let stand for 5 minutes, then lightly fluff with a fork.

Make the salad: In a large bowl, mix together all the salad ingredients.

SERVE NOW: Divide the couscous, salad, and meatballs among 4 dishes.

MEAL PREP: Divide the couscous and meatballs among 4 meal prep containers. Place the salad in a separate container and store everything in the fridge. Reheat the couscous and meatballs in the microwave for 2 to 3 minutes, then top with the cold salad and serve.

SKINNY SCOOP To make this a gluten-free meal, swap the couscous for quinoa or brown rice and make sure to use gluten-free broth.

Per Serving (3/4 cup couscous + 1/2 cup salad + 3 meatballs) ● Calories 396 Fat 13.5 g ● Saturated Fat 3 g ● Cholesterol 98 mg ● Carbohydrate 42 g Fiber 4 g ● Protein 28 g ● Sugars 3 g ● Sodium 644 mg

Korean Beef and Rice Bowls

Q **DF** **FF**

SERVES 4

¼ cup reduced-sodium soy sauce

2 teaspoons light brown sugar

1 teaspoon toasted sesame oil

½ teaspoon crushed red pepper flakes

Cooking spray

1 pound 93% lean ground beef

¼ cup chopped yellow onion

2 garlic cloves, crushed

1 teaspoon grated fresh ginger

3 cups cooked brown rice

1 small sliced cucumber, skin on

2 tablespoons *gochujang* sauce

½ tablespoon sesame seeds

2 scallions, sliced

FRIDGE: UP TO 4 DAYS

FREEZER: STORE BEEF AND RICE FOR UP TO 6 MONTHS (THAW OVERNIGHT IN THE FRIDGE BEFORE REHEATING)

When I worked full-time in Manhattan I loved exploring the cuisine of Koreatown when lunching with co-workers. After I quit my job in the city I really missed the Korean food (it's not as readily available here on Long Island), so I started to make my favorite dishes at home. The one essential ingredient you'll need here is *gochujang* sauce. It's a delicious Korean ingredient that has a very distinct spicy and sweet flavor. I use Annie Chun's Gochujang Sauce since it's available in my local supermarket, but you can also buy it online.

Combine the soy sauce, 2 tablespoons water, brown sugar, sesame oil, and pepper flakes in a small bowl.

Heat a large, deep, nonstick skillet over high heat. When the pan is hot, spray with oil. Brown the ground beef, using a wooden spoon to break it into small pieces as it cooks, until cooked through, about 5 minutes.

Add the onion, garlic, and ginger and cook for about 1 minute, until soft.

Pour the sauce over the beef, cover, and simmer on low heat for about 10 minutes to allow the flavors to meld.

SERVE NOW: To assemble the bowls, place ¾ cup rice in each bowl, and top with a scant ⅔ cup beef, cucumber, *gochujang*, sesame seeds, and scallions.

MEAL PREP: Divide the beef and rice into 4 meal prep containers and store the toppings separately. When ready to eat, reheat and top with the cucumber, *gochujang*, sesame seeds, and scallions.

SKINNY SCOOP Using frozen brown rice here is super convenient—you can make your own (see page 23) or you can buy it precooked in many supermarkets, such as Trader Joe's. It takes about 3 minutes to heat up in the microwave.

Per Serving (1 bowl) • Calories 411 • Fat 11.5 g • Saturated Fat 3.5 g
Cholesterol 70 mg • Carbohydrate 48 g • Fiber 4.5 g • Protein 30 g
Sugars 8 g • Sodium 733 mg

Roasted Veggie and Barley Buddha Bowls

SERVES 4

Olive oil spray

4 cups cauliflower florets, cut into bite-size pieces

4 cups broccoli florets, cut into bite-size pieces

6 long skinny carrots, cut crosswise into ¾-inch pieces

1 pound mini rainbow peppers, cut into 1½-inch pieces

Kosher salt

Freshly ground black pepper

2 tablespoons plus 1 teaspoon olive oil

1 cup pearled barley

3 cups low-sodium chicken or vegetable broth

Juice of ½ lemon

2 scallions, white parts only

1 (15-ounce) can chickpeas, drained and rinsed

DRESSING

¼ cup 2%-fat plain Greek yogurt

¼ teaspoon kosher salt

Freshly ground black pepper

Juice of ½ lemon

2 tablespoons thinly sliced scallion greens

10 large fresh basil leaves

2 tablespoons chickpeas (reserved from can)

FRIDGE: UP TO 4 DAYS

Who doesn't love a Buddha bowl? These versatile, healthy, and hearty one-dish meals are packed with colorful vegetables, whole grains, and fresh flavors. Here, chewy, nutty barley pairs beautifully with the sweetness of the roasted veggies. The yogurt dressing and chickpeas provide a boost of creamy flavor and protein to tie it all together.

Preheat the oven to 400°F. Spray two large sheet pans with oil.

Spread the cauliflower and broccoli in an even layer on one pan, then spread the carrots and peppers on the other. Season all the veggies with ¾ teaspoon salt and pepper to taste. Drizzle each pan with 1 tablespoon olive oil and toss the veggies to make sure they are evenly coated.

Roast the broccoli and cauliflower for about 10 minutes, then add the peppers and carrots to the oven. Roast, tossing halfway through, until all the veggies are browned on the edges and crisp-tender, about 20 minutes more.

Meanwhile, combine the barley and broth in a medium pot. Bring to a boil over high heat, then reduce the heat to low to simmer. Cover and cook until the barley has tripled in volume and is soft yet chewy, about 25 minutes. (If the barley is cooked but there is still liquid left, cover the pot and let it sit for 10 minutes.) Add the lemon juice, scallion whites, ¼ teaspoon salt, and pepper to taste and gently mix to combine. Fluff with a fork.

Make the dressing: In a small blender or food processor, combine the yogurt, salt, pepper, lemon juice, scallion greens, basil, and reserved chickpeas. Blend until smooth. Add water, 1 tablespoon at a time, to thin the dressing to a pourable consistency.

SERVE NOW: Divide the barley evenly among 4 bowls (¾ cup each). Top each one with one-fourth of the veggies, one-fourth of the chickpeas, and about 2 tablespoons of the dressing.

MEAL PREP: Let the barley cool, then divide evenly among 4 airtight containers. Top each with one-fourth of the veggies and one-fourth of the chickpeas. Divide the dressing (2 tablespoons each) among 4 small containers.

Per Serving (1 bowl) • Calories 537 • Fat 12.5 g • Saturated Fat 1.5 g
Cholesterol 1 mg • Carbohydrate 92 g • Fiber 22 g • Protein 21 g
Sugars 14 g • Sodium 789 mg

California Roll Bowls

Q GF DF

SERVES 4

3 cups cooked short-grain brown rice

2 tablespoons unseasoned rice vinegar

2 (6-ounce) cans wild lump crabmeat, drained, or imitation crabmeat

1⅓ cups diced cucumber

1 cup chopped red cabbage

Sliced pickled ginger (optional)

4 teaspoons furikake or sesame seeds

4 ounces (from 1 small) Hass avocado, sliced

SOY-WASABI DRESSING

2 tablespoons reduced-sodium soy sauce* or gluten-free tamari

1 teaspoon wasabi (I like the type that comes in a tube)

2½ tablespoons mirin

2 tablespoons unseasoned rice vinegar

½ tablespoon toasted sesame oil

*Read the label to be sure this product is gluten-free.

FRIDGE: UP TO 4 DAYS

These bowls are super easy to whip up when a sushi craving strikes—which for me is several times a week! They're made with canned lump crabmeat, but you can swap it for imitation crab, cooked shrimp, salmon, tuna, or even shelled cooked edamame to make it meatless. For maximum freshness, prep the vegetables and dressing and wait to add the crab and avocado until the day you plan on eating it.

Reheat the rice, then transfer to a mixing bowl, add the rice vinegar, and stir. Let cool.

Make the dressing: In another small bowl, whisk together the soy sauce, wasabi, mirin, rice vinegar, and sesame oil.

SERVE NOW: Place ¾ cup rice in each of 4 bowls and divide the crab, cucumber, cabbage, and ginger (if using) over the rice. Top with the furikake and sliced avocado, and drizzle each with 2 tablespoons dressing.

MEAL PREP: Divide the dressing into 4 airtight dressing containers. Assemble the bowls in 4 airtight containers by adding ¾ cup rice to each and dividing the cucumber, cabbage, and ginger (if using) over the rice. Top with the furikake. When ready to eat, add the crab and 1 ounce sliced avocado to each bowl, and drizzle each with 2 tablespoons dressing.

SKINNY SCOOP You can use frozen brown rice (I like Trader Joe's) or any quick brown rice to make this come together in minutes.

Per Serving (1 bowl) ● Calories 364 ● Fat 9 g ● Saturated Fat 1.5 g Cholesterol 76 mg ● Carbohydrate 46 g ● Fiber 5.5 g ● Protein 22 g Sugars 6 g ● Sodium 717 mg

Roasted Cauliflower Shawarma Lettuce Wraps

SERVES 4

WHITE YOGURT SAUCE (MAKES 1¼ CUPS)

1 cup whole-milk plain yogurt (not Greek)

2 tablespoons mayonnaise

1 tablespoon apple cider vinegar

1 teaspoon fresh lemon juice

½ teaspoon kosher salt

½ teaspoon sugar

⅛ teaspoon freshly ground black pepper

CAULIFLOWER

3 tablespoons extra-virgin olive oil

1 tablespoon fresh lemon juice

3 garlic cloves, crushed through a garlic press

1 teaspoon smoked paprika

1 teaspoon ground cumin

¾ teaspoon ground turmeric

¼ teaspoon ground cinnamon

1¼ teaspoons kosher salt

1 large head cauliflower, cut into 1-inch florets

1 medium white onion, sliced ¼ inch thick

SERVING

16 large Bibb lettuce leaves (from 2 heads)

⅓ cup mild red harissa sauce (I love Mina)

2 cups sliced red cabbage

1 cup fresh cilantro leaves

1 cup fresh mint leaves

FRIDGE: UP TO 4 DAYS

I love this vegetarian take on a classic Turkish street food typically made with meat. While roasted cauliflower is one of my favorite vegetables, it's definitely not Tommy's. However, he completely changed his mind once he tasted this dish. While happily gobbling up a wrap he said, "If you didn't tell me this was cauliflower I would have never known!" Fresh herbs and red cabbage add color, freshness, and texture; the harissa sauce adds the perfect amount of heat; and the tangy, magic, white yogurt sauce tastes good on, well, everything! The cauliflower would also be excellent over brown rice.

Prepare the white sauce: Combine all the ingredients in a medium bowl and whisk until thoroughly combined. Set aside.

Prepare the cauliflower: Preheat the oven to 450°F.

In a large mixing bowl add the olive oil, lemon juice, garlic, paprika, cumin, turmeric, cinnamon, and salt. Whisk to combine.

Add the cauliflower and onion to the bowl and toss to coat.

Spread the cauliflower and onion out on a large rimmed baking sheet. Roast, stirring occasionally and rotating the pan halfway through, until tender and browned on the edges, 20 to 25 minutes.

SERVE NOW: Fill each lettuce leaf with ¼ cup cauliflower, then drizzle each with 1 generous tablespoon white sauce. Top with 1 teaspoon harissa and garnish with sliced red cabbage, cilantro, and mint leaves.

MEAL PREP: Divide the cauliflower, sauces, and toppings into separate containers and store in the refrigerator. To eat, reheat the cauliflower in the microwave for about 1 minute (or enjoy at room temperature) and assemble the wraps.

Per Serving (4 lettuce wraps) ● Calories 290 ● Fat 19 g ● Saturated Fat 3.5 g Cholesterol 11 mg ● Carbohydrate 26 g ● Fiber 8 g ● Protein 9 g Sugars 13 g ● Sodium 720 mg

Smashed Broccoli Pecorino Farro Bowls

SERVES 4

Kosher salt

1½ cups pearled farro

1¼ pounds broccoli florets

2 tablespoons olive oil

4 garlic cloves, crushed with the side of a knife and then roughly chopped

⅛ teaspoon crushed red pepper flakes, plus more for serving, to taste (optional)

¼ cup freshly grated Pecorino Romano cheese, plus more for serving (optional)

FRIDGE: UP TO 4 DAYS

These nutrient-packed veggie-and-grain bowls are a huge hit with my picky family! You can serve them as a meatless main dish, and they also make a great side dish. They're delicious warm or at room temperature, and they're ready in less than 15 minutes! Farro is a nutrient-rich ancient grain that has a soft, chewy texture and a nutty flavor. Rather than following the directions on the package, I treat the farro like pasta and boil it in water, which is easier and tastier!

Bring a large pot of salted water to boil over high heat. Once boiling, add the farro and cook for about 6 minutes, then add the broccoli and cook for about 6 minutes more, until the broccoli and farro are tender and cooked through. Drain in a colander, reserving ¼ cup liquid.

Heat 1 tablespoon olive oil in the pot over medium-high heat. Add the garlic and pepper flakes and cook for about 1 minute, stirring until golden. Add the cooked broccoli and farro, season with ½ teaspoon salt, and cook, stirring frequently, for 1 to 2 minutes more, roughly smashing any large chunks of broccoli with a wooden spoon. Add a little of the reserved liquid if it's too dry. Stir in the remaining olive oil and the Pecorino.

SERVE NOW: Serve warm or at room temperature with more grated cheese and crushed red pepper flakes (if using).

MEAL PREP: Divide among 4 meal prep containers. Reheat in the microwave for 2 to 3 minutes or on the stove with a little water for 3 to 5 minutes.

SKINNY SCOOP Pearled farro takes less time to cook than semi-pearled, which takes less time to cook than whole farro.

Per Serving (1½ cups) ● Calories 395 ● Fat 10.5 g ● Saturated Fat 2 g
Cholesterol 6 mg ● Carbohydrate 63 g ● Fiber 11.5 g ● Protein 17 g
Sugars 3 g ● Sodium 283 mg

Roasted Winter Veggie Quinoa Bowls

V **GF** **DF**

SERVES 4

DRESSING

2 tablespoons fresh lemon juice

2 tablespoons extra-virgin olive oil

1 tablespoon unseasoned rice vinegar

Pinch of kosher salt

BOWLS

Olive oil spray

1 large (12-ounce) sweet potato, peeled and cut into 1/2-inch pieces

4 cups (18 ounces) trimmed and halved Brussels sprouts

3 teaspoons olive oil

Kosher salt

1 (6-ounce) package baby spinach

4 large eggs

2 cups cooked tri-color quinoa

FRIDGE: UP TO 4 DAYS

My favorite way to meal prep when the weather turns cold is to roast a bunch of veggies on two sheet pans, and serve them with whatever grains I happen to have already cooked. These vegetables pair perfectly with cooked quinoa, wilted spinach, and an egg with a runny yolk. Of course, if you want your eggs hard-boiled, that's fine, too. The dressing is a simple lemon vinaigrette, but a drizzle of tahini would also be great.

Make the dressing: Whisk all of the ingredients together and set aside.

Preheat the oven to 425°F. Spray a sheet pan with oil.

Place the sweet potato and Brussels sprouts on the sheet pan and toss with 2 teaspoons olive oil and 1/2 teaspoon salt. Bake for about 40 minutes, turning halfway through, until the vegetables are tender and golden.

Meanwhile, in a large skillet over medium heat, heat the remaining oil and add the spinach. Cover and cook until the spinach wilts, 2 to 3 minutes. Season with 1/8 teaspoon salt.

Bring a small pot of water to a boil over high heat. Add the eggs and cook for about 6 minutes for a perfectly runny yolk, or about 12 minutes for a firm yolk. Run under cold water to stop the eggs from cooking, then peel. Cut the eggs in half.

SERVE NOW: To make the bowls, place 1/2 cup quinoa into each of 4 bowls. Divide the spinach among the bowls, and top each with 3/4 cup roasted vegetables and 1 egg. Serve drizzled with the dressing.

MEAL PREP: Place 1/2 cup quinoa into each of 4 meal prep containers. Divide the spinach among the 4 containers, and top each with 3/4 cup roasted vegetables and 1 egg. Pack the dressing in separate containers. Serve chilled or at room temperature.

Per Serving (1 bowl) ● Calories 431 ● Fat 19 g ● Saturated Fat 3.5 g Cholesterol 186 mg ● Carbohydrate 51 g ● Fiber 11 g ● Protein 17 g Sugars 8 g ● Sodium 391 mg

Smart Snacks

Deviled Eggs
with Lox

Q **GF**

SERVES 4

4 hard-boiled eggs, peeled

¼ cup whipped cream cheese

4 teaspoons chopped fresh chives,
   plus more for garnish

¼ teaspoon kosher salt

Freshly ground black pepper

4 ounces nova lox or smoked salmon

8 slices unpeeled cucumber

2 small tomatoes (such as Campari),
   sliced

8 small red onion rings

FRIDGE: UP TO 4 DAYS

I always keep hard-boiled eggs on hand for a quick snack or breakfast, but when you add lox, cream cheese, tomato, and cucumber slices, basic eggs are transformed into a truly crave-worthy treat. These also make a perfect snack when you need something to hold you over between meals.

Cut the eggs in half and remove the yolks. Place the yolks in a medium bowl and set the whites aside.

Mash the yolks, then add the cream cheese, chives, salt, and pepper to taste. Evenly distribute the mixture among the egg white halves. Top each half with ½ ounce lox, 1 slice cucumber, 1 slice tomato, and 1 slice onion. Poke a toothpick through each half to keep the toppings in place if needed. Garnish with chives and serve.

MEAL PREP: Store the deviled eggs upright in an airtight container in the refrigerator.

Per Serving (2 egg halves + toppings) ● Calories 150 ● Fat 9 g
Saturated Fat 3.5 g ● Cholesterol 225 mg ● Carbohydrate 5 g ● Fiber 1 g
Protein 13 g ● Sugars 3 g ● Sodium 479 mg

Buffalo Chicken–Stuffed Celery Sticks

(Q) (GF)

SERVES 4

2 tablespoons ⅓-less-fat cream cheese

1 tablespoon nonfat Greek yogurt or sour cream

1 tablespoon crumbled blue cheese, plus more for garnish (optional)

3 tablespoons cayenne pepper hot sauce, such as Frank's RedHot, plus more for garnish (optional)

1 (5-ounce) can chicken breast, drained (or leftover chicken breast from Paprika Roasted Whole Chicken, page 248, shredded)

4 large celery stalks, trimmed and cut into 8 (3½-inch-long) pieces

> FRIDGE: UP TO 4 DAYS

These Buffalo chicken celery sticks take celery to a whole new level! Honestly, I'm not a big fan of raw celery as I find it just overpowers whatever I'm eating . . . except when it comes to Buffalo chicken salad. Celery and Buffalo-sauce are a magical combo! If you don't have celery, you can serve this with cucumber or carrot sticks instead. It's also great on crackers.

In a small bowl, stir together the cream cheese, yogurt, blue cheese, and hot sauce until smooth. Mix in the chicken until smooth.

SERVE NOW: Spoon about 1¾ tablespoons chicken mixture into each piece of celery. Drizzle each with a few more drops of hot sauce and sprinkle with more blue cheese (if using).

MEAL PREP: Prep the celery and salad and store in separate containers in the refrigerator. Assemble when ready to serve.

SKINNY SCOOP This would also make a great appetizer. Simply slice a sliver off the bottom of each celery stick to create a flat bottom that will keep the sticks from rolling.

Per Serving (2 pieces) • Calories 92 • Fat 4.5 g • Saturated Fat 2 g
Cholesterol 22 mg • Carbohydrate 2 g • Fiber 0.5 g • Protein 10 g
Sugars 1 g • Sodium 555 mg

California Tuna Salad–Stuffed Cucumbers

Q GF DF

SERVES 4

1 (5-ounce) can chunk light tuna in water, drained

3 tablespoons chopped broccoli florets

2 tablespoons minced carrot

2 tablespoons diced red bell pepper

1 teaspoon grated fresh ginger

2 tablespoons Hellmann's Light mayonnaise

1 teaspoon toasted sesame oil

8 small Persian cucumbers

FRIDGE: UP TO 4 DAYS

I'm not much of a sandwich person; in fact, I rarely buy sliced bread. But I love having tuna salad, egg salad, or chicken salad in my fridge for snacking or a quick lunch. This tuna salad recipe is inspired by a California sushi roll, with hints of sesame and fresh ginger. It's delicious served in a cored Persian cucumber (their skins are so thin, you don't need to bother peeling them) or with Japanese rice crackers. And if you have guests for lunch, you can just double the recipe.

In a medium bowl, combine the tuna, broccoli, carrot, bell pepper, ginger, mayonnaise, and sesame oil.

Cut the cucumbers in half lengthwise and use a small spoon to scoop a well out of the center of each half.

SERVE NOW: Spoon 1 tablespoon tuna salad into each cucumber half and enjoy!

MEAL PREP: Transfer the tuna salad and cucumber halves to separate airtight containers. When ready to serve, assemble the stuffed cucumbers.

Per Serving (4 cucumber halves) ● Calories 116 ● Fat 4 g ● Saturated Fat 0.5 g Cholesterol 13 mg ● Carbohydrate 10 g ● Fiber 4.5 g ● Protein 9 g Sugars 0.5 g ● Sodium 175 mg

Zucchini Chips

V **GF** **DF**

SERVES 2

2 medium (7-ounce) zucchini

½ teaspoon kosher salt

Olive oil spray (I like my Misto or Bertolli)

PANTRY: UP TO 7 DAYS

I'm not going to lie: making these chips is time-consuming, and the yield is very small for the amount of time they take to crisp up in the oven . . . but trust me, they are worth it! They're so much lighter and tastier than regular potato chips. And zucchini is so naturally flavorful, I didn't even add seasoning besides the salt! Baking them on a rack helps the air circulate all around the chips, making them extra crispy. If you don't have a rack, using parchment paper will also work. And when you use a mandoline slicer, all the slices are uniform, so they cook evenly and come out perfectly crunchy.

Adjust two oven racks closest to the center of your oven. Preheat the oven to 225°F. Place two baking racks on two large sheet pans and set aside.

Using a mandoline, slice each zucchini into ⅛-inch slices. Place the slices in a medium bowl and sprinkle with the salt. Gently mix and separate the slices with your hands. Allow to sit for 5 minutes (this helps release moisture), then transfer the slices to a kitchen towel or paper towel in a single layer. Lay another towel (or paper towels) on top and gently press to remove excess moisture.

Lightly spritz the top of the zucchini with olive oil spray, then transfer to the sheet pans, oil side down, in an even layer without overlapping. Lightly spritz the other side of the zucchini with olive oil spray so they are evenly coated.

Place the pans in the oven and bake for about 1 hour. Remove the pans from the oven. Flip the slices over, then place the pans back in the oven on opposite racks, and bake for 45 to 55 minutes, until crisp and golden.

Remove the chips from the oven and let them cool on wire racks. Store in an airtight container.

Per Serving (generous ½ cup) ● Calories 34 ● Fat 0.5 g ● Saturated Fat 0 g Cholesterol 0 mg ● Carbohydrate 6 g ● Fiber 2 g ● Protein 2 g Sugars 5 g ● Sodium 296 mg

BBQ Roasted Green Peas

(V) (GF) (DF)

SERVES 4

Olive oil spray

1 (16-ounce) package frozen green peas (not petite), thawed

1 tablespoon onion powder

1 tablespoon garlic powder

1 teaspoon smoked paprika

1½ teaspoons kosher salt

½ teaspoon mustard powder

1 tablespoon packed brown sugar

⅛ teaspoon cayenne pepper

1 tablespoon olive oil

PANTRY: UP TO 1 WEEK

True story, I hate peas. Or should I say, I strongly dislike them—in fact, I never cook them unless they are mixed in a recipe with so many other ingredients that you can't really taste them. Surprisingly though, I'm completely addicted to these BBQ roasted peas! They're an ideal crunchy snack, but they would also make a great topper for salads or soups.

Preheat the oven to 350°F. Adjust two oven racks to the second position from the top and the second position from the bottom. Spray two large sheet pans with oil.

Lay the thawed peas out on a kitchen towel or paper towels. Top with another towel and gently roll the peas between the towels to remove excess moisture.

In a small bowl, combine the onion powder, garlic powder, paprika, salt, mustard powder, brown sugar, and cayenne. Set aside.

Lay the peas out in an even layer on the prepared sheet pans and spritz all over with oil spray. Cook for about 20 minutes to partially roast them, then remove from the oven.

Drizzle the peas with the olive oil and gently toss to evenly coat. Sprinkle the seasoning mix over the top and toss again to evenly coat the peas.

Place the sheet pans back in the oven, rotating them on the racks for even cooking. Roast until crispy and golden, 45 to 50 minutes. Allow to cool completely on the sheet pans, then transfer to an airtight container.

Per Serving (generous ½ cup) ● Calories 147 ● Fat 4 g ● Saturated Fat 0.5 g
Cholesterol 0 mg ● Carbohydrate 22 g ● Fiber 6 g
Protein 7 g ● Sugars 9 g ● Sodium 547 mg

Air-Popped Popcorn with Sea Salt

SERVES 2

⅓ cup popcorn kernels

Olive oil spray (I like my Misto or Bertolli)

Coarse sea salt in an adjustable grinder (I like McCormick's) or popcorn salt

Did you know you can pop popcorn on the stove with no oil? Yup, no fancy machines or equipment required! We snack on popcorn a lot in my house—it's a whole grain loaded with fiber, which makes it the perfect light snack when you're watching a movie or just craving something savory. Many store-bought popcorns are loaded with butter or oil or, worse, "natural flavorings," but when you make your popcorn at home it's healthier (and cheaper!) than the store-bought stuff. Just a few spritzes of olive oil and finely ground sea salt is our favorite way to eat it.

If you are using coarse sea salt in an adjustable grinder, set the grinder to the fine setting.

In the bottom of a large heavy-bottomed pot or Dutch oven over medium heat, place the popcorn kernels in an even layer (if you add more kernels, the saucepan will not have room for them once they pop!) and cover. Stay close to the stove as you'll need to listen to the kernels as they pop. Listen for the kernels to start popping. At first, they will pop vigorously. After 6 to 7 minutes, when there is an interval of 1 to 2 seconds between the popping, remove from the heat.

While the popcorn is still hot, spritz with olive oil and a few grinds of salt, tossing the popcorn to evenly coat. Eat right away or store in large zip-top bags.

SKINNY SCOOP Popcorn salt is a finely textured salt that adheres to kernels more easily than a coarse salt. For my popcorn I like to use sea salt that comes with a built-in grinder so that it comes out super fine.

More Popcorn Seasoning Variations:

- Coconut oil spray with confectioners' sugar and cinnamon
- Finely grated Parmesan cheese
- Nutritional yeast (a dairy-free alternative to Parmesan cheese)
- Sea salt and freshly ground black pepper
- Taco seasoning
- Vermont cheese powder (by King Arthur)

Per Serving (3½ cups) ● Calories 120 ● Fat 1.5 g ● Saturated Fat 0 g
Cholesterol 0 mg ● Carbohydrate 24 g ● Fiber 4 g ● Protein 3 g
Sugars 0 g ● Sodium 64 mg

"Everything" Nuts

Q V GF DF

SERVES 8

1 large egg white

2 cups raw, unsalted mixed nuts (such as almonds, pecans, and walnuts)

EVERYTHING BAGEL SEASONING

1 teaspoon white sesame seeds

1 teaspoon black sesame seeds

1 teaspoon dried minced onion

1 teaspoon dried minced garlic

½ teaspoon poppy seeds

½ teaspoon kosher salt

PANTRY: UP TO 1 WEEK

I'm nuts about everything bagel seasoning, and not only on my bagels! I use it wherever I can—from eggs to salmon to chicken, you name it. So, naturally, when I added it to nuts, my new favorite snack was born. Rather than using premade seasoning, I make mine from scratch so I can control the amount of sodium.

Preheat the oven to 325° F. Line a medium rimmed baking sheet with parchment paper.

In a medium bowl, use a fork to whisk the egg white until it is broken up. Add the nuts and toss until evenly coated. Add the sesame seeds, onion, garlic, poppy seeds, and salt and mix well.

Spread the seasoned nuts out on the baking sheet and roast for 13 to 15 minutes, until golden, tossing and breaking up the pieces halfway through. Let cool completely and store in an airtight container at room temperature.

Per Serving (¼ cup) ● Calories 212 ● Fat 18 g ● Saturated Fat 2.5 g
Cholesterol 0 mg ● Carbohydrate 9 g ● Fiber 3.5 g ● Protein 7 g
Sugars 0 g ● Sodium 81 mg

PB+J Healthy Oatmeal Cookies

Q V GF DF FF

SERVES 4

Cooking spray

2 medium extra-ripe bananas, mashed with a fork

2 tablespoons chunky peanut butter

1 cup uncooked quick-cooking oats*

4 teaspoons reduced-sugar fruit jam (grape, raspberry, strawberry, or any flavor you like)

*Read the label to be sure this product is gluten-free.

FRIDGE: UP TO 4 DAYS

FREEZER: UP TO 3 MONTHS

When I have overripe bananas on the counter, I whip up a batch of these easy-to-make cookies. These are best when the bananas are super ripe as their natural sugars sweeten the cookies. Keep in mind that they aren't crisp like a dessert cookie, but are moist and chewy. Ready in just minutes, they're great as an afternoon snack or even as a quick breakfast. I like using chunky peanut butter since it adds texture, and you can play around with different jam flavors. They're best eaten warm, right out of the oven or popped in the microwave for just a few seconds.

Preheat the oven to 350°F. Spray a nonstick baking sheet with cooking spray or use a silicone baking mat.

In a medium bowl, combine the mashed bananas and peanut butter and mix well. Add the oats and mix until thoroughly combined.

Place generous tablespoons of the batter on the baking sheet (you'll have about 16 cookies). Make an indent in the center of each with the back of the measuring spoon.

Bake until golden, about 15 minutes. Remove from the oven.

SERVE NOW: Immediately top each cookie with ¼ teaspoon jam. Enjoy while warm.

MEAL PREP: To refrigerate or freeze, transfer the cookies, without the jam, to a zip-top plastic bag. When ready to eat, pop them in the microwave for a few seconds to reheat. Top with the jam and serve.

Per Serving (4 cookies) • Calories 188 • Fat 5 g • Saturated Fat 1 g
Cholesterol 0 mg • Carbohydrate 32 g • Fiber 4 g • Protein 5 g
Sugars 11 g • Sodium 41 mg

DIY Protein Bistro Snack Boxes

4 SERVINGS

2 medium apples, washed, cored, and halved

8 large hard-boiled eggs, peeled and halved

2 cups red grapes, washed

4 Mini Babybel light cheese wheels

1 teaspoon Everything Bagel Seasoning (see page 150)

½ cup peanut butter or your favorite nut or seed butter

FRIDGE: UP TO 5 DAYS

This easy bistro box is perfect for a light lunch or post-workout snack, or anytime you need an energy boost. I was inspired by Starbucks Protein Boxes, one of my favorite healthy on-the-go lunch ideas. My DIY version is easy to prep and more affordable than buying the pre-packaged variety. And since there's no need to heat them up, they are great for packing for work and school lunches and snacks.

Slice the apples, then transfer them to 4 meal prep containers, keeping the halves intact and pressed together face down to prevent browning (or cut them just before you eat). Arrange the eggs, grapes, and cheese in the containers and sprinkle the eggs with the everything bagel seasoning. Portion the peanut butter into 2-tablespoon containers and store refrigerated.

SKINNY SCOOP If packing for school, I love using peanut-free Wow Butter.

Per Serving (1 box) ● Calories 484 ● Fat 30 g ● Saturated Fat 8.5 g
Cholesterol 432 mg ● Carbohydrate 31 g ● Fiber 4.5 g ● Protein 27 g
Sugars 23 g ● Sodium 616 mg

Pumpkin Hummus

Q V GF DF

SERVES 8

3 garlic cloves

2 teaspoons kosher salt

⅓ cup tahini

1 (15-ounce) can chickpeas,* drained and rinsed

Juice of 3 lemons

½ teaspoon ground cumin

½ teaspoon ground coriander

2 teaspoons grated fresh ginger

1 (15-ounce) can unsweetened pumpkin puree

1 teaspoon olive oil

Sweet paprika, for garnish

Raw veggies, for dipping

*Read the label to be sure this product is gluten-free.

FRIDGE: UP TO 4 DAYS

Don't let the name fool you! This hummus doesn't taste like pumpkin pie—it's light and lemony with a hint of ginger. Serve it as a dip for crudités, tortilla chips, or whole wheat pita, or add it to your favorite mezze platter. Using canned pumpkin adds a healthy dose of vitamin A and antioxidants. This recipe makes a lot of hummus; to make less, simply halve all of the ingredients.

Place the garlic, salt, and tahini in a food processor and process until smooth. Add the chickpeas, lemon juice, cumin, coriander, and ginger and process until smooth. Add the pumpkin puree and process until all the ingredients are well combined, about 2 minutes.

SERVE NOW: Transfer to a bowl and drizzle with the olive oil and sprinkle with paprika. Serve with the cut-up veggies.

MEAL PREP: Transfer to airtight containers with the cut-up veggies in separate containers.

Per Serving (⅓ cup) ● Calories 161 ● Fat 7 g ● Saturated Fat 1 g
Cholesterol 0 mg ● Carbohydrate 21 g ● Fiber 5 g ● Protein 6 g
Sugars 2 g ● Sodium 403 mg

Freezer Favorites: Vegetarian

Ribollita Soup

Q V FF

SERVES 5

1 tablespoon olive oil

1 large onion, cut into ¼-inch dice

1 large carrot, cut into ¼-inch dice

1 celery stalk, trimmed and cut into ¼-inch dice

2 garlic cloves, finely minced

¼ teaspoon kosher salt

⅛ teaspoon crushed red pepper flakes

2 cups roughly chopped lacinato kale, ribs removed

2 sprigs of fresh thyme (leaves only)

1 (15-ounce) can no-salt-added white beans (such as cannellini or Great Northern), undrained

4 cups vegetable broth

1 (14-ounce) can diced tomatoes

2 cups ½-inch-diced stale whole wheat, rustic bread

Freshly grated Parmesan cheese, for serving (optional)

> FRIDGE: UP TO 4 DAYS

> FREEZER: FREEZE KITS FOR UP TO 6 MONTHS

Ribollita is a hearty Tuscan bread soup, made with stale bread, cannellini beans, kale, and vegetables. You can play around with the ingredients and add pancetta, diced potatoes, or even sausage, but quite honestly, I think it's perfect as is. Robin, a Skinnytaste reader, actually shared with me how she freezer preps her version of this soup, multiplies the recipe by four, and turns it into individual freezer "kits." Here's how: Prep the soup without the broth and bread so it's less bulky for the freezer, then label each kit with the remaining pantry staples you will need. It only takes about 15 minutes to go from kit to table (and zero "watch time"). Grab a kit and dump it in a big pot on the stove, add the broth, read the mail, take the dog out for a walk, add the bread cubes, add a handful of canned goods, and then it's time for dinner. Easy-peasy!

In a large pot or Dutch oven set over medium heat, combine ½ tablespoon oil, onion, carrot, and celery. Cook, stirring occasionally, until tender, 8 to 10 minutes. Add the garlic, salt, and pepper flakes. Cook until fragrant, about 1 minute.

To serve now, in a blender, purée half of the beans in their liquid along with ½ cup water. Add the broth, puréed beans, remaining whole beans, kale, thyme, and diced tomatoes to the pot and bring to a boil over high heat.

Add the bread and simmer for about 10 minutes, until the bread thickens the soup. Drizzle with the remaining ½ tablespoon olive oil and serve with Parmesan (if using).

> **Make It a Freezer Kit!** If you are preparing your soup in advance to freeze and serve later, after the first step, cool the vegetables completely, then transfer them to a freezer-safe container, along with the kale and thyme. Label your container with the remaining ingredients to add later, including the white beans, vegetable broth, diced tomatoes, and stale bread. When ready to cook, place the kit in a pot and proceed with the recipe. Multiply the recipe by 4 or more to make multiple kits.

Per Serving (scant 1½ cups) ● Calories 195 ● Fat 4 g ● Saturated Fat 0.5 g Cholesterol 0 mg ● Carbohydrate 33 g ● Fiber 7 g ● Protein 7 g Sugars 6 g ● Sodium 935 mg

Tomato Basil Soup with Broccoli Grilled Cheese

SERVES 6

2 pounds fresh plum tomatoes

1 medium onion, roughly chopped

1 large carrot, roughly chopped

1 celery stalk, roughly chopped

3 garlic cloves

1 tablespoon unsalted butter

¼ teaspoon kosher salt

32 ounces chicken or vegetable broth

Rind from a wedge of Pecorino Romano cheese (optional)

3 sprigs of fresh parsley

10 fresh basil leaves, plus more for garnish

2 bay leaves

¼ cup freshly grated Pecorino Romano cheese, plus more for serving (optional)

Grilled Cheese with Broccoli (recipe follows)

> **FRIDGE:** UP TO 4 DAYS

> **FREEZER:** UP TO 3 MONTHS (BOTH FINISHED SOUP AND KIT)

Soup and a sandwich is my go-to meal on nights when I'm craving something warm and comforting . . . and easy! This tomato soup is made from scratch with fresh plum tomatoes, grated cheese, and fresh basil. Freeze the soup in portions so you can pop individual servings into the microwave for a quick lunch. There's no better side dish for tomato soup than a crisp, golden, grilled cheese sandwich, but if you prefer you can serve it with some crusty bread on the side.

To peel the tomatoes, bring a large pot of water to boil. Slice an X on the bottom of each tomato. When the water is boiling, drop the tomatoes in and blanch for 1 to 2 minutes, until the skin cracks. Quickly remove from the water and transfer to a colander. Let them cool for a few minutes until they are cool enough to handle, and then the skin will come right off.

Finely chop the onion, carrot, celery, and garlic using a small food processor.

Melt the butter in a large heavy pot or Dutch oven over medium heat. Add the onion, carrot, celery, and garlic. Add ¼ teaspoon salt and cook, stirring often, until soft, 8 to 10 minutes.

Add the broth, tomatoes, and cheese rind (if using). Tie the parsley, basil, and bay leaves together with kitchen string or a rubber band and drop them into the soup (so they are easy to remove later). Bring to a boil and then lower the heat and simmer, covered, for about 30 minutes for the flavors to meld.

Remove the herbs and Pecorino rind and discard. Blend the soup with an immersion blender until smooth. Stir in the Pecorino.

SERVE NOW: Ladle into bowls and top with more freshly grated Pecorino (if using). Serve with 1 sandwich.

FREEZE AND SERVE LATER: Freeze the soup in 1¼-cup portions. Thaw overnight in the refrigerator or reheat from frozen in the microwave. Prepare the grilled cheese sandwiches while you thaw and reheat the soup.

> *Make It a Freezer Kit!* When your garden is overflowing with tomatoes, turn this into a freezer kit. Blanch and peel the tomatoes as directed. Sauté the veggies, then combine with the tomatoes and the remaining ingredients except for the broth and transfer to freezer-safe containers or gallon zip-top plastic bags. When ready to cook, transfer to a pot with the broth and cook as directed.

Per Serving (1¼ cups) • Calories 93 Fat 4 g • Saturated Fat 2 g Cholesterol 9 mg • Carbohydrate 11 g Fiber 2.5 g • Protein 5 g Sugars 7 g • Sodium 1,433 mg

Broccoli Grilled Cheese

SERVES 2

This grown-up grilled cheese is quick to prepare and delicious, made on a crusty Tuscan loaf, filled with chopped broccoli infused with garlic and Parmesan cheese, then lightly toasted with Havarti cheese. I love Havarti for its creamy, semisoft, buttery texture, but mozzarella would also work. You can easily double or triple the recipe as needed.

1¾ cups (5 ounces) broccoli florets
1 teaspoon olive oil
1 tablespoon chopped garlic
¼ teaspoon kosher salt
Freshly ground black pepper
2 tablespoons freshly grated Pecorino Romano cheese
Pinch of crushed red pepper flakes
Olive oil spray (I like my Misto or Bertolli)
4 slices (4 ounces total) Tuscan bread,* cut ¼ inch thick
4 ounces light Havarti cheese, grated

* Read the label to be sure this product is gluten-free.

Steam the broccoli with a little water in a microwave-safe bowl in the microwave until crisp-tender, about 2 minutes. Finely chop.

Heat the oil a medium skillet over medium-high heat. Add the garlic and sauté until soft, about 1 minute. Add the broccoli, salt, and pepper to taste. Cook, stirring, until the flavors meld, about 2 minutes. Remove from the heat and add the Pecorino and pepper flakes.

Spray one side of each slice of bread with oil. Heat a large nonstick skillet over medium-low heat. Place 2 slices of bread, oil side down, on the skillet. Top each piece of bread with 1 ounce of Havarti, divide the broccoli on top, and add the remaining Havarti. Top with the remaining bread, oil side up, and cook until the bottom piece of bread is golden, 4 to 5 minutes. Use a spatula to carefully flip the sandwich over. Cook until the other slice of bread is golden brown, 3 to 4 minutes. Cut in half on an angle and serve with the soup.

Per Serving (1 sandwich) ● Calories 365 ● Fat 20 g ● Saturated Fat 7.5 g
Cholesterol 34 mg ● Carbohydrate 35 g ● Fiber 3.5 g ● Protein 25 g
Sugars 2 g ● Sodium 972 mg

Slow Cooker Coconut Red Curry Butternut Soup

(V) (GF) (DF) (FF) (SC)

SERVES 4

2 pounds (1 small) butternut squash

2 large shallots, quartered

1-inch (½-ounce) piece fresh ginger, peeled

2 tablespoons Thai red curry paste

2 cups chicken or vegetable broth*

½ cup canned full-fat coconut milk, plus more for drizzling (optional)

Chopped fresh cilantro, for garnish

Lime wedges, for serving

*Read the label to be sure this product is gluten-free.

> FRIDGE: UP TO 5 DAYS

> FREEZER: UP TO 3 MONTHS

Thanks to the pureed butternut squash and coconut milk, this soup is super creamy but also surprisingly light. Thai curry flavors pair perfectly with butternut squash, and honestly, this recipe was a total accident! On a whim, I doctored up my basic butternut soup with Thai red curry paste, fresh cilantro, and a squeeze of lime, and the results were just amazing. Since peeling a butternut is such a chore, I just scoop the flesh out of the skin after it's cooked (using pre-cut butternut would also work).

Cut the squash in half and remove the seeds. Place the squash cut side down in the slow cooker with the shallots, ginger, and red curry paste. Add the broth and cook on high for 4 to 5 hours or on low for 8 to 9 hours, until the squash is very soft and cooked through (a knife should be easily inserted).

Remove the squash from the slow cooker. Scoop the flesh out from the skin and return to the slow cooker (discard the peel). Stir in the coconut milk. Blend with an immersion blender until smooth. (A regular blender will work, but be sure to let the soup cool before blending and fill only halfway in the blender so it doesn't explode on you.)

SERVE NOW: Transfer the soup to 4 bowls and drizzle with more coconut milk and cilantro. Serve with lime wedges.

FREEZE AND SERVE LATER: Transfer to individually portioned airtight containers or 1 large container. To reheat, thaw overnight in the refrigerator, then reheat in the microwave or stove.

> *Make It a Freezer Kit!* Prep the butternut squash and transfer to a gallon-size zip-top plastic bag or container with the shallots, ginger, and red curry paste. Label, date, and freeze for up to 3 months. When ready to prepare, thaw overnight in the refrigerator, then transfer to the slow cooker and proceed with the recipe.

Per Serving (1¼ cups) • Calories 195 • Fat 6.5 g • Saturated Fat 5.5 g
Cholesterol 0 mg • Carbohydrate 35 g • Fiber 6 g • Protein 5 g
Sugars 8 g • Sodium 621 mg

Carrot Tomato Ginger Soup

V GF DF FF

SERVES 6

1 tablespoon unsalted butter

1 medium onion, chopped

1 celery stalk, chopped

2 tablespoons grated fresh ginger

3 garlic cloves, minced

4 cups vegetable or chicken broth*

1 pound carrots, roughly chopped

1 pound plum tomatoes, peeled (see page 163)

4 sprigs of fresh parsley

2 bay leaves

1 teaspoon kosher salt

Freshly ground black pepper

Low-fat plain yogurt, for serving (optional)

* Read the label to be sure this product is gluten-free.

FRIDGE: UP TO 5 DAYS

FREEZER: UP TO 3 MONTHS

Carrot confession: I'm not the biggest fan of the orange veggie. But I do love them in this rich, creamy soup, which actually requires no cream at all. The vegetables themselves thicken the soup once they're cooked, and then it all gets puréed. I personally love my bowl of soup served with a dollop of yogurt on top, but that's totally optional. Truth be told, it's great with or without. This soup is perfect for lunch served with a salad, half a sandwich, or a crusty piece of bread on the side.

In a large pot, melt the butter over medium-low heat. Add the onion, celery, ginger, and garlic. Cook, stirring often, until soft, 5 to 8 minutes. Add the broth, carrots, and tomatoes, stirring well.

Using kitchen string, tie the herbs together and drop them into the soup (this will make them easy to remove later). Season with the salt and black pepper to taste. Reduce the heat to low and simmer, covered, until the carrots are tender, about 30 minutes.

Remove the herbs and discard. Blend the soup with an immersion blender until smooth. (A regular blender will work, but be sure to let the soup cool before blending and fill only halfway in the blender so it doesn't explode on you.)

SERVE NOW: Transfer the soup to 6 bowls and top with yogurt (if using).

FREEZE AND SERVE LATER: Cool the soup, divide it among airtight containers, and freeze. Remove your containers from the freezer and thaw in the refrigerator overnight. Heat the soup in a large saucepan over medium-low heat, stirring occasionally and adding a little broth or water if necessary. To serve, top with yogurt (if using).

Per Serving (generous 1 cup) ● Calories 85 ● Fat 2.5 g ● Saturated Fat 1.5 g Cholesterol 5 mg ● Carbohydrate 15 g ● Fiber 4.5 g ● Protein 2 g Sugars 8 g ● Sodium 586 mg

Baked Spinach Stuffed Shells

(V) (FF)

SERVES 9

Kosher salt

9 ounces jumbo pasta shells (27 shells)

2 large eggs

1 (15-ounce) container part-skim ricotta cheese (I like Polly-O)

1 (8-ounce) package frozen chopped spinach, thawed and squeezed well

1 cup (3 ounces) finely grated Parmesan cheese, plus more for serving (optional)

¼ cup finely chopped fresh parsley

2 cups (8 ounces) shredded part-skim mozzarella cheese

Freshly ground black pepper

3 cups Basil Pomodoro Sauce (page 294) or store-bought marinara sauce

FRIDGE: UP TO 5 DAYS (BOTH BAKED AND UNBAKED)

FROZEN: UP TO 3 MONTHS

When you need a family-friendly freezer casserole to welcome a new neighbor, or to drop off to a friend who's going through a hard time, this is my go-to because it checks all the boxes: It freezes great, requires no prep of any kind, pleases even the pickiest of palates, satisfies vegetarians, and meat-eaters never miss the meat (Tommy loves it!). It even swaps out some of the cheese filling for a healthy dose of greens. When I'm making it for my family, I usually bake half in a 9 × 9-inch baking dish and freeze the other half for another night. Serve it with a big green salad on the side.

Preheat the oven to 375°F.

Bring a large pot of salted water to a boil. Cook the shells, stirring occasionally to prevent sticking, until al dente, about 3 minutes less than the package instructions. Drain well, run under cold water to stop the cooking, and drain again.

In a large bowl, lightly whisk the eggs. Stir in the ricotta, spinach, Parmesan, parsley, and 1½ cups mozzarella. Season with ¼ teaspoon salt and pepper to taste. Transfer the filling to a large resealable plastic bag.

Spread 1½ cups marinara sauce in a 9 × 13-inch baking dish. Snip off a corner of the plastic bag and squeeze the filling into the shells, arranging the shells over the sauce in a single layer as you go. Top with the remaining marinara sauce and remaining mozzarella. Cover the pan tightly with foil.

SERVE NOW: Bake until heated through and bubbling on the edges, 35 to 40 minutes. Uncover and continue baking until any liquid around the edges of the pan dries up, 10 to 15 minutes more. Let stand 10 minutes before serving. Serve with more grated Parmesan on top, if using.

REFRIGERATE AND SERVE LATER: Before baking, the dish can be prepared up to 5 days in advance and refrigerated. Bake from the fridge, covered, at 375°F for 40 to 45 minutes, until heated through.

FREEZE AND SERVE LATER: Before baking, the dish can be prepared in a freezer-to-ovenproof baking dish, covered tightly, and frozen for up to 3 months. Bake from frozen (no need to thaw) at 375°F, covered, until heated through in the center and bubbling on the edges, about 1 hour 15 minutes. Uncover and bake until any liquid on the edges dries up, 15 to 20 minutes more.

Per Serving (3 shells) • Calories 322 • Fat 12.5 g • Saturated Fat 7 g Cholesterol 79 mg • Carbohydrate 33 g • Fiber 4 g • Protein 23 g Sugars 4 g • Sodium 615 mg

Chickpea Spinach Tomato Curry

(Q) (V) (GF) (DF) (FF)

SERVES 4

½ tablespoon coconut oil

½ medium yellow onion, finely chopped

1 teaspoon ground cumin

1½ teaspoons ground turmeric

1 teaspoon Madras curry powder*

½ teaspoon chili powder*

1 teaspoon kosher salt

1 tablespoon minced fresh ginger

2 garlic cloves, minced

1 (15-ounce) can diced tomatoes

2 (15-ounce) cans low-sodium chickpeas,* rinsed and drained

2 cups baby spinach

¾ cup canned unsweetened full-fat coconut milk

2 cups cooked basmati rice, for serving

*Read the label to be sure this product is gluten-free.

> FRIDGE: UP TO 4 DAYS

> FREEZER: UP TO 6 MONTHS

I love meat and dairy, but I also love to give my body a break and eat plant-based dishes like this ready-in-a-hurry curry, which takes less than 15 minutes to prepare. This back-pocket dinner, made with a few cans from the pantry, can be whipped up with almost no notice any night of the week. You can use any greens you happen to have in your refrigerator, such as spinach, kale, or Swiss chard. To make it a meal, serve it over basmati rice or with naan bread. Leftovers reheat nicely for lunch, and if you're making this as a freezer meal, just leave the coconut milk out and add it when you reheat the curry.

Heat the oil in a large, deep skillet over medium heat. Add the onion, cumin, turmeric, curry powder, chili powder, and ½ teaspoon salt. Cook for 4 to 5 minutes, stirring occasionally, until the onion is soft and golden. Add the ginger and garlic and cook for 1 to 2 minutes more, until fragrant.

Add the tomatoes, chickpeas, and ¼ cup water and stir. Cook uncovered, stirring occasionally, for about 5 minutes, to let the flavors meld.

Stir in the spinach, coconut milk, and remaining salt, and stir over medium-low heat until the spinach wilts, about 2 minutes.

SERVE NOW: Place 1 cup curry in each shallow bowl and serve with ½ cup rice alongside.

FREEZE AND SERVE LATER: Make the curry without the coconut milk and transfer to a large freezer-safe container or 4 smaller containers. To reheat, thaw the curry overnight in the refrigerator, then heat on the stove in a saucepan, stirring in the coconut milk.

Per Serving (generous 1 cup curry + ½ cup rice) ● Calories 453 ● Fat 14.5 g Saturated Fat 9.5 g ● Cholesterol 0 mg ● Carbohydrate 67 g Fiber 12.5 g ● Protein 16 g ● Sugars 6 g ● Sodium 971 mg

Eggplant Parmesan

SERVES 8

Olive oil spray

2 pounds eggplant (1 large or 2 medium), peeled

1 teaspoon kosher salt

12 ounces part-skim ricotta cheese (I like Polly-O)

1 large egg, lightly beaten

¼ cup fresh parsley, chopped

¼ cup plus 2 tablespoons freshly grated Pecorino Romano cheese

4 cups Basil Pomodoro Sauce (page 294) or store-bought marinara sauce

2½ cups part-skim shredded mozzarella cheese

FRIDGE: UP TO 4 DAYS

FREEZER: UP TO 3 MONTHS (UNBAKED)

This lighter eggplant Parmesan is one of my favorite ways to eat eggplant. My mom always made eggplant Parmesan this way, and I've always preferred it over the deep-fried breaded version. It does take some time to make, but it's so worth it! The eggplant is layered with sauce and cheese, and it almost becomes like a noodle-less eggplant lasagna. It's so good it literally melts right in your mouth with each bite. For best flavor, I always use a good Parmesan cheese, such as Parmigiano-Reggiano, or Pecorino Romano cheese, such as Locatelli. Either can be used here.

Preheat the oven to 450°F. Spray two sheet pans with oil.

Slice the eggplant into ¼-inch-thick rounds. Transfer them to the prepared pans (it's OK if they overlap slightly). Season both sides with salt. Bake for about 20 minutes, turning halfway through, until the eggplant is golden.

Meanwhile, in a medium bowl, combine the ricotta, egg, parsley, and ¼ cup Pecorino.

When the eggplant has finished baking, put ½ cup sauce on the bottom of a 9 × 12-inch baking dish and add one-third of the eggplant to cover the bottom of the dish. Top with a third of the ricotta mixture, ¾ cup mozzarella, and ¾ cup sauce. Add another layer of eggplant and repeat the layers of ricotta, mozzarella, and sauce two more times. Finish with the remaining sauce, remaining mozzarella, and remaining 2 tablespoons Pecorino. Cover the pan tightly with foil until ready to bake.

SERVE NOW: Preheat the oven to 400°F. Bake, covered, for 40 to 45 minutes. Uncover and bake for about 10 minutes more to help thicken the sauce. Remove from the oven and let it rest for 10 minutes before serving.

REFRIGERATE AND SERVE LATER: You can prep this dish 24 hours before baking. Tightly wrap before refrigerating.

FREEZE AND SERVE LATER: Prepare the unbaked Eggplant Parmesan in a freezer-to-ovenproof baking dish or foil dish. Cover tightly and freeze. There is no need to thaw: bake from frozen in a preheated oven at 350°F for 2¼ to 2½ hours, until heated through in the center. Uncover and bake for 10 to 15 minutes more. Remove from the oven and let rest for 15 minutes before serving.

MEAL PREP: Cut slices of the cooked eggplant Parmesan into individual servings and store in the refrigerator in meal prep containers. Reheat in the microwave or in the oven for lunches and dinners.

Per Serving (1 slice) ● Calories 266 ● Fat 13.5 g ● Saturated Fat 7.5 g
Cholesterol 59 mg ● Carbohydrate 20 g ● Fiber 6 g ● Protein 20 g
Sugars 8 g ● Sodium 732 mg

Zucchini Rollatini

SERVES 6

2 cups Basil Pomodoro Sauce
(page 294) or store-bought
marinara sauce

4 large (14-ounce) zucchinis

Kosher salt

Freshly ground black pepper

2 large eggs

1⅓ cups part-skim ricotta cheese
(I like Polly-O)

1 cup grated Pecorino Romano
cheese, plus more for serving

½ cup chopped fresh basil

2 garlic cloves, minced

1½ cups (6 ounces) shredded
mozzarella cheese (I like Polly-O)

> FRIDGE: UP TO 4 DAYS

> FREEZER: UP TO 3 MONTHS

On days when I want to go meatless and low-carb, I make this much-loved, cheesy, veggie-loaded dish! Similar to eggplant rollatini, this is made with strips of grilled zucchini stuffed with a basil-cheese filling and finished with tomato sauce and even more cheese. I usually make two batches—one for dinner and one to freeze for later. You'll want to use two large zucchinis so that the strips are large enough to stuff. To make the zucchini pliable, and to reduce the liquid when they bake, I grill the strips first on my grill pan before filling and rolling. This dish can be prepped a day ahead, then baked when ready to eat.

Preheat the oven to 400°F. Spread ½ cup marinara sauce on the bottom of a 9 × 13-inch baking dish.

Cut the zucchinis lengthwise into ¼-inch-thick slices until you have a total of 24 slices of about the same size.

Preheat a grill pan over high heat (or preheat a grill to high) and oil the pan or grates. Season both sides of the zucchini slices with 1 teaspoon salt and black pepper to taste, then grill until pliable and grill marks form, but not fully cooked through, about 2 minutes on each side.

In a medium bowl, beat the eggs, then mix together with the ricotta, Pecorino, basil, garlic, ¼ teaspoon salt, and ¼ teaspoon black pepper.

Spread about 1½ tablespoons of the ricotta mixture onto each zucchini slice, spreading to evenly cover.

Roll up the zucchini slices and arrange them seam side down in the prepared dish. Top each with 1 tablespoon marinara sauce and 1 tablespoon mozzarella cheese and tightly cover with foil. Bake for about 20 minutes, or until the cheese is hot and melted.

FREEZE AND SERVE LATER: Before baking, the rollatini can be prepared in a foil pan or freezer-to-ovenproof dish. Cover tightly with foil and freeze. Bake from frozen, covered, in a preheated 400°F oven for about 45 minutes, then uncover and cook for about 5 minutes more, until heated through in the center.

MEAL PREP: Store individual servings in meal prep containers and refrigerate. Reheat in the microwave for 2 to 3 minutes, until heated through.

SKINNY SCOOP For best results, use a mandoline to slice the zucchini so they are all the same thickness.

Per Serving (4 rolls) ● Calories 320 ● Fat 16.5 g ● Saturated Fat 9.5 g
Cholesterol 112 mg ● Carbohydrate 19 g ● Fiber 4 g ● Protein 26 g
Sugars 10 g ● Sodium 960 mg

Torta Pasqualina (Spinach Pie)

(V) (GF) (FF)

SERVES 6

½ tablespoon olive oil

1 large onion, diced

3 garlic cloves, chopped

11 ounces fresh baby spinach

1¼ teaspoons kosher salt

¼ teaspoon crushed red pepper flakes

¼ teaspoon freshly ground black pepper

6 large eggs

½ cup part-skim ricotta cheese

¼ cup freshly grated Parmesan cheese

¼ cup shredded part-skim mozzarella cheese

8-ounce sheet (½ package) frozen puff pastry, thawed (I like Pepperidge Farm)*

All-purpose flour, for dusting*

1 tablespoon fat-free milk

*Use gluten-free puff pastry and flour to make this gluten-free.

FRIDGE: UP TO 4 DAYS

FREEZER: UP TO 4 MONTHS

SKINNY SCOOP A slice of this pie is pretty filling thanks to the eggs and cheese. If you wish, you can serve it with a small green salad on the side.

This savory Italian Easter pie is also popular in Argentina, where my Aunt Milda is from. Growing up I always loved when she made this spinach pie, and I was thrilled when she shared her recipe with me. She makes hers double-crusted, but using only one crust is an easy way to lighten up the dish. You can swap the spinach for chard or another green, but the most important aspect of *torta pasqualina* is the eggs that are baked inside. When you cut the pie, you should see the egg sliced through the middle, which looks beautiful and festive.

Prepare the torta filling: Heat the oil in a large, deep skillet over medium heat. Add the onion and cook for about 5 minutes, until soft. Add the garlic and cook for about 2 minutes more, until fragrant. Add the spinach, salt, pepper flakes, and black pepper. Cook, stirring frequently, for 4 to 5 minutes, until the spinach is wilted. Remove the skillet from the heat. Once cooled, transfer the spinach mixture to a mixing bowl.

Preheat the oven to 375°F.

In a small bowl, whisk 2 of the eggs. Once the spinach is cool, add the 2 beaten eggs, ricotta, Parmesan, and mozzarella, and mix well.

Prepare the torta crust: You will need a standard 9-inch pie plate that is about 1½ inches deep. Lay out the puff pastry sheet on a lightly floured surface and slightly roll it out so it's larger than the top diameter of the pie plate. Place the pie plate upside down on the pastry sheet as a stencil and use a knife to cut around it to make a circle. Set the rest of the dough aside for later.

Lay the pastry sheet in your pie plate (the dough should come up the sides to the top edges).

Put half the spinach mixture into the pie plate. Make four large wells in the spinach—one in each quarter of the pie—and then gently crack one of the remaining eggs into each well. Using your hands, carefully top with the remaining spinach, being careful not to crack the yolk.

Roll out the remaining dough and cut it into long strips to lay across the top of the spinach in a crisscross pattern (about four rows in each direction). Brush the milk over the top of the pie crust with a pastry brush.

Bake for about 50 minutes, until the crust is golden. Serve hot or at room temperature.

Per Serving (1 slice) ● Calories 371 ● Fat 24 g ● Saturated Fat 7.5 g Cholesterol 197 mg ● Carbohydrate 24 g ● Fiber 2.5 g ● Protein 16 g Sugars 2 g ● Sodium 544 mg

FREEZE AND SERVE LATER: Wrap the cooked pie tightly in plastic wrap and then foil and store in the freezer. To reheat, thaw in the refrigerator overnight, uncover, and reheat in the microwave in 30-second intervals until heated through.

MEAL PREP: Cut the pie in individual servings and transfer to meal prep containers and refrigerate. Reheat in the microwave.

FRIDGE: UP TO 24 HOURS
BEFORE BAKING, UP TO
4 DAYS ONCE COOKED

FREEZER: UP TO 3 MONTHS
AFTER BAKING

Roasted Vegetable Lasagna

(V) (FF)

SERVES 8

ROASTED VEGETABLES

Olive oil spray

1 red bell pepper, seeded and cut into 1/2-inch pieces

1 yellow bell pepper, seeded and cut into 1/2-inch pieces

1 large (12-ounce) zucchini, cut into 1/4-inch-thick rounds

4 ounces sliced mushrooms

1 medium (8-ounce) fennel bulb, stalks and fronds removed, cut into 1/2-inch pieces

1 medium red onion, sliced into 1/2-inch pieces

6 garlic cloves, smashed lightly

1 tablespoon balsamic vinegar

1 tablespoon extra-virgin olive oil

1/2 teaspoon dried oregano

1/2 teaspoon dried basil

1/2 teaspoon kosher salt

Freshly ground black pepper

LASAGNA

1 (15-ounce) container part-skim ricotta cheese (I like Polly-O)

1/2 cup freshly grated Pecorino Romano or Parmesan cheese

1/4 cup chopped fresh basil, plus more for garnish

5 cups Basil Pomodoro Sauce (page 294) or store-bought marinara sauce

1 (9-ounce) box no-boil lasagna noodles (I like Barilla)

3 cups shredded part-skim mozzarella cheese

You'll need a deep baking dish to make this lasagna, which is bursting with roasted vegetables between each layer. Although it will take time to assemble, it's worth every second because it's outstanding. I always make my own marinara sauce, but to save time, you can use your favorite jarred version. I highly recommend doubling this recipe and freezing the second batch. You'll thank me later! You can bake this uncooked, straight from the freezer, so make sure you use a freezer-to-ovenproof baking dish.

Adjust the oven racks to the center and bottom positions. Preheat the oven to 450°F. Spray two large baking sheets with oil.

Place the bell peppers, zucchini, mushrooms, fennel, onion, and garlic on the sheets and toss with the balsamic vinegar, olive oil, oregano, dried basil, salt, and black pepper to taste. Roast on the lower oven rack, stirring halfway through, until tender and slightly browned, 30 to 35 minutes. Remove the vegetables from the oven and reduce the oven temperature to 400°F.

In a medium bowl, combine the ricotta, Pecorino, and fresh basil.

In a 9 × 13 × 3-inch freezer-to-ovenproof baking dish, spread 1/2 cup marinara on the bottom of the dish. Arrange 3 lasagna noodles across the dish (they will expand as they cook) and top with 3/4 cup sauce, one-fourth of the roasted vegetables, one-fourth of the ricotta cheese mixture, and 1/2 cup mozzarella. Repeat 3 more times, starting with the pasta. Arrange the last 3 sheets of pasta noodles on top and spread with the remaining marinara sauce.

Cover with foil and bake on the center rack until the lasagna is cooked through in the center, about 45 minutes. Uncover and cook until bubbling and hot, about 10 minutes more. Add the remaining mozzarella and bake until melted, about 5 minutes. Remove from the oven and let rest for 15 minutes before serving. Cut into 8 slices and serve.

REFRIGERATE AND SERVE LATER: Tightly wrap the assembled and unbaked lasagna in foil and refrigerate for up to 24 hours before baking. Follow the directions above, adding an extra 10 minutes to the initial bake time to account for it being cold from the refrigerator.

FREEZE AND SERVE LATER: Bake the lasagna as directed and let it cool completely. Tightly wrap with foil, or cut into portions and transfer to separate airtight containers, and freeze. To reheat, transfer to the refrigerator for at least 24 to 48 hours to completely thaw, then reheat in a 375°F oven until heated through, 1 hour to 1 hour 15 minutes.

Per Serving (1 slice) ● Calories 453 ● Fat 18.5 g ● Saturated Fat 9.5 g Cholesterol 54 mg ● Carbohydrate 46 g ● Fiber 6 g ● Protein 28 g Sugars 13 g ● Sodium 827 mg

Zucchini Pupusas

(V) (GF) (FF)

SERVES 8

DOUGH

2 cups corn flour (masa), plus more for dusting

1 teaspoon kosher salt

2 cups warm water

1 teaspoon vegetable or canola oil, plus more for your hands

FILLING

1 teaspoon unsalted butter

1/3 cup minced onion

2 garlic cloves, minced

1 1/2 cups coarsely grated zucchini (don't squeeze out the excess water)

1 teaspoon kosher salt

3/4 cup plus 2 tablespoons shredded part-skim mozzarella cheese*

1 1/2 tablespoons freshly grated Parmesan cheese

Olive oil spray

Shredded cabbage and sliced avocado, for serving (optional)

*Read the label to be sure this product is gluten-free.

> FRIDGE: UP TO 4 DAYS. REHEAT ON THE SKILLET.

> FREEZER: UP TO 6 MONTHS

Walk into any Salvadorian restaurant and chances are you'll find *pupusas* (say it: poo-POO-sa—yes, it's fun!), a savory cross between a tortilla and a tamale stuffed with just about anything: pork, cheese, beans, and more. It's kind of like a Salvadorian grilled cheese, and it's awesome. One of my favorites is the *queso con loroco*, a filling made with an edible green flower native to Central America—I re-created the filling here with zucchini instead and totally nailed it. You can eat it with sliced avocado and a quick cabbage slaw, or use it place of a tostada shell and pile it high with taco meat, cabbage, and pico de gallo. If you want to make this as part of a large dinner, serve it with yellow rice and Colombian beans (see page 276) on the side—delish!

Make the dough: In a large bowl, combine the flour and salt. Whisk to combine. Add the warm water and the oil and mix with a spatula until a dough forms. Cover with a damp towel while you make the filling.

Make the zucchini filling: Melt the butter in a medium skillet over medium heat. Add the onion and garlic and cook until soft, 2 to 3 minutes. Add the zucchini and season with the salt. Cook over medium-high heat, stirring frequently, until the zucchini is soft and all the liquid has evaporated, 2 to 3 minutes. Transfer to a medium bowl and let cool for 5 minutes. Once cool, add the mozzarella and Parmesan cheese.

To make pupusas: With a spatula, knead the dough in the bowl for about 20 seconds. Turn the dough out onto a lightly floured surface and form it into a slightly flattened ball. If the dough seems dry and cracks, add a little more water, 1 tablespoon at a time. Cut the dough into 8 equal pieces. Cover with a damp towel.

(recipe continues)

Per Serving (1 *pupusa*) ● Calories 162 ● Fat 5 g ● Saturated Fat 2 g Cholesterol 9 mg ● Carbohydrate 24 g ● Fiber 2 g ● Protein 7 g Sugars 1 g ● Sodium 363 mg

In a small bowl, mix ¾ cup water and ½ teaspoon oil. Use this to help you work the dough and prevent it from sticking to your hands. Lightly moisten your hands with the water-oil mixture and, working with one piece at a time, roll the dough into a ball and place on your left palm. Flatten it into a ¼-inch-thick disk, using your fingers pressed onto the palm of your hand.

Scoop 3 tablespoons of the filling into the middle of the disk, making sure not to overfill. Bring all the edges to the center to cover the filling completely. Dampen your hands once again and start flattening to form a 5- to 5½-inch disk, being careful not to squish out the filling. Repeat with the remaining dough and filling. Discard the water with oil.

SERVE NOW: When ready to cook, heat a large skillet over medium-low heat and spray with oil. Cook one *pupusa* at a time for 7 to 10 minutes, turning halfway through, until browned and crisp on the outside. To keep the cooked *pupusas* warm, place them on a sheet pan in a 200°F oven while you make the rest.

FREEZE AND SERVE LATER: Form the *pupusas* and freeze them uncooked, with parchment in between them. Transfer to a freezer-safe bag or airtight container. To cook from frozen, heat a skillet over medium-low heat and cook until the bottom is browned, about 7 minutes. Flip with a spatula and cook for about 5 minutes more, or until browned and crisp.

SKINNY SCOOP For a bean-and-cheese version, combine 1 cup leftover Colombian beans (see page 276) with ⅔ cup part-skim mozzarella cheese and use in place of the zucchini.

Black Bean and Butternut Enchilada Bake

V **GF** **FF**

SERVES 6

1 teaspoon olive oil

1 small onion, chopped

2 fresh jalapeño peppers, 1 chopped, 1 thinly sliced for topping

3 garlic cloves, finely minced

4 cups cubed (fresh or frozen) butternut squash, ½-inch dice

1 (15-ounce) can low-sodium black beans,* rinsed and drained

¼ cup chopped fresh cilantro, plus more for serving

1 teaspoon ground cumin

½ teaspoon chili powder

1 teaspoon kosher salt

2 cups (16 ounces) enchilada sauce (see recipe below, or use jarred sauce)

¼ cup sour cream, plus more for serving (optional)

6 corn tortillas, torn into quarters

1 cup (4 ounces) shredded cheese, such as a Mexican blend or Monterey Jack

5 ounces (from 1 medium) Hass avocado, sliced, for topping

*Read the label to be sure this product is gluten-free.

> FRIDGE: UP TO 4 DAYS

> FREEZER: UP TO 6 MONTHS

This cheesy enchilada bake gets dinner on the table fast. Unlike traditional enchiladas, this is essentially a tortilla casserole, which makes the preparation much simpler. No rolling and no stuffing—everything gets mixed right in the skillet and then poured into one dish. I use my homemade enchilada sauce, which I usually have in the freezer because it's so dang good, but you can use jarred if you wish (I won't judge!). You can also store individual portions of this casserole in the freezer rather than in one big dish, making meal prep even easier.

Preheat the oven to 500°F.

Heat the oil in a large, deep nonstick skillet over medium heat.

Add the onion, chopped jalapeño, and garlic and cook, stirring frequently, until the onion has softened, about 5 minutes. Add the butternut squash, black beans, ½ cup water, the cilantro, cumin, chili powder, and salt. Cover and cook over medium-low heat, stirring occasionally, until the squash is tender, about 20 minutes.

Add the enchilada sauce, sour cream, and ¼ cup water and stir. Fold in the tortillas and mix well until thoroughly coated. Cook over medium heat until warmed through, about 3 minutes, then transfer to a 9 × 12-inch baking dish. Sprinkle the cheese all over the top and cover with foil.

SERVE NOW: Bake (covered) in the center of the oven until hot and the cheese is melted and bubbling, about 10 minutes. Let cool slightly, then top with avocado, sour cream, jalapeño slices, and cilantro. Cut into 6 slices.

FREEZE AND SERVE LATER: Assemble the casserole in a freezer-to-ovenproof or foil baking dish and let the ingredients cool. Sprinkle the cheese over the top, cover tightly, and freeze. For best results, thaw the casserole and then bake, covered with foil, in a 350°F oven until heated through, 25 to 30 minutes.

> *To make your own enchilada sauce,* heat ½ teaspoon olive oil in a saucepan and sauté 4 minced garlic cloves. Add 1½ cups reduced-sodium chicken broth, 3 cups tomato sauce, 3 tablespoons chopped chipotle peppers in adobo with sauce, 1 teaspoon each of Mexican hot chili powder and ground cumin, ¼ teaspoon kosher salt, and freshly ground black pepper to taste. Bring to a boil, then reduce the heat to low and simmer, uncovered, for 7 to 10 minutes. Makes about 4 cups. Freeze whatever you don't use for another night.

Per Serving (1 slice) ● Calories 326
Fat 13 g ● Saturated Fat 5.5 g
Cholesterol 24 mg ● Carbohydrate 43 g
Fiber 12.5 g ● Protein 13 g
Sugars 6 g ● Sodium 571 mg

Falafel Chickpea Burgers

(V) (GF) (FF)

SERVES 4

1 (15-ounce) can chickpeas,* rinsed and drained

½ red bell pepper, roughly chopped

½ cup roughly chopped onion

¼ cup packed roughly chopped fresh cilantro

¼ cup packed roughly chopped fresh parsley

¼ cup packed roughly chopped fresh mint

3 garlic cloves

½ cup quick-cooking oats*

1 large egg

1½ tablespoons fresh lemon juice

1 tablespoon ground cumin

1 teaspoon kosher salt

¼ teaspoon crushed red pepper flakes

Olive oil spray

SERVING

4 whole wheat 100-calorie buns (I like Martin's) or gluten-free buns

½ cup tzatziki, store-bought or homemade (see page 256)

1 medium tomato, thinly sliced

12 thin slices cucumber

¼ cup sliced red onion

Hot sauce (optional)

*Read the label to be sure this product is gluten-free.

> FREEZER: UP TO 3 MONTHS

Inspired by Middle Eastern falafel, these burgers are made with canned chickpeas, oats, and lots of fresh herbs and spices. They're the perfect freezer meal, because freezing them actually helps them hold their shape when it comes time to cook. Although you can certainly serve them in a pita, I prefer them on buns with tzatziki, tomatoes, and cucumbers.

Using paper towels, dry the chickpeas well after rinsing (extra moisture will keep the burgers from holding together well). In a medium bowl, mash the chickpeas with a fork or potato masher until thick and pasty.

In a food processor, add the bell pepper, onion, cilantro, parsley, mint, and garlic and process until fine. Add the oats, followed by the egg, lemon juice, cumin, salt, and pepper flakes and pulse a few times until well mixed. Transfer to the bowl with the chickpeas and fold until thoroughly combined.

Place a large sheet of wax paper on a work surface. Use your hands (slightly oiled or wet) to divide the mixture into 4 patties, about ½ cup each, and place on the wax paper. (If the mixture is too wet, add another tablespoon of oats.) Wrap tightly in plastic and freeze. (Freeze for a minimum of 2 hours before cooking.)

To cook, spray a large skillet with olive oil and place it over medium heat. Add the frozen burgers and cook until golden brown and heated through, about 7 minutes on each side. If grilling, preheat the grill over medium heat, lightly spray a sheet of foil with oil, and place on the grill. Grill the frozen burgers until lightly browned and heated through, 7 to 8 minutes on each side.

To serve, place each patty on a bun and top with 2 tablespoons tzatziki, sliced tomato, cucumber, red onion, and hot sauce (if using).

SKINNY SCOOP Have fun with the toppings! Try the burgers with hummus instead of tzatziki, or make an easy harissa mayonnaise by combining equal parts mayo and harissa. For more crunch, add lettuce or chopped cabbage. Or you can turn them into salad bowls by skipping the buns and serving them on a big Greek salad.

Per Serving (1 burger) ● Calories 316 ● Fat 7 g ● Saturated Fat 1.5 g
Cholesterol 52 mg ● Carbohydrate 48 g ● Fiber 8 g ● Protein 17 g
Sugars 9 g ● Sodium 668 mg

Freezer Favorites: Meat & Seafood

5 Freezer Chicken Marinades

Q GF DF FF

SERVES 6

1½ pounds chicken (boneless, skinless chicken breasts, chicken tenders, and/or boneless, skinless chicken thighs)

Marinade of your choice (recipes follow)

FRIDGE: UP TO OVERNIGHT (UNCOOKED)

FREEZER: UP TO 6 MONTHS (UNCOOKED)

Is there anything easier than grabbing marinated and ready-to-cook chicken from the freezer for busy weeknights? Just thaw the individually wrapped portions overnight in the fridge, then prepare them on the grill or grill pan or in an air fryer. Each of these marinades is good for about 1½ pounds of chicken—you can use boneless chicken breasts, chicken tenders, and/or boneless chicken thighs. Use gallon-size heavy-duty freezer bags, or if you're cooking for one or two, portion the servings out into smaller bags. Be sure to write the name of the recipe in permanent marker along with the date *before* filling the bags.

Trim the fat off the chicken. If using chicken breasts, place them on a work surface and cut each horizontally into two cutlets. Transfer to a labeled gallon-size, heavy-duty freezer bag.

In a medium bowl, combine the marinade ingredients of your choice and transfer to the bag with the chicken.

SERVE NOW: If serving now, let marinate for at least 4 hours or overnight in the refrigerator.

To grill, preheat a grill pan over medium-high heat (or preheat a grill to medium-high). Discard the marinade in the bag and grill the chicken on the oiled pan or grate for about 5 minutes per side, or until cooked through.

To air-fry, preheat the air fryer to 400°F and cook the breasts as directed for about 10 minutes, turning halfway through. For thighs, cook at 400°F for 16 to 18 minutes, turning halfway through.

FREEZE AND SERVE LATER: Squeeze the air out of the bag with the chicken and marinade and freeze. To thaw, transfer to the refrigerator the day before serving and grill or air-fry as directed.

SKINNY SCOOP For best results, always start with organic chicken that has not been previously frozen.

Italian Marinade

Perfect served over some pasta, salad, or rice.

3 tablespoons olive oil

3 tablespoons red wine vinegar

2 garlic cloves, minced

1½ teaspoons kosher salt

½ teaspoon onion powder

½ teaspoon dried oregano

½ teaspoon dried basil

¼ teaspoon dried thyme

½ teaspoon sugar

⅛ teaspoon freshly ground black pepper

Per Serving (½ cooked breast)
Calories 141 ● Fat 4 g
Saturated Fat 1 g
Cholesterol 73 mg
Carbohydrate 0 g ● Fiber 0 g
Protein 24 g ● Sugars 0 g
Sodium 179 mg

Maple-Dijon Soy Marinade

Simple and delicious; slice this chicken up and serve over a salad for a protein and veggie feast.

¼ cup reduced-sodium soy sauce or gluten-free tamari

3 tablespoons pure maple syrup

3 tablespoons Dijon mustard

3 garlic cloves, crushed

Per Serving (½ cooked breast)
Calories 140 ● Fat 3 g
Saturated Fat 3 g
Cholesterol 73 mg
Carbohydrate 2 g ● Fiber 0 g
Protein 24 g ● Sugars 1 g
Sodium 241 mg

Honey-Soy Marinade

Sweet and savory, this marinade is inspired by Japanese yakitori and is delicious with steamed rice and sliced cucumbers.

⅓ cup reduced-sodium soy sauce or gluten-free tamari

3 tablespoons honey

3 tablespoons mirin

3 garlic cloves, crushed

½ teaspoon grated fresh ginger

Per Serving (½ cooked breast)
Calories 149 ● Fat 3 g
Saturated Fat 0.5 g
Cholesterol 73 mg
Carbohydrate 5 g ● Fiber 0 g
Protein 24 g ● Sugars 4 g
Sodium 303 mg

Greek Lemon Marinade

Try pairing this with orzo, roasted lemon potatoes, or Greek salad.

3 tablespoons fresh lemon juice

2 tablespoons extra-virgin olive oil

1 tablespoon red wine vinegar

6 garlic cloves, minced

2 teaspoons dried oregano

½ teaspoon ground turmeric

2 teaspoons kosher salt

⅛ teaspoon freshly ground black pepper

Per Serving (½ cooked breast)
Calories 134 ● Fat 3.5 g
Saturated Fat 0.5 g
Cholesterol 73 mg
Carbohydrate 0 g ● Fiber 0 g
Protein 24 g ● Sugars 0 g
Sodium 162 mg

Shawarma Marinade

This Middle Eastern–inspired chicken is delicious served over salad with feta and tzatziki or stuffed into gyro bread with red onions and tomatoes.

2 tablespoons extra-virgin olive oil

Juice of 2 medium lemons

6 garlic cloves, minced

2 teaspoons ground cumin

2 teaspoons smoked paprika

½ teaspoon ground turmeric

½ teaspoon curry powder

¼ teaspoon ground cinnamon

Pinch of red pepper flakes

2 teaspoons kosher salt

⅛ teaspoon freshly ground black pepper

Per Serving (½ cooked breast)
Calories 136 ● Fat 3.5 g
Saturated Fat 0.5 g
Cholesterol 73 mg
Carbohydrate 0.5 g ● Fiber 0 g
Protein 24 g ● Sugars 0 g
Sodium 179 mg

Freezer-to-Instant-Pot Chicken and Dumpling Soup

FF IP

SERVES 7

PREP AHEAD AND FREEZE

½ cup diced onion

1 cup chopped celery

1 cup chopped carrots

1 garlic clove, minced

1¼ pounds boneless, skinless chicken breasts

2 fresh sage leaves, chopped

2 bay leaves

8 ounces frozen ricotta cavatelli

ADD LATER

1 tablespoon unsalted butter

2 tablespoons all-purpose flour

6 cups water

2 tablespoons organic chicken bouillon (I like Better Than Bouillon)

¼ teaspoon kosher salt

Chopped fresh parsley, for garnish

> FRIDGE: UP TO 4 DAYS. THE PASTA WILL SOAK UP A LOT OF THE LIQUID. ADD MORE WATER AS NEEDED WHEN REHEATING.

> FREEZER: UP TO 6 MONTHS

SKINNY SCOOP Cavatelli is an Italian pasta, sometimes made with ricotta, sometimes without. The ones I use here are made with ricotta and are sold frozen in some supermarkets or Italian specialty stores. Frozen gnocchi could also be used in their place.

When the weather turns cool, I crave comfort foods—the kind of dishes that stick to your bones and warm you up like a big hug or a cozy sweater. Most comfort foods, however, are loaded with calories and fat . . . so my solution is always a big pot of soup! This chicken and dumpling soup is perfect to prep ahead and freeze, so you can whip it up anytime you're craving comfort in a bowl. To streamline the recipe, I used frozen ricotta cavatelli rather than making the dumplings from scratch. (Note: If you want to make this with fresh ingredients rather than frozen, the same cook times will apply.)

Add the onion, celery, carrots, and garlic to a gallon-size zip-top plastic bag or freezer-safe container. Wrap the chicken, sage, and bay leaves separately in plastic, then place in the same bag or container with the vegetables.

When ready to cook, remove from the freezer.

Press the sauté button on the Instant Pot (or any electric pressure cooker). Add the butter. Once melted, add the onion, celery, carrots, and garlic. Cook, stirring occasionally, until the vegetables are soft, about 5 minutes. Add the flour and cook, stirring constantly, for about 1 minute to cook out the raw taste of the flour. Press cancel. Add the water and stir with a wooden spoon to deglaze, scraping any browned bits stuck to the bottom of the pot. Add the frozen chicken, the bouillon, and the frozen herbs. Cover and cook on high pressure for 20 minutes. Natural release. Remove the chicken and discard the bay leaves. Shred the chicken with two forks, then return to the pot.

Add the frozen cavatelli, cover, and cook on high pressure for 2 minutes. Quick release. Stir in the salt.

SERVE NOW: Divide among 7 serving bowls, and garnish with parsley.

FREEZE AND SERVE LATER: If you want to freeze the cooked soup, cook as directed above without adding the cavatelli, then freeze. Reheat on the stove until heated through, then add the cavatelli and cook until tender and thawed.

No Instant Pot, No Problem! *If you don't have an electric pressure cooker, no problem. Add an additional ½ cup water and simmer this soup in a covered large pot or Dutch oven on low for about 1 hour before adding the cavatelli. Cook according to the package directions until the cavatelli is tender.*

Per Serving (scant 1½ cups) ● Calories 203 ● Fat 4 g ● Saturated Fat 1.5 g Cholesterol 58 mg ● Carbohydrate 17 g ● Fiber 1.5 g ● Protein 21 g Sugars 2 g ● Sodium 742 mg

Freezer Chicken Black Bean Burritos

FF **SC**

MAKES 10

CHICKEN

- 1 cup canned reduced-sodium black beans, rinsed and drained
- 1 (10-ounce) can diced tomatoes with mild green chilies
- 1 pound boneless, skinless chicken breast
- ½ teaspoon kosher salt
- ¾ teaspoon ground cumin
- ½ teaspoon garlic powder
- ¼ teaspoon cayenne pepper
- 1¼ cups jarred mild or spicy chunky salsa
- 1¼ cups cooked brown rice
- ¼ cup chopped fresh cilantro

BURRITOS

- 10 (8-inch) low-carb flour tortillas (I like Olé Xtreme Wellness)
- 1¼ cups shredded cheddar or pepper Jack cheese
- Cooking spray
- Hot sauce, salsa, guacamole, and/or sour cream, for serving (optional)

FRIDGE: UP TO 4 DAYS

FREEZER: UP TO 3 MONTHS

On those crazy-busy weeknights when there's zero time to cook, you'll be happy to have these burritos tucked away in your freezer! Using the slow cooker to make the chicken and bean filling, and buying frozen brown rice (I'm obsessed with Trader Joe's brand!), makes the prep super simple. Since this recipe makes ten burritos, you can serve some for dinner when you make them, then freeze the rest for another night. To make it a more substantial meal, serve them with refried beans, guacamole, and pico de gallo on the side.

Make the chicken: In a slow cooker, combine the beans and tomatoes with chilies. In a medium bowl, season the chicken with the salt, cumin, garlic powder, and cayenne. Place the chicken over the beans in the slow cooker and top with the salsa. Cover and cook on low for about 4 hours, or until the chicken is tender. In the slow cooker, shred the chicken with two forks and mix well with the sauce to let the flavors combine. Pour the chicken mixture into a large colander to drain (you don't want any liquid) and return to the slow cooker. Mix in the rice and cilantro.

Assemble the burritos: On a hot griddle or over an open flame, lightly char both sides of the tortillas. (Keep them warm under a towel covering if eating right away.)

On a clean work surface, spread out the tortillas and scoop ½ cup of the chicken and bean mixture onto the center of each. Top each with 2 tablespoons cheese. To assemble, roll a tortilla from the bottom up and fold the left and right edges in toward the center. Continue rolling into a tight cylinder. Repeat with the remaining tortillas and filling.

SERVE NOW: Heat a skillet over medium heat. When hot, spray the skillet with oil and add the burritos, seam side down. Cook, covered, until the bottom of the burritos are golden brown, about 3 minutes on each side. Serve with hot sauce, salsa, and other optional toppings.

FREEZE AND SERVE LATER: After assembling the burritos, place a piece of foil on a work surface vertically, then place a burrito at the bottom center. Fold the sides of the foil over the burrito and roll it up. Transfer to a labeled freezer-safe bag to prevent freezer burn.

Per Serving (1 burrito) ● Calories 225 ● Fat 8 g ● Saturated Fat 3.5 g Cholesterol 44 mg ● Carbohydrate 29 g ● Fiber 13.5 g ● Protein 20 g Sugars 2 g ● Sodium 785 mg

How to Reheat

Thawing overnight in the refrigerator (best results): Transfer the burritos to the refrigerator the night before you plan to eat them.

Preheat the oven to 425° F. Place the burritos, still in their foil, on a baking sheet. Bake for about 20 minutes, turning them over halfway through. Carefully remove the foil and bake uncovered for about 5 minutes more, until browned. Let cool for 2 minutes before serving.

Reheating directly from freezer to oven (best results): Preheat the oven to 425°F. Bake the wrapped burritos for about 45 minutes, turning over halfway through. Carefully remove the foil and bake uncovered for about 5 minutes, until browned. Let cool for 2 minutes before serving.

Reheating from freezer to microwave (least favorite results): Remove a burrito from the foil, place on a microwave-safe dish, cover with a paper towel, and microwave for 1 minute. Flip the burrito, then cook for an additional 1 to 1½ minutes. Let cool for 2 minutes before serving.

Freezer-to-Instant-Pot Cream of Chicken and Wild Rice Soup

GF FF IP

SERVES 6

PREP AHEAD AND FREEZE

2 cups sliced shiitake mushrooms (about 4 ounces)

1 cup chopped celery

1 cup chopped carrots

¼ cup chopped shallots

2 tablespoons chopped fresh parsley

1 pound boneless, skinless chicken breasts

6 ounces uncooked wild rice

1½ teaspoons fresh thyme leaves

2 bay leaves

ADD LATER

¼ cup all-purpose flour

2 tablespoons chicken bouillon* (I like Better Than Bouillon)

½ cup reduced-fat sour cream

¼ teaspoon kosher salt

* Read the label to be sure this product is gluten-free.

> FRIDGE: UP TO 4 DAYS. ADD BROTH OR WATER TO LOOSEN WHEN REHEATING IF THE SOUP IS TOO THICK.

> FREEZER: FREEZE UNCOOKED PREPPED INGREDIENTS UP TO 6 MONTHS.

I literally crave this hearty soup when the weather begins to chill. It's thick, creamy, and so warming on a cold day. This soup also works great as a freezer-to-Instant-Pot meal—just prep all your veggies and herbs and freeze them with the chicken and rice. When a soup craving strikes, simply pop it in the Instant Pot, adding the flour and sour cream after. It makes enough for dinner, with leftovers for lunch the next day. I find that chicken thighs are more tender and flavorful here, but I used chicken breasts for this recipe.

Add the mushrooms, celery, carrots, shallots, and parsley to a gallon-size zip-top plastic bag or freezer-safe container (make sure the container fits in your Instant Pot (or any electric pressure cooker) so you don't have to thaw it before cooking) along with the chicken, rice, thyme, and bay leaves. Label with the remaining ingredients you will need for later.

When ready to cook, remove from the freezer.

Add the frozen ingredients to the Instant Pot with 5 cups water. In a small bowl, add the flour to an additional 1 cup water and whisk well. Add to the pot along with the bouillon. Cover and cook on high pressure for 25 minutes. Natural release. Remove the chicken and discard the bay leaves. Shred the chicken with two forks and return the chicken to the pot. Stir in the sour cream and salt.

SERVE NOW: Divide the soup among 6 bowls (1½ cups each) and eat right away.

No Instant Pot, No Problem! *You can prepare this soup in a Dutch oven, adding an additional ¼ cup water. Simmer on low heat for 45 to 55 minutes, until the wild rice is tender.*

Per Serving (1½ cups) • Calories 282 • Fat 5.5 g • Saturated Fat 2.5 g Cholesterol 56 mg • Carbohydrate 32 g • Fiber 3.5 g • Protein 24 g Sugars 4 g • Sodium 862 mg

Freezer-to-Instant-Pot Thai Chicken Stew with Butternut Squash

SERVES 5

STEW

2¼ pounds boneless, skinless chicken thighs (about 10), fat trimmed

1½ pounds peeled butternut squash, 1-inch cubes

3 medium scallions, cut into 1-inch pieces

1 medium red bell pepper, diced

4 medium garlic cloves, thinly sliced

1 tablespoon grated fresh ginger

2 teaspoons toasted sesame oil

1 tablespoon red curry paste

1½ teaspoons kosher salt

1 tablespoon Sriracha sauce

⅓ cup reduced-sodium soy sauce*

¼ cup fresh lime juice (from about 2 limes)

2 tablespoons chopped fresh cilantro, plus 1 tablespoon for garnish

½ cup canned unsweetened full-fat coconut milk

SERVING

2½ cups cooked basmati rice

*Read the label to be sure this product is gluten-free.

FRIDGE: UP TO 4 DAYS

FREEZER: UP TO 9 MONTHS (UNCOOKED) OR 3 MONTHS (COOKED)

This Thai-inspired stew is a great contender for prepping and freezing the ingredients ahead of time. This way, you can cook the ingredients from frozen right in an Instant Pot (or any electric pressure cooker) whenever the mood strikes. Just be sure to freeze the stew ingredients in a freezer-safe container that fits in the Instant Pot. With curry paste, a hint of coconut milk, Sriracha, and lime, this flavorful stew is perfect over basmati rice.

In a large bowl, combine all of the stew ingredients except for the coconut milk and mix well (I like to wear gloves to mix with my hands). Transfer to a large freezer-safe container (use one that will fit in your Instant Pot, or any electric pressure cooker, so it fits when frozen) or a gallon-size freezer bag, pressing out all the air out. Seal and freeze. (If using a freezer bag, I place the bag in a container that will fit in my Instant Pot rather than laying it flat, so it fits frozen.)

When ready to cook, remove from the freezer and run under warm water to make it easy to take out.

Place all of the stew ingredients plus the coconut milk and ½ cup water in an electric pressure cooker. Seal and cook on high pressure for 15 minutes. Let the pressure release for 10 minutes before quick releasing.

Transfer to 5 bowls and scoop ½ cup rice over each bowl. Garnish with cilantro.

No Instant Pot, No Problem! *Make this on the stove by adding an additional ¼ cup water and cooking on low for about 40 minutes, or until the chicken is tender and cooked through.*

Per Serving (2 cups stew + ½ cup rice) ● Calories 501 ● Fat 15.5 g Saturated Fat 6.5 g ● Cholesterol 194 mg ● Carbohydrate 46 g Fiber 4 g ● Protein 45 g ● Sugars 6 g ● Sodium 1,209 mg

Instant Pot Cajun Red Beans and Rice

(GF) (DF) (FF) (IP)

SERVES 8

1 pound dried kidney beans

1 tablespoon kosher salt

½ tablespoon extra-virgin olive oil

1 large onion, diced

1 green bell pepper, diced

2 celery stalks, diced

6 garlic cloves, minced or pressed through a garlic press

1 teaspoon Cajun or Creole seasoning (I like Tony Chachere's Creole Seasoning)

¼ teaspoon cayenne pepper

12 ounces cooked chicken andouille sausage,* sliced (I like Aidells or Al Fresco)

1½ teaspoons chopped fresh sage

4 sprigs of fresh thyme

2 bay leaves

SERVING

4 cups cooked white rice

Sliced scallions or chopped fresh parsley, for garnish

Hot sauce (optional)

* Read the label to be sure this product is gluten-free.

FRIDGE: UP TO 4 DAYS

FREEZER: UP TO 3 MONTHS

In New Orleans, it's a Monday tradition to simmer a big pot of red beans and rice in the kitchen all day long—but using an Instant Pot makes this classic Cajun dish cook up a whole lot faster! The beans are seasoned with onions, bell peppers, and celery (the "holy trinity" of Cajun cooking), along with garlic, herbs, spices, and smoky andouille sausage. If you can't find chicken or turkey andouille sausage, any smoked sausage, or even a smoked turkey leg, would also work. Puréeing some of the beans at the end in a blender is the key as it creates a creamy consistency.

Rinse the beans and place them into the Instant Pot (or any electric pressure cooker) with 8 cups water and 1 teaspoon salt. Seal and cook on high pressure for 4 minutes. Let natural release for 10 minutes, then quick release. Drain and rinse the beans.

Press the sauté button on the Instant Pot. Add the oil, onion, bell pepper, celery, garlic, 1 teaspoon salt, Cajun seasoning, and cayenne. Cook, stirring occasionally, until the vegetables are soft, 5 to 7 minutes. Stir in 3½ cups water, the parcooked beans, sausage, sage, thyme, bay leaves, and remaining 1 teaspoon salt.

Seal and cook on high pressure for 15 minutes. Natural release.

Discard the thyme sprigs and bay leaves. Pour 1½ cups of the beans and liquid (without the sausage) into a regular blender, process until smooth, then pour back into the pot to thicken the mixture.

Press the sauté button. Bring the entire mixture to a boil and cook, stirring occasionally, until thickened, 4 to 5 minutes.

SERVE NOW: Divide the beans and sausage among 8 bowls and top each with ½ cup rice. Garnish with scallions or parsley and serve with hot sauce on the side.

FREEZE AND SERVE LATER: Divide among 8 airtight containers and refrigerate or freeze. To reheat, thaw overnight in the refrigerator and reheat on the stove or in the microwave.

No Instant Pot, No Problem! To make this in a Dutch oven, soak the beans overnight and discard the water. Cook covered with 6 cups water over medium-low heat for 1 hour 45 minutes, stirring occasionally. Discard the herbs and purée 1½ cups of the beans and liquid (not sausage) in a blender. Cook 10 to 15 minutes more, until thickened.

Per Serving (generous 1 cup beans and sausage + ½ cup rice) ● Calories 402 Fat 5.5 g ● Saturated Fat 1.5 g ● Cholesterol 33 mg ● Carbohydrate 66 g Fiber 10 g ● Protein 23 g ● Sugars 3 g ● Sodium 707 mg

Instant Pot Chicken and Shrimp Gumbo

GF FF IP

SERVES 6

1 tablespoon unsalted butter

1 large onion, chopped

1 green bell pepper, chopped

2 celery stalks, chopped

3 garlic cloves, minced

1½ cups chicken broth*

1 (14.5-ounce) can petite diced tomatoes, undrained

½ (10-ounce) can diced tomatoes with green chilies, undrained

24 ounces boneless, skinless chicken thighs (about 6 total), fat trimmed

9 ounces chicken andouille sausage, sliced

2 cups sliced fresh or frozen okra (fresh is best)

¾ cup fresh or frozen corn kernels

¼ teaspoon cayenne pepper

½ teaspoon kosher salt

Freshly ground black pepper

¾ pound peeled and deveined raw medium shrimp, tails removed

2 teaspoons ground gumbo filé powder (I like Zatarain's)

2 cups cooked brown rice

Chopped scallions, for garnish

*Read the label to be sure this product is gluten-free.

FRIDGE: UP TO 3 DAYS

FREEZER: UP TO 3 MONTHS

This lightened-up gumbo is loaded with so many delicious ingredients: chicken thighs, shrimp, sausage, okra, and lots of veggies. While many Louisiana recipes start with a roux (a mixture of flour and fat used to thicken sauces, stews, and gravies), this gumbo is actually roux-free. The result is a quicker dish that is lighter in calories, but certainly not in flavor! The base of this stew is made with onions, bell pepper, and celery, plus garlic and filé powder (made with ground sassafras leaves, it's available online). I like to serve this over brown rice, but you can skip the rice if you prefer to keep it low-carb.

Press the sauté button on the Instant Pot. Add the butter. Once melted, add the onion, bell pepper, and celery. Cook, stirring occasionally, until the vegetables are tender, about 5 minutes. Stir in the garlic and cook until fragrant, about 1 minute. Press cancel. Add the broth and stir with a wooden spoon to deglaze, scraping up any browned bits stuck to the bottom of the pot. Add the diced tomatoes, tomatoes with green chilies, chicken, sausage, okra, corn, cayenne, salt, and pepper to taste. Cook on high pressure until the chicken easily shreds, about 25 minutes. Natural release.

Shred the chicken coarsely with two forks, then return to the pot and add the shrimp. Press the sauté button and bring the mixture to a boil. Simmer until the shrimp is opaque and cooked through, 4 to 5 minutes. Press cancel, and when it stops boiling, stir in the filé powder.

SERVE NOW: Divide among 6 bowls and serve topped with the rice and scallions.

FREEZE AND SERVE LATER: Let the gumbo cool to room temperature, then transfer to freezer-safe containers. Thaw overnight in the refrigerator before reheating on the stove or in the microwave.

No Instant Pot, No Problem! *Make this on the stove by increasing the broth to 1¾ cups and cook, covered, over low heat for about 50 minutes, until the chicken is tender, then add the shrimp and cook for about 3 minutes more, until the shrimp is opaque and cooked through.*

Per Serving (1⅔ cups gumbo + ⅓ cup rice) ● Calories 419 ● Fat 11.5 g Saturated Fat 3.5 g ● Cholesterol 213 mg ● Carbohydrate 34 g Fiber 5 g ● Protein 43 g ● Sugars 6 g ● Sodium 1,188 mg

Chicken and Chickpea Stew

GF DF FF IP

SERVES 4

4 large bone-in, skinless chicken thighs, fat trimmed (1½ pounds)

1½ teaspoons kosher salt

½ teaspoon garlic powder

1 teaspoon olive oil

1 large onion, chopped

¼ cup chopped fresh parsley

3 garlic cloves, minced

2 tablespoons tomato paste

½ cup white wine

2 (15-ounce) cans chickpeas,* rinsed and drained

2 cups chopped collard greens or Swiss chard

1 teaspoon sweet paprika

Freshly ground black pepper

1 bay leaf

*Read the label to be sure this product is gluten-free.

FRIDGE: UP TO 4 DAYS

FREEZER: UP TO 3 MONTHS

Some days call for a rustic and cozy meal that fills your belly and warms your soul. That's where this simple chicken stew comes in—it's the kind of dish you can eat with a fork *and* a spoon. This unfussy one-pot recipe is made with bone-in thighs, white wine, canned chickpeas, and collard greens, and my family actually prefers it over beef stew. I often double the recipe and freeze the other half for another night; the cook time remains the same and it gives me a night off later in the month.

Season the chicken with ½ teaspoon salt and garlic powder. Set aside.

Heat a large pot or Dutch oven over medium heat. Add the oil, onion, parsley, and garlic and sauté until soft, about 2 minutes. Stir in the tomato paste and cook until slightly darkened, about 1 minute. Add the wine and let reduce for about 2 minutes. Add the chicken, chickpeas, greens, and 2½ cups water (enough to just cover the chicken), the remaining 1 teaspoon salt, paprika, pepper to taste, and bay leaf. Mix to combine. Cover and cook until the chicken is tender, 45 to 50 minutes. Discard the bay leaf and serve.

FREEZE AND SERVE LATER: Let the stew cool to room temperature. Divide into freezer-safe containers and freeze. To reheat, transfer to the refrigerator to thaw completely or reheat from frozen in 30-second intervals in the microwave until heated through.

For an Instant Pot: Reduce the water to 2 cups and cook for 20 minutes on high pressure, then quick release.

For a Slow Cooker: Reduce the water to 2 cups and cook on low for 8 hours.

Per Serving (1 thigh + 1 cup chickpeas + greens) ● Calories 510
Fat 12 g ● Saturated Fat 2 g ● Cholesterol 119 mg ● Carbohydrate 57 g
Fiber 12 g ● Protein 41 g ● Sugars 3 g ● Sodium 1,000 mg

Chicken Orzo Soup with Dill

GF DF FF IP

SERVES 8

1½ pounds boneless, skinless chicken thighs, fat trimmed

½ teaspoon kosher salt, plus more if needed

2 teaspoons extra-virgin olive oil

1 cup diced leeks, white and pale green parts only, rinsed well

1 cup diced celery

1 cup diced carrot

5 garlic cloves, minced

11 cups reduced-sodium chicken broth (canned or homemade)*

2 bay leaves

⅛ teaspoon freshly ground black pepper

1 cup orzo pasta, wheat or gluten-free

4 cups baby spinach

½ cup chopped fresh dill

Lemon wedges, for serving (optional)

* Read the label to be sure this product is gluten-free.

FRIDGE: UP TO 4 DAYS

FREEZER: UP TO 3 MONTHS

This weeknight chicken soup is Greek-inspired—I use orzo in place of noodles, flavor it with a handful of fresh dill, and finish it off with a squeeze of lemon juice. It's hearty enough to stand on its own as a meal, but you can also serve a small salad or piece of crusty bread on the side if you'd like. It's easy, inexpensive, and great for lunch or dinner. Or better yet, enjoy half for dinner and freeze the rest for another night alongside an entrée.

Season the chicken with the salt. Set aside.

In a large pot or Dutch oven, heat the oil over medium heat. Add the leeks, celery, carrot, and garlic and sauté until soft, about 5 minutes. Add the chicken, broth, bay leaves, and pepper and bring to a boil. Cover, reduce the heat to medium-low, and cook until the chicken is tender and cooked through, 25 to 30 minutes. Discard the bay leaves.

Transfer the chicken to a plate and shred with two forks. Set aside.

Bring the soup to a boil over high heat. Add the pasta and cook according to package directions. Add the baby spinach during the last minute of cooking to wilt. Return the chicken to the pot along with the dill and adjust the salt to taste. Serve with lemon wedges for squeezing over (if using).

FREEZE AND SERVE LATER: Let the soup cool, then transfer to airtight, freezer-safe containers. To reheat from frozen, let thaw in the refrigerator the night before, then reheat on the stove or in the microwave.

For an Instant Pot: Prepare the soup in an Instant Pot (or any electric pressure cooker). Seal and cook on high pressure for 20 minutes. Natural release, then add the orzo and cook on high pressure for 2 minutes (or press sauté and cook uncovered according to package directions). Quick release and serve.

SKINNY SCOOP Leeks are mild and delicious in this soup, but chopped onions would also work well.

Per Serving (1¾ cups) ● Calories 238 ● Fat 6.5 g ● Saturated Fat 1.5 g
Cholesterol 81 mg ● Carbohydrate 20 g ● Fiber 2 g ● Protein 23 g
Sugars 3 g ● Sodium 1,062 mg

Slow Cooker White Bean Chicken Chili

SERVES 8

2 (15.5-ounce) cans small Great Northern or navy beans,* undrained

2 (4-ounce) cans chopped green chile peppers, undrained

4 medium scallions, chopped

1/3 cup chopped fresh cilantro, plus more for topping

3 tablespoons reduced-sodium taco seasoning* (from 1 packet)

1 1/2 pounds boneless, skinless chicken breasts (3 breasts)

OPTIONAL TOPPINGS

Sour cream, sliced avocado, pepper Jack cheese, poblano cream (page 217)

*Read the label to be sure this product is gluten-free.

FRIDGE: UP TO 4 DAYS

FREEZER: UP TO 3 MONTHS

I always prefer white beans over red, pink, or black beans—*especially* in chili! This white bean chicken chili is light but also substantial, and the prep couldn't be easier since nothing has to precook. Just dump all of the ingredients into the slow cooker and then set it and forget it—my favorite type of slow cooker recipe! This chili is also tasty with boneless chicken thighs if you prefer dark meat.

Combine the beans and their liquid, 3/4 cup water, green chiles and their liquid, scallions, cilantro, and taco seasoning in the slow cooker and mix well. Add the chicken and cook on high for 5 to 6 hours or on low for 8 to 10 hours. (To make in an Instant Pot, or any electric pressure cooker, cook for 20 minutes on high pressure with quick release.)

Shred the chicken with two forks and mix to combine.

SERVE NOW: Top with fresh cilantro and serve with your favorite chili toppings.

FREEZE AND SERVE LATER: Transfer the cooked chili to freezer-safe containers. To reheat, thaw overnight in the refrigerator and reheat on the stove or in the microwave.

> ***Make It a Freezer Meal Kit!*** Combine all of the ingredients except the beans and water in a freezer-safe bag. Label, date, and freeze the bag. When ready to prepare, transfer to the refrigerator to thaw overnight, then empty the contents of the bag into the slow cooker. Add the beans and water and cook as directed.

Per serving (about 1 cup) • Calories 194 • Fat 3 g • Saturated Fat 0.5 g Cholesterol 54 mg • Carbohydrate 20 g • Fiber 8.5 g • Protein 24 g Sugars 0 g • Sodium 682 mg

Pollo Guisado

GF DF FF IP

SERVES 4

4 chicken drumsticks, on the bone,
  skin removed (14 ounces total)

4 bone-in chicken thighs, skin
  removed and fat trimmed
  (1¼ pounds total)

½ teaspoon kosher salt

½ teaspoon garlic powder

1 teaspoon olive oil

4 medium scallions, chopped

1 plum tomato, diced

2 garlic cloves, minced

¼ cup chopped fresh cilantro,
  plus 2 tablespoons for garnish

1 (8-ounce) can tomato sauce

1 tablespoon chicken bouillon* (I like
  Better Than Bouillon)

½ teaspoon ground cumin

2 bay leaves

*Read the label to be sure this
  product is gluten-free.

FRIDGE: UP TO 4 DAYS

FREEZER: UP TO 3 MONTHS

If you've ever lived in or visited Colombia, you probably know that stews are the most common type of food eaten there, especially at lunchtime, when they're served with a slice of avocado and a side of white rice to soak up the sauce. If I eat this with rice and avocado, a single piece of chicken is usually enough. It's also great served over cauliflower rice, which is not very Colombian but still a great way to add more vegetables to the meal and cut your carbs, to boot. Any part of the chicken works—you can even use a whole cut-up chicken (just be sure to remove the skin). I also prefer to use bone-in chicken because the bones add more flavor and collagen that thickens the soup.

Season the chicken with the salt and garlic powder. Set aside.

In a large pot or Dutch oven, heat the olive oil over medium heat. Add the scallions and sauté until soft, 2 to 3 minutes. Add the tomato and garlic and cook until soft, 2 to 3 minutes. Stir in the cilantro and cook for about 1 minute more. Add the tomato sauce, 1 cup water, bouillon, and cumin. Stir well to combine.

Add the chicken and bay leaves to the sauce. Bring to a boil, then reduce the heat to medium-low. Cover and cook until the chicken is tender, about 50 minutes. Uncover the pot and increase the heat to high. Cook until the sauce is thickened, 5 to 10 minutes. Discard the bay leaves, top with the remaining 2 tablespoons cilantro, and serve.

FREEZE AND SERVE LATER: Let the soup cool to room temperature, then transfer to freezer-safe containers. To reheat, thaw in the fridge the night before and reheat on the stove or in the microwave until heated through.

For an Instant Pot: Prepare the ingredients in an Instant Pot (or any electric pressure cooker). Seal and cook on high pressure for 20 minutes. Natural release, then open when the pressure subsides. Serve as directed.

SKINNY SCOOP If you want to make this a one-pot meal, add peeled, diced yellow potatoes or yucca along with the chicken. You can also add a few corncobs cut in half in the last 5 minutes of cooking.

Per Serving (2 pieces chicken + ⅓ cup sauce) ● Calories 290 ● Fat 9.5 g
Saturated Fat 2 g ● Cholesterol 90 mg ● Carbohydrate 6 g ● Fiber 1.5 g
Protein 41 g ● Sugars 4 g ● Sodium 1,158 mg

DIY Chicken Taco Kits

(Q) (GF) (FF)

SERVES 4

CHICKEN

1¼ pounds boneless, skinless chicken thighs, fat trimmed, cut into ½-inch-thick strips

1 large yellow onion, cut into ¼-inch-thick slices

1 tablespoon extra-virgin olive oil

3 tablespoons fresh lime juice

1 tablespoon ground cumin

1 tablespoon dried oregano

1 teaspoon chili powder*

2 garlic cloves, crushed

Kosher salt

Freshly ground black pepper

Olive oil spray

ROASTED POBLANO CREAM

¼ poblano pepper, with seeds

Olive oil spray

1 cup light sour cream

2 tablespoons fresh lime juice

2 tablespoons chopped fresh cilantro

½ teaspoon kosher salt

Freshly ground black pepper

SERVING

8 (6-inch) corn tortillas

2 cups shredded green cabbage

¼ cup chopped red onion

1 lime, cut into 8 wedges

Chopped fresh cilantro, for garnish

*Read the label to be sure this product is gluten-free.

> FRIDGE: UP TO 4 DAYS
> (CHICKEN AND SAUCE)

> FREEZER: UP TO 3 MONTHS
> (MARINATED RAW CHICKEN)

Inspired by Costco's Street Taco Dinner kits, which are pretty genius, I set out to make my own homemade chicken tacos to pack for lunch or make ahead for dinner. Easy-peasy—the chicken and caramelized onions cook at the same time all in one skillet and I use boneless chicken thighs because they have more flavor and are juicer than chicken breasts. The whole thing takes just about 30 minutes—make the sauce and prep the rest while the chicken cooks. This recipe makes extra poblano sauce; you can use the rest drizzled over chili or frozen taquitos (see page 225).

Preheat the oven to 350°F.

Make the chicken: In a medium bowl, toss the chicken and onion with the olive oil, lime juice, cumin, oregano, chili powder, and garlic. Season with 1¼ teaspoons salt and black pepper to taste. (If making the chicken ahead, you can freeze at this point. Thaw overnight in the refrigerator before cooking.)

Heat a large, deep nonstick skillet over high heat until very hot. When hot, spray with oil and add the chicken and onion along with any marinade and cook, stirring occasionally, until the liquid evaporates and the chicken and onion are tender and browned on the edges, 20 to 25 minutes. Set aside.

Make the poblano cream: Place the poblano on a small baking sheet and spritz with oil. Roast until slightly charred, flipping halfway through, about 12 minutes. Transfer to a food processor with the sour cream, lime juice, cilantro, salt, and black pepper to taste and process until smooth.

SERVE NOW: Heat the tortillas on an open flame for 30 seconds. Divide the chicken among the charred tortillas and top with the cabbage, red onion, 1 teaspoon cream, a squeeze of lime juice, and cilantro. (You'll have about 1 cup cream left over; store up to 4 days in an airtight container.)

MEAL PREP: Roll up each tortilla and place in an airtight container with ¾ cup chicken and onion, ½ cup cabbage, 1 tablespoon red onion, 2 lime wedges, cilantro, and 1 teaspoon cream. When ready to serve, warm the tortillas on an open flame for about 30 seconds, and reheat the chicken in a skillet over medium heat for about 3 minutes or in the microwave. Top as directed.

Per Serving (2 tacos) ● Calories 366 ● Fat 12.5 g ● Saturated Fat 3 g Cholesterol 139 mg ● Carbohydrate 33 g ● Fiber 6 g ● Protein 32 g Sugars 4 g ● Sodium 558 mg

Italian Stuffed Jalapeño Peppers

GF FF

SERVES 4

16 large fresh jalapeño peppers

1 pound 93% lean ground turkey

¾ cup cooked brown rice (I like Trader Joe's frozen brown rice)

⅓ cup seasoned bread crumbs, whole wheat or gluten-free

3 cups Basil Pomodoro Sauce (page 294) or store-bought marinara sauce

¼ cup minced onion

3 tablespoons chopped fresh parsley

1 large egg, beaten

1 garlic clove, minced

¼ cup freshly grated Pecorino Romano or Parmesan cheese

2 teaspoons tomato paste

¾ teaspoon kosher salt

Freshly ground black pepper

FRIDGE: UP TO 5 DAYS

FREEZER: UP TO 3 MONTHS

Eating these stuffed jalapeños filled with ground turkey and rice is a little bit like playing Russian roulette—some are mild, some are spicy, and you just don't know what you're going to get! No matter what you end up with, you're sure to enjoy it because they are incredibly delicious. Most of the heat comes from the seeds and the membrane of the peppers, so make sure to clean them well before stuffing.

Preheat the oven to 375°F.

Using gloves, slice off the top of the jalapeño peppers, cut out the membranes, and remove the seeds. Cut a slit along one edge to make them easier to stuff.

In a large bowl, combine the turkey, rice, bread crumbs, ¼ cup marinara sauce, onion, parsley, egg, garlic, Pecorino, tomato paste, salt, and pepper to taste. Mix thoroughly.

Stuff the ground turkey mixture (about ¼ cup) into each pepper.

Pour ½ cup marinara sauce into the bottom of a 9 × 13-inch baking dish. Place the peppers on top and cover with the remaining sauce. Cover tightly with foil.

SERVE NOW: Bake until the peppers are tender, 1 to 1½ hours.

REFRIGERATE AND SERVE LATER: Before baking, the dish can be prepared up to 24 hours ahead and refrigerated. Bake for 1 to 1½ hours.

FREEZE AND SERVE LATER: Before baking, the dish can be prepared in a freezer-to-ovenproof baking dish, covered tightly, and frozen. Bake from frozen (no need to thaw) in a preheated 350°F oven for about 2 hours, until heated through and tender.

Per Serving (4 peppers + sauce) ● Calories 375 ● Fat 15 g ● Saturated Fat 4.5 g Cholesterol 136 mg ● Carbohydrate 33 g ● Fiber 6.5 g ● Protein 31 g Sugars 10 g ● Sodium 971 mg

Autumn Stuffed Acorn Squash

GF DF FF

SERVES 6

3 small acorn squashes (22 ounces each), washed, halved lengthwise, and seeds removed

Olive oil spray

½ teaspoon kosher salt

Freshly ground black pepper

½ cup (3 ounces) uncooked wild rice

1 tablespoon olive oil

1 small yellow onion, chopped

1 medium carrot, chopped

1 medium celery stalk, chopped

2 garlic cloves, minced

4 links (11 ounces total) sweet Italian chicken sausage, casings removed

1 Granny Smith apple, chopped into ¼-inch pieces

1½ tablespoons chopped fresh sage

½ tablespoon chopped fresh thyme

½ cup chicken broth*

¼ cup dry white wine

2 cups chopped kale

*Read the label to be sure this product is gluten-free.

FRIDGE: UP TO 5 DAYS

FREEZER: UP TO 3 MONTHS

Acorn squash, the star of this dish with its deep orange color, makes the perfect edible bowl. I pack it with a wild rice stuffing featuring chicken sausage, sage, apples, and thyme. You can serve it for dinner, then pack the extras for lunch, or make it ahead to freeze for the month. And don't toss those squash seeds! Just like pumpkin seeds, you can toast the seeds of an acorn squash with a few spritzes of olive oil and a little salt for easy snacking.

Preheat the oven to 375°F.

Spritz both sides of the squash with olive oil spray. Season the insides with the salt and black pepper to taste.

Place the squash on a large baking sheet, skin side up, and bake until soft and tender, 45 to 50 minutes.

Meanwhile, cook the wild rice according to the package directions and set aside.

In a large skillet, heat the olive oil over medium heat. Add the onion and carrot and cook until beginning to soften, about 3 minutes. Add the celery and cook until softened, about 2 minutes more. Add the garlic and cook until fragrant, about 1 minute.

Add the chicken sausage, breaking it up as it cooks, until cooked through, about 6 minutes. Add the apple, sage, thyme, broth, wine, and kale. Mix well and cook until the liquid evaporates, 10 to 15 minutes. Mix in the wild rice and remove from the heat.

Fill the acorn squash cavities with the rice and sausage mixture, about a generous ¾ cup each. Transfer to a large casserole dish, cover with foil, and bake until heated through, about 15 minutes. Serve hot.

FREEZE AND SERVE LATER: After stuffing the cavities, transfer to airtight containers or a large covered baking dish and transfer to the refrigerator or freezer. If reheating from frozen, let thaw in the refrigerator for 1 to 2 days. Reheat in the microwave for 3 to 4 minutes or in a 375°F oven for 20 to 30 minutes, until heated through.

SKINNY SCOOP To make your "bowl" sit flat, simply slice the squash in half lengthwise and slice off a tiny piece of the skin at the bottom of each half.

Per Serving (1 stuffed half) ● Calories 295 ● Fat 7 g ● Saturated Fat 1.5 g Cholesterol 39 mg ● Carbohydrate 47 g ● Fiber 7 g ● Protein 15 g Sugars 12 g ● Sodium 553 mg

Sofrito-Stuffed Cabbage Rolls

GF DF FF

SERVES 8

SOFRITO

1 small onion, roughly chopped

2 Cubanelle peppers, seeded and roughly chopped

1 large bunch fresh cilantro, ends trimmed, roughly chopped

8 garlic cloves, roughly chopped

1/2 tablespoon olive oil

ROLLS

1 large head cabbage

1 pound 93% lean ground beef

1 pound 93% lean ground turkey

2 cups cooked brown rice

2/3 cup chopped pitted green olives, plus 2 tablespoons of the brine

1 teaspoon dried oregano

1 large egg, beaten

1 3/4 teaspoons kosher salt

Freshly ground black pepper

SAUCE

1 teaspoon olive oil

1/4 teaspoon kosher salt

3 (8-ounce) cans tomato sauce

1 cup reduced-sodium beef broth*

*Read the label to be sure this product is gluten-free.

FRIDGE: UP TO 4 DAYS

FREEZER: UP TO 3 MONTHS

I grew up eating my dad's Czech-style stuffed cabbage, but since I'm also half-Colombian, I can't help but put a Latin spin on them here by adding lots of sofrito and green olives. Although they're a labor of love, once they're made, you can easily get two meals out of them for a family of four or freeze them in portioned servings for meals for the month. They can be prepped a day ahead and refrigerated until they're ready to bake. Freeze them cooked, then thaw overnight in the refrigerator and reheat in the oven or microwave.

Preheat the oven to 350°F.

Make the sofrito: Working in 3 to 4 batches, add the onion, peppers, cilantro, garlic, and olive oil to a blender and pulse a few times until chopped, but not puréed. You should have about 1 3/4 cups.

Bring a large pot of water to a boil over high heat. Remove the entire core of the cabbage with a paring knife. Immerse the whole head of cabbage in the boiling water for a few minutes, peeling off each leaf with tongs as soon as it becomes flexible, about 3 minutes. Set the leaves aside to dry and cool. You will need 16 outer leaves.

When cool, shave or cut out the thick rib of the cabbage leaves with a knife to make them easy to roll.

Make the sauce: Heat a medium pot over medium heat. Add the oil, 1/2 cup sofrito, and salt and cook until soft, about 5 minutes. Add the tomato sauce and broth and simmer until the flavors meld, about 5 minutes.

In a large bowl, combine the ground beef, ground turkey, remaining sofrito, brown rice, olives and brine, oregano, egg, salt, and pepper to taste. Add 1/3 cup sauce and mix well.

Scoop about 1/2 cup ground meat mixture onto the center of each cabbage leaf. Roll up the leaves, tucking in the ends.

Ladle 1 cup tomato sauce on the bottom of a 9 × 13-inch casserole dish in an even layer. Transfer the cabbage rolls, seam side down, to the dish, tightly packing them into 2 rows of 8 each. Top with the remaining sauce. Tightly cover with foil and bake until the cabbage is tender enough to cut with a spoon, 1 1/2 to 2 hours.

FREEZE AND SERVE LATER: Let the rolls cool completely before transferring a few at a time into separate freezer bags with the sauce, squeezing out any air, and freeze. To reheat, remove from the bag and transfer to a baking dish. Thaw in the refrigerator overnight. Bake in a 350°F oven until heated through, 40 to 50 minutes.

Per Serving (2 rolls + sauce) ● Calories 341 ● Fat 13.5 g ● Saturated Fat 3.5 g Cholesterol 100 mg ● Carbohydrate 30 g ● Fiber 7.5 g ● Protein 29 g Sugars 10 g ● Sodium 1,070 mg

Turkey Taquitos

Q GF FF

SERVES 8

TAQUITOS

Cooking spray

1 teaspoon garlic powder

1½ teaspoons ground cumin

1¼ teaspoons kosher salt

1 teaspoon chili powder*

½ teaspoon dried oregano

1 pound 93% lean ground turkey

½ small yellow onion, diced

½ cup tomato sauce

16 (6-inch) corn tortillas

1 cup (4 ounces) shredded
   reduced-fat Mexican cheese
   blend*

SERVING

2 medium (8 ounces total) Hass
   avocados

Juice of 1 small lime

¼ teaspoon kosher salt

½ cup light sour cream

8 cups shredded iceberg lettuce

*Read the label to be sure this
   product is gluten-free.

> FREEZER: UP TO 3 MONTHS

Whether you want a quick snack for the kids when they're hanging out with their friends or a main dish they won't complain about, you'll be happy to have a batch of these easy, crispy taquitos stashed in your freezer. The protein-packed filling made with ground turkey and Mexican cheese is so flavorful, and the taquitos reheat great in the oven or air fryer. As an appetizer, I usually just serve them with salsa for dipping, but to make it a meal, serve them over a bed of lettuce with guacamole and a drizzle of sour cream.

Preheat the oven to 400°F. Line a sheet pan with foil and spray with cooking spray.

In a small bowl, combine the garlic powder, cumin, salt, chili powder, and oregano.

Heat a large skillet over medium heat. Spray with oil. Brown the ground turkey, using a wooden spoon to break it into smaller pieces as it cooks, until no longer pink, 5 to 6 minutes. Stir in the spice mixture and mix well. Add the onion, tomato sauce, and ¼ cup water. Reduce the heat to low and simmer until the flavors meld and the sauce thickens, about 20 minutes. Let cool slightly.

Working in batches, place 3 tortillas between two paper towels and microwave until they are warm and pliable, about 30 seconds. Place a tortilla on a work surface and spread 2 tablespoons filling onto the bottom third of the tortilla and top with 1 tablespoon cheese. Roll the tortilla up from the bottom to surround the filling and place on the prepared baking sheet, seam side down. Repeat with the remaining filling and tortillas, arranging them in the pan about ½ inch apart. Spray the tops with oil, then bake until the tortillas are golden and crispy, about 15 minutes.

SERVE NOW: In a small bowl, mash the avocados. Stir in the lime juice and salt. Place the sour cream in a small bowl and stir in a small amount of water to achieve a drizzling consistency. Divide the shredded lettuce on serving plates and top with the taquitos, mashed avocado, and sour cream drizzle.

FREEZE AND SERVE LATER: Allow the taquitos to cool completely, then place in an airtight container or zip-top plastic bag and freeze. To reheat in an oven: Preheat the oven to 400°F. Place the frozen taquitos on a sheet pan and bake for 15 to 18 minutes, until heated through. To reheat in an air fryer: Preheat the air fryer to 380°F for 3 minutes. Cook the frozen taquitos for about 8 minutes, flipping halfway through, until heated through.

Per Serving (2 taquitos + ¼ cup guacamole + 1 tablespoon sour cream)
Calories 317 ● Fat 15 g ● Saturated Fat 5 g ● Cholesterol 55 mg ● Carbohydrate 30 g
Fiber 6.5 g ● Protein 20 g ● Sugars 3 g ● Sodium 467 mg

Sicilian Rice Ball (Arancini) Casserole

GF FF

SERVES 8

2 cups uncooked long-grain white rice

1 teaspoon kosher salt

14 ounces sweet Italian chicken sausage, casings removed

¼ cup minced onion

5 ounces frozen peas

2 cups Basil Pomodoro Sauce (page 294) or store-bought marinara sauce, plus more for serving (optional)

½ cup freshly grated Pecorino Romano cheese

2 large eggs, lightly beaten

Olive oil spray

¼ cup seasoned bread crumbs, regular or gluten-free

1¼ cups shredded part-skim mozzarella cheese*

Chopped fresh parsley or basil, for garnish (optional)

*Read the label to be sure this product is gluten-free.

FRIDGE: UP TO 4 DAYS

FREEZER: UP TO 3 MONTHS

This comforting casserole takes one of my favorite Italian appetizers (arancini) and turns it into a weeknight meal. It's an idea from my Italian friend Julia that is pure genius—I originally shared the recipe on my blog a few years ago and it's been a huge hit! A simple green salad on the side completes the meal. Julia usually makes two casseroles—one for dinner and one for the freezer to save for another night. It's basically the same amount of work to make two, so why not?

Cook the rice with the salt according to the package directions. Set aside to cool.

Heat a large nonstick skillet over medium-high heat. Add the sausage and cook, breaking it up into small pieces with a wooden spoon, until browned, about 5 minutes. Stir in the onion and cook until browned, 4 to 5 minutes more. Add the peas and 1 cup marinara sauce. Reduce the heat to low and cover. Cook until the flavors meld, about 20 minutes.

Preheat the oven to 400°F.

In a large bowl, combine the cooked rice, Pecorino, eggs, and ½ cup marinara sauce and mix well. (The mixture should be a bit sticky.)

Spray the bottom and sides of a 9 × 13-inch baking dish with oil. Add 2 tablespoons bread crumbs to the dish and roll around to coat the bottom and sides.

Take half the rice mixture (or a little more if needed) and cover the bottom and sides of the dish, pressing the rice down to form an even bottom layer. Add the meat-pea mixture and spread into an even layer. Top with ¾ cup mozzarella. Cover with the remaining rice mixture, pressing until even. Top with the remaining ½ cup marinara, 2 tablespoons bread crumbs, and ½ cup mozzarella.

SERVE NOW: Cover with foil and bake until hot, about 30 minutes. Garnish with parsley or basil (if using). Cut into 8 pieces and serve with more marinara (if using).

FREEZE AND SERVE LATER: Before baking, cover the uncooked dish tightly with plastic wrap, then foil, and freeze. Let completely thaw in the refrigerator 24 hours before cooking. Preheat the oven to 350°F. **Remove the plastic wrap** and cover tightly with foil. Bake until heated through in the center, 40 to 50 minutes.

Per Serving (1 piece) • Calories 391 • Fat 11.5 g • Saturated Fat 5 g • Cholesterol 98 mg • Carbohydrate 49 g • Fiber 3 g • Protein 22 g • Sugars 4 g • Sodium 913 mg

Turkey Cheeseburger Egg Rolls

FF **AF**

SERVES 7

1 teaspoon olive oil

1 cup white mushrooms, chopped

1¼ pounds 93% lean ground turkey

1 teaspoon kosher salt

1 small onion, chopped

3 garlic cloves, chopped

1 teaspoon yellow mustard

1 cup shredded cheddar cheese

14 egg roll wrappers (I like Nasoya)

5 tablespoons finely chopped pickles, drained on paper towels

Olive oil spray

Ketchup, mustard, or special sauce, for dipping (optional)

> FRIDGE: YOU CAN MAKE THE FILLING AHEAD AND REFRIGERATE FOR UP TO 3 DAYS BEFORE ASSEMBLING. EGG ROLLS ARE BEST WHEN EATEN RIGHT AWAY BUT CAN BE REFRIGERATED OVERNIGHT.

> FREEZER: UP TO 6 MONTHS

SKINNY SCOOP To make a special sauce for dipping, in a small bowl combine ¼ cup light mayonnaise, 1½ tablespoons ketchup, 1 teaspoon yellow mustard, and 1 teaspoon dill pickle juice.

These egg rolls are filled with everything you love about your favorite burger—pickles, mushrooms, and cheddar. They're perfect for snacking while watching a game, but if you're not a sports fan, like me, they're great for lunch or dinner, served with lettuce and tomatoes on the side. You can also swap your favorite burger mix-ins such as chopped bacon or jalapeño! My best advice for making egg rolls is to be sure there is no extra moisture in the filling. You can cook them all at one time if you're entertaining, or you can freeze the ones you don't cook—they bake from frozen beautifully.

Heat the oil in a large skillet over medium-high heat and add the mushrooms. Cook for 2 to 3 minutes, stirring occasionally, until soft. Add the turkey and salt. Brown the meat, using a wooden spoon to break it into small pieces, until just cooked through, 4 to 5 minutes. Add the onion, garlic, and mustard, and cook for 2 to 3 minutes, stirring occasionally, until soft.

Drain the meat in a colander, then transfer to a mixing bowl and mix in the cheese.

One at a time, place an egg roll wrapper on a clean surface, positioning it in a diamond shape in front of you. Spoon ¼ cup turkey mixture onto the bottom third of the wrapper. Top with about 1 teaspoon pickles. Dip your finger in a small bowl of water and run it along the edges of the wrapper. Carefully lift the bottom point nearest to you and wrap it around the filling. Fold the left and right corners in toward the center and continue to roll into a tight cylinder. Repeat with the remaining wrappers and filling.

SERVE NOW: Spray all sides of the egg rolls with oil and rub with your fingers to evenly coat. Preheat an air fryer to 370°F. Cook the egg rolls in batches for about 7 minutes, turning halfway through, until golden brown. Serve immediately, with dipping sauce on the side (if using).

FREEZE AND SERVE LATER: Before cooking the egg rolls, transfer to freezer bags, squeeze out as much air as possible, and seal. To cook from frozen, preheat an air fryer to 320°F and cook for 12 to 14 minutes, turning halfway through, until golden brown and crisp. Serve immediately, with dipping sauce on the side (if using).

No Air Fryer, No Problem! Bake for 12 to 16 minutes in a 400°F oven, flipping halfway through. From frozen, cook for 18 to 20 minutes at 375°F, flipping halfway through.

Per Serving (2 egg rolls) ● Calories 322 ● Fat 13 g ● Saturated Fat 5.5 g Cholesterol 77 mg ● Carbohydrate 26 g ● Fiber 0.5 g ● Protein 24 g Sugars 1 g ● Sodium 621 mg

Indian-Inspired Shepherd's Pie

This samosa-inspired savory pie is hearty and flavor-packed, and comes together pretty quickly thanks to the lean ground turkey that is used in place of lamb. It takes nearly the same amount of time to make two pies, so if you want to double the recipe, you can eat one now and freeze one for later. Baking from frozen does require some additional time (at least 2½ hours), so if you want something quick for dinner, it's best to thaw it in the refrigerator the night before.

Place the potatoes and 1 tablespoon salt in a medium saucepan. Cover with water, bring to a boil, and cook for 16 to 18 minutes, until tender. Drain and return to the saucepan. Add ½ teaspoon salt, the sour cream, ½ teaspoon turmeric, ¼ teaspoon garam masala, ¼ teaspoon cumin, and ¼ teaspoon chili powder, and mash with a potato masher. Set aside.

Heat a large, deep nonstick skillet over medium heat and melt the ghee. Add the onion and cook until golden, 6 to 8 minutes. Add the garlic and ginger and cook until fragrant, about 2 minutes.

Add the ground turkey and 1 teaspoon salt to the skillet. Brown the meat, using a wooden spoon to break it until small pieces, until cooked through, 4 to 5 minutes. Add the tomato sauce, ¼ cup water, cilantro, chile pepper, remaining ¾ teaspoon garam masala, remaining ½ teaspoon cumin, remaining ½ teaspoon chili powder, and remaining ½ teaspoon turmeric, and stir well. Cover and cook on low heat for 20 to 25 minutes, then stir in the frozen peas and cook for about 3 minutes more, until the peas are warmed through.

Transfer the meat mixture to an 8- or 9-inch baking dish or deep pie plate, spreading it across in an even layer. Dollop the potatoes across the top and gently push them around until they cover the entire top of the casserole, then run the tines of a fork across the top for texture. Dust with the chili powder for color.

SERVE NOW: Position an oven rack in the center of the oven and preheat to 375°F. Place the pie on a sheet pan and bake for 25 to 30 minutes, until heated through. Adjust an oven rack 4 to 6 inches from the heating element and turn the broiler to high. Finish under the broiler for 2 to 3 minutes. Serve as is or sprinkled with cilantro, if using.

FREEZE AND SERVE LATER: Assemble the unbaked pie in a foil or freezer-to-ovenproof baking dish or pie plate. Cover the pie with foil and freeze. When ready to bake, transfer the baking dish to a sheet pan and bake, covered, in a 350°F oven until heated through in the center, about 2½ hours. (If you thawed it the night before, bake for 30 to 35 minutes.) Adjust an oven rack 4 to 6 inches from the heating element and turn the broiler to high. Finish under the broiler for 2 to 3 minutes.

SERVES 6

1½ pounds Yukon Gold potatoes, peeled and diced into 1-inch pieces

Kosher salt

¼ cup sour cream or full-fat yogurt

1 teaspoon ground turmeric

1 teaspoon garam masala*

¾ teaspoon ground cumin

¾ teaspoon chili powder,* plus more for dusting

2 teaspoons ghee or unsalted butter

1 large yellow onion, minced

3 garlic cloves, minced

1 teaspoon grated fresh ginger

1 pound ground 93% lean turkey

¾ cup tomato sauce

2 tablespoons chopped fresh cilantro, plus more for garnish (optional)

1 red chile pepper, seeded and minced

¾ cup frozen peas

*Read the label to be sure this product is gluten-free.

FRIDGE: UP TO 4 DAYS

FREEZER: UP TO 6 MONTHS

Per Serving (1 cup) ● Calories 271 ● Fat 10 g ● Saturated Fat 3.5 g Cholesterol 65 mg ● Carbohydrate 28 g ● Fiber 4.5 g ● Protein 19 g Sugars 5 g ● Sodium 534 mg

Moussaka Makeover

GF FF

SERVES 8

Olive oil spray

1 pound 90% lean ground beef

1 pound 93% lean ground turkey

Kosher salt

1 large yellow onion, chopped

6 garlic cloves, minced

8 ounces white mushrooms, finely chopped

2 (8-ounce) cans tomato sauce

1 teaspoon ground cinnamon

1 tablespoon dried oregano

1 teaspoon dried basil

3 bay leaves

4 large eggplants (1¼ pounds each), peeled and sliced lengthwise, ¼ inch thick

BÉCHAMEL SAUCE

¼ cup unsalted butter

¼ cup all-purpose flour, wheat or gluten-free

2½ cups 2% milk, warmed (don't use fat-free)

½ teaspoon kosher salt, plus more to taste

5 tablespoons freshly grated kefalotyri or Pecorino Romano cheese

Pinch of ground nutmeg

2 large eggs, beaten

FRIDGE: UP TO 4 DAYS

FREEZER: UP TO 3 MONTHS

SKINNY SCOOP Kefalotyri is a hard, salty, white cheese made from sheep's and/or goat's milk in Greece and Cyprus. If it's not easy to find near you, Pecorino Romano works fine in its place.

Moussaka is a rich Mediterranean casserole similar to an Italian lasagna, except it's layered with eggplant, cinnamon-spiced ground meat, and béchamel sauce. Like any good lasagna, it takes time to prepare, but it's worth the work! It's ideal to make ahead—just refrigerate or freeze until ready to bake. I lightened up the classic by roasting the eggplant instead of frying it, mixing chopped mushrooms and ground turkey in with the ground beef, and reducing the amount of béchamel sauce on top. It's still every bit as delish as the original.

Preheat the oven to 450°F. Spray four large sheet pans with oil.

Heat a large, deep skillet over high heat. Add the beef, turkey, and 1½ teaspoons salt. Brown the meat, using a wooden spoon to break it into small pieces, until cooked through, about 5 minutes. Add the onion and garlic and cook until soft, 4 to 5 minutes. Reduce the heat to low and stir in the mushrooms, tomato sauce, ½ cup water, cinnamon, oregano, basil, and bay leaves. Simmer, stirring occasionally, until thickened, about 20 minutes. Remove the bay leaves.

While the sauce simmers, transfer the eggplant slices to the prepared sheet pans (it's OK if they overlap slightly). Spray both sides with olive oil and season with 1 teaspoon salt. Bake until the eggplant is golden, flipping halfway through, 15 to 16 minutes.

Make the béchamel sauce: In a medium pot, melt the butter over medium heat. Add the flour, stirring quickly with a wooden spoon to prevent lumps from forming. Cook, stirring constantly, until the mixture turns golden, about 2 minutes. While constantly stirring, pour in the milk, then add the salt. When the mixture thickens, turn off the heat and stir in 3 tablespoons kefalotyri and the nutmeg. Slowly pour in the eggs and continue stirring until combined.

To assemble: In a 9 × 13-inch baking dish, spread 1 cup meat mixture on the bottom of the dish. Top with half the eggplant, then half the meat mixture. Add the second layer of eggplant and the remaining meat mixture. Pour the béchamel sauce on top and sprinkle the remaining 2 tablespoons cheese over the top. (At this point, you can refrigerate for up to 1 day before baking.)

Bake until the top is golden brown, 30 to 35 minutes. Let cool for 10 minutes before cutting into 8 pieces and serving.

FREEZE AND SERVE LATER: Let cool completely, then cover tightly with foil and freeze. To reheat from frozen, bake, still covered with foil, in a 350°F oven until heated through, 50 to 60 minutes.

Per Serving (1 piece) ● Calories 420 ● Fat 20.5 g ● Saturated Fat 9 g Cholesterol 149 mg ● Carbohydrate 30 g ● Fiber 11.5 g ● Protein 33 g Sugars 14 g ● Sodium 954 mg

Low-Country Boil Foil Packets

Q GF DF FF

SERVES 4

32 peeled and deveined jumbo shrimp, tails on (18 ounces total)

2 garlic cloves, minced

4 teaspoons Old Bay seasoning

12 ounces baby red potatoes, washed and sliced 1/4 inch thick

2 medium ears corn, husked and kernels removed from cob (about 2 cups)

6 ounces turkey kielbasa, sliced

1/4 cup beer

4 teaspoons olive oil

8 thin lemon slices

1/4 cup chopped parsley

FRIDGE: UP TO 1 DAY (UNCOOKED)

FREEZER: UP TO 2 MONTHS (UNCOOKED)

You can bake just about anything in a foil packet! Filled with everything you'd find in a classic shrimp boil—Old Bay seasoning, shrimp, potatoes, corn, and sausage—these delicious packets make it so much easier to serve this dish any night of the week.

In a medium bowl, toss the shrimp with the garlic and 1 teaspoon of the Old Bay seasoning. In a separate medium bowl, toss the potatoes with 2 teaspoons of the Old Bay.

Place four large (12 x 18-inch) pieces of heavy-duty aluminum foil on a flat surface.

Place one-fourth of the potatoes in a single layer in the center of each foil piece, then top with the corn, kielbasa, and shrimp. Drizzle each with 1 tablespoon of the beer and 1 teaspoon of the oil, followed by the remaining teaspoon Old Bay and the lemon slices. Sprinkle each with 1 tablespoon of the parsley.

Fold each piece of the foil to form a packet, sealing tightly and leaving a little room inside for air to circulate in the packet.

SERVE NOW: Preheat the oven to 425°F. Arrange the packets on a baking sheet and cook until the shrimp are cooked through and the potatoes are tender, about 25 minutes. Open the packets slowly, being careful of the hot steam. Transfer to plates and eat hot.

FREEZE AND SERVE LATER: Place the assembled, uncooked foil packets into sealable gallon plastic bags (2 should fit in each one). Keep upright and freeze for up to 2 months. Cook from frozen on a baking sheet in a cold oven set to 425°F. Once the oven comes to temperature, continue to cook until the potatoes are tender and the shrimp is opaque, 40 minutes.

SKINNY SCOOP: If you prefer spicier packets, just use a little (or a lot!) more Old Bay. Andouille chicken sausage can also be used in place of kielbasa.

Per Serving (1 foil packet) • Calories 333 • Fat 9 g • Saturated Fat 2 g Cholesterol 183 mg • Carbohydrate 27 g • Fiber 3 g • Protein 33 g Sugars 4 g • Sodium 1,369 mg

Slow Cooker BBQ Brisket

GF DF FF SC

SERVES 8

2½ pounds lean beef brisket, trimmed of all fat

1¾ teaspoons kosher salt

1 teaspoon smoked paprika

1 teaspoon garlic powder

Freshly ground black pepper

3 teaspoons olive oil

1 tablespoon mesquite liquid smoke

2 medium onions, sliced lengthwise

¾ cup BBQ sauce of choice, plus more for serving (optional)

1 tablespoon chopped fresh parsley, for garnish

FRIDGE: UP TO 4 DAYS

FREEZER: UP TO 3 MONTHS

I just love the smoky taste of BBQ brisket, and with this easy slow cooker recipe, you can have it any time of the year—no smoker or charcoal grill required! The slow cooker transforms one of the toughest cuts of beef (brisket) into something so tender and delicious, you can cut it with a fork. Just rub the brisket with smoked paprika and liquid smoke, add caramelized onions and BBQ sauce, then let the slow-cooking magic begin. Slicing the beef before it's completely cooked, then arranging the slices like a fallen stack of dominoes inside the slow cooker to finish cooking, is a pro trick. This not only keeps the slices from falling to shreds, it allows all of the delicious smoky flavor to seep into every slice as it finishes cooking. Serve this with mashed potatoes or cauliflower mash and corn on the cob. Any leftovers are great on a roll with coleslaw.

Season the brisket with 1½ teaspoons salt, paprika, garlic powder, and pepper to taste.

Heat 2 teaspoons oil in a large cast iron or heavy skillet over medium-high heat. Add the brisket and cook until browned on both sides, about 5 minutes per side. Transfer to a 5- to 6-quart slow cooker (an oval cooker is ideal). Pour the liquid smoke over the brisket.

Heat the skillet over medium-low heat. Add the remaining 1 teaspoon oil and the onions and cook, stirring constantly, until soft and golden, about 15 minutes. Place the onions on top of the brisket in the slow cooker and sprinkle with ¼ teaspoon salt and more pepper to taste. Pour the BBQ sauce on top. Cover and cook on low for about 8 hours, until tender.

Remove the brisket and transfer to a cutting board. Using a sharp knife, slice the meat across the grain into approximately ¼-inch-thick slices. Place the sliced meat back into the slow cooker, arranging the meat like fallen dominoes and submerging it in the liquid and onions. Cook for about 1 hour more, until very tender. Keep warm until ready to serve.

SERVE NOW: Top with the fresh parsley just before serving. Serve with more BBQ sauce (if using). (To freeze, store cooked brisket and sauce in an airtight container.)

REFRIGERATE AND SERVE LATER: To prep the night ahead, follow all the steps up to turning on the slow cooker. Refrigerate, covered, until ready to cook. In the morning, remove from the refrigerator. Cook on low for about 8 hours 30 minutes before continuing with the recipe (the extra 30 minutes accounts for starting with cold ceramic). Note: Never place your stoneware (whether it has been refrigerated or is at room temperature) in a preheated slow cooker.

Per serving (3.25 ounces [generous ½ cup] beef + sauce) • Calories 275 Fat 10 g • Saturated Fat 3 g • Cholesterol 95 mg • Carbohydrate 17 g • Fiber 0.5 g Protein 31 g • Sugars 13 g • Sodium 584 mg

Winter Brisket and Barley Soup

SERVES 6

1 tablespoon olive oil

1¼ pounds beef brisket, trimmed and cut into 4 pieces

1 large onion, chopped

2 medium carrots, chopped

2 leeks, rinsed well, white part only, chopped

1 celery stalk, diced

2 tablespoons tomato paste

6 cups beef broth

8 ounces sliced white mushrooms

1 bay leaf

¼ cup chopped fresh parsley, plus more for garnish

2 ounces uncooked pearled barley

½ teaspoon kosher salt

Freshly ground black pepper

FRIDGE: UP TO 5 DAYS

FREEZER: UP TO 3 MONTHS

When I was growing up, my parents made soup almost every day (beef and barley was always one of my favorites—it's the perfect cold-weather comfort soup). We either started our meal with a light soup or enjoyed a more substantial soup, like this, as our main course. Soup was one of my mom's go-to recipes because it allowed her to stretch her dollar and feed a crowd. Anyone who knows us knows there was always someone staying for dinner. Even today, if you were to show up at my mom's house hungry, she'd have food ready and waiting for you. And, of course, soup makes the best leftovers for lunch or dinner a second night—it's always better the next day.

Heat a heavy pot or Dutch oven over high heat. When hot, add ½ tablespoon oil, then add the brisket and brown on both sides, 3 to 4 minutes on each side. Remove from the pot.

Add the remaining oil, onion, carrots, leeks, and celery. Reduce the heat and cook until the vegetables soften, 4 to 5 minutes. Add the tomato paste and cook, stirring often, until tender, about 2 minutes.

Return the beef to the pot. Add the broth, mushrooms, bay leaf, parsley, and barley and bring to a boil. Reduce the heat to low, cover, and simmer until the beef is very tender, 2 to 2½ hours. Discard the bay leaf. Remove the beef from the pot and shred it with two forks. Return the beef to the pot, season with the salt and pepper to taste, garnish with parsley, and serve.

FREEZE AND SERVE LATER: Let the soup cool, then divide among airtight freezer-safe containers. To reheat from frozen, transfer to the refrigerator the night before to thaw, then reheat on the stovetop or in the microwave.

For an Instant Pot: Reduce the broth amount to 5¾ cups and cook on high pressure for 1 hour. Natural release, then open when the pressure subsides.

Per Serving (1½ cups) ● Calories 249 ● Fat 8 g ● Saturated Fat 2.5 g
Cholesterol 63 mg ● Carbohydrate 20 g ● Fiber 4 g ● Protein 26 g
Sugars 5 g ● Sodium 1,037 mg

Lentil Soup with Bacon

GF DF FF

SERVES 10

1½ cups chopped carrots

1 pound uncooked small green lentils, rinsed well

1 (48-ounce) carton reduced-sodium chicken broth*

2 bay leaves

3 slices center-cut bacon, chopped

¾ cup chopped scallions (from 5 to 6)

4 garlic cloves, minced

1½ cups diced tomatoes (from 2 medium)

1 tablespoon sazón seasoning (I like Badia)

½ cup chopped fresh cilantro

*Read the label to be sure this product is gluten-free.

FRIDGE: UP TO 4 DAYS

FREEZER: UP TO 3 MONTHS

Every time I make lentil soup, I always wonder why I don't make it more often. It's healthy, filling, and super budget-friendly; it freezes perfectly; and it's seriously delish. I make mine over-the-top flavorful by adding bacon, scallions, cilantro, and sazón seasoning, which infuses so much flavor into the soup that everyone will be begging for seconds. Plus, you'll feel good about serving it because it's packed with vegetables and nutrients. Add a big salad and warm crusty bread and dinner is done!

Combine the carrots, lentils, broth, bay leaves, and 2 cups water in a large pot or Dutch oven. Bring to a boil, cover, and reduce the heat to low. Cook until the lentils are tender, about 30 minutes.

Meanwhile, heat a large skillet over medium heat and add the bacon. Cook, stirring occasionally, until browned, 4 to 5 minutes, then remove with a slotted spoon to a paper towel to drain. Add the scallions and garlic to the skillet and cook until they begin to soften, 2 to 3 minutes. Add the tomatoes and sazón seasoning, and cook, stirring frequently, until the tomatoes are soft, 2 to 3 minutes.

Once the lentils are cooked, stir the tomato mixture into the pot along with the cilantro. Cover and cook until the flavors meld, 8 to 10 minutes. Discard the bay leaves, stir the bacon into the soup, and serve.

FREEZE AND SERVE LATER: Let cool and then transfer to one large or individual containers and freeze. Thaw overnight in the refrigerator, then reheat on the stove or in the microwave.

Per Serving (1¼ cups) ● Calories 206 ● Fat 1.5 g ● Saturated Fat 0.5 g
Cholesterol 1 mg ● Carbohydrate 32 g ● Fiber 15 g ● Protein 16 g
Sugars 4 g ● Sodium 939 mg

Frozen Fish Sticks with Dill Tartar Sauce

(Q) (GF) (FF) (AF)

SERVES 4

DILL TARTAR SAUCE

1 tablespoon chopped fresh dill

2 tablespoons drained capers, minced

¼ cup fat-free Greek yogurt

¼ cup light mayonnaise

Juice of ½ lemon

FISH

28 ounces skinless wild cod or haddock fillets (thawed, if frozen)

1 teaspoon kosher salt

2 teaspoons finely chopped fresh dill

1 teaspoon lemon zest

2 large egg whites, lightly beaten

1 cup plus 2 tablespoons plain or gluten-free panko bread crumbs

Olive oil spray

> FREEZER: UP TO 3 MONTHS (UNBAKED)

Forget the frozen aisle! Make your own healthy fish sticks from scratch with cleaner, fresh ingredients that taste so much better than packaged. Guys, these are so easy to make and so delicious, you'll be very happy you tried them. The dill tartar sauce is a must-make when you're ready to serve them, but a squeeze of fresh lemon would also be great in a pinch. Everyone in my home thought they actually taste even better cooked from frozen (the texture is firmer). But if you don't have time to freeze them and want them for dinner tonight, they will still be tasty. Another option is to double the batch: one for dinner tonight and one for the freezer.

Prepare the sauce: Combine the ingredients for the dipping sauce in a small bowl and refrigerate until ready to eat.

Prepare the fish: Cut the fish into 16 sticks, about 4 x 1 inches. Season with ½ teaspoon salt, the 2 teaspoons dill, and the lemon zest.

Place the egg whites in a shallow bowl. In a second shallow bowl, combine the panko with the remaining ½ teaspoon salt. Dip the fish into the egg whites, then the panko. Set aside.

SERVE NOW: Preheat the oven to 450°F. Line a sheet pan with foil and spray with oil. Lay the fish sticks on the sheet pan, making sure they don't touch. Spray the tops of the fish sticks with oil and bake in the center of the oven for 14 to 16 minutes, turning halfway, until golden and crisp. Serve hot with tartar sauce.

FREEZE AND SERVE LATER: Place the sheet pan with the uncooked breaded fish sticks in the freezer for about 2 hours to flash freeze them. Once frozen, transfer them carefully into a freezer bag or container, squeezing out all the air. To serve, preheat the oven to 475°F. Place the frozen fish sticks on a sheet pan lined with foil and spray with oil. Bake from frozen for 12 to 14 minutes, turning halfway or until they flake easily and are cooked in the center and golden and crisp.

Per Serving (4 sticks + scant 2 tablespoons sauce) • Calories 298 • Fat 6.5 g • Saturated Fat 1 g • Cholesterol 91 mg • Carbohydrate 17 g • Fiber 1 g • Protein 41 g • Sugars 2 g • Sodium 685 mg

Southwest Salmon Burgers

DF **FF** **AF**

SERVES 5

SLAW

2 cups shredded red cabbage

¼ cup thinly sliced red onion

¼ cup fresh cilantro leaves

1 tablespoon fresh lime juice

1 tablespoon extra-virgin olive oil

1 teaspoon apple cider vinegar

½ teaspoon kosher salt

SALMON PATTIES

1 pound wild salmon fillet, skin and bones removed

6 tablespoons panko bread crumbs, wheat or gluten-free

4 scallions, green parts finely chopped, white parts thinly sliced

1 garlic clove, minced

1 large egg, lightly beaten

1 tablespoon light mayonnaise

1 tablespoon fresh lime juice

1 tablespoon chopped fresh cilantro

½ teaspoon ground cumin

½ teaspoon chili powder

1 teaspoon smoked paprika

¼ teaspoon chipotle chile powder

⅛ teaspoon cayenne pepper

1 teaspoon kosher salt

Olive oil spray

5 whole wheat potato buns

5 ounces (from 1 medium) Hass avocado, sliced, for serving

> FRIDGE: COOKED PATTIES UP TO 3 DAYS

> FREEZER: COOKED PATTIES UP TO 6 MONTHS; UNCOOKED PATTIES UP TO 3 MONTHS

Salmon burgers are my new favorite way to eat salmon! The simple base for my burgers is usually wild salmon fillet and some type of binder such as bread crumbs or panko and egg. Then I just mix in different spice blends, herbs, and aromatics. These Southwest-style burgers are smoky with a little kick, and I pair them with a limey, crunchy cabbage slaw with cilantro and some creamy avocado in place of mayo. The burgers retain the salmon flavor and texture but don't have an overpowering fishy taste, making it a great recipe for introducing salmon to kids or the non-fish eater in your life. You can also make the patties ahead of time and keep them frozen until you're ready to cook.

Prepare the slaw: Combine the cabbage with the onion, cilantro, lime juice, olive oil, apple cider vinegar, and salt. Refrigerate until ready to eat the burgers.

Prepare the salmon patties: Cut off a 4-ounce piece of salmon and transfer it to a food processor. Pulse until it becomes pasty. This consistency will help hold the burgers together. With a knife, chop the remaining salmon into a small dice.

In a medium bowl, combine the salmon with the panko, scallions, garlic, egg, mayo, lime juice, cilantro, cumin, chili powder, paprika, chipotle chile powder, cayenne, and salt. Toss gently to combine. Form the mixture into 5 patties. Refrigerate for at least 30 minutes before cooking.

To cook the patties in a skillet, heat a large skillet over medium-low heat and spray with oil. When hot, cook for 5 to 6 minutes on each side, until browned and cooked through.

To air-fry, preheat an air fryer to 400°F and cook the burgers in batches for 5 to 6 minutes on each side, until golden and cooked through.

SERVE NOW: Transfer each patty to a bun and serve with ⅓ cup cabbage slaw and 1 ounce avocado.

FREEZE AND SERVE LATER: Store uncooked patties in an airtight freezer bag or container in single layers, separated by parchment paper, and freeze. Thaw the patties for 24 hours in the refrigerator before cooking and serving according to the recipe instructions.

Per Serving (1 burger) • Calories 360 • Fat 16.5 g • Saturated Fat 2.5 g Cholesterol 88 mg • Carbohydrate 27 g • Fiber 5.5 g • Protein 27 g Sugars 6 g • Sodium 567 mg

Big Batches & Planned-Overs

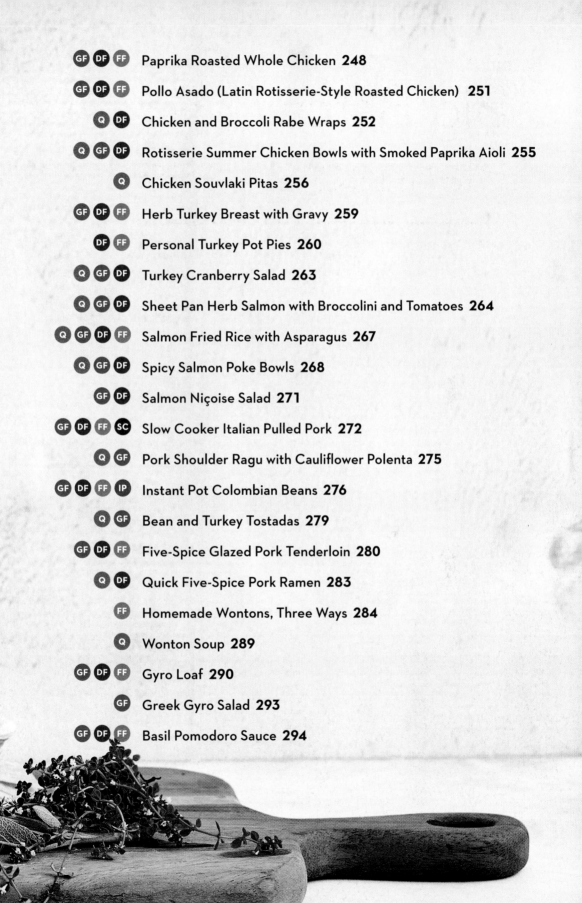

Paprika Roasted Whole Chicken

SERVES 4

1 (3½- to 4-pound) whole chicken, giblets removed, patted dry with paper towels

2 teaspoons kosher salt

1 teaspoon sweet paprika

½ teaspoon garlic powder

¼ teaspoon black pepper

2 sprigs of fresh rosemary

2 sprigs of fresh thyme

2 sprigs of fresh sage

2 medium shallots, quartered

FRIDGE: UP TO 4 DAYS

When I want a crispy-skinned, golden, and juicy roasted chicken for dinner, this is my go-to, tried-and-true recipe. Of course, nothing beats the convenience of picking up a rotisserie chicken from the grocery store, but making it from scratch is so much tastier and more satisfying. And this recipe is so simple that after making it a few times you'll know it by heart. One of my favorite meal-prep tricks is cooking two birds at the same time; one for dinner that night, and the other to transform into weeknight dishes. This trick maximizes time and money without sacrificing a drop of flavor. The following pages have lots of suggestions to make planned-overs if you cook a second bird.

Season the chicken inside and out with the salt, paprika, garlic powder, and pepper. Refrigerate it uncovered for at least 1 hour or up to overnight.

When ready to roast the chicken, preheat the oven to 425°F.

Transfer the chicken, breast side up, to a roasting pan or large rimmed sheet pan, and stuff the cavity with the rosemary, thyme, sage, and shallots.

Roast the chicken with the feet toward the back of the oven for about 50 minutes. Remove and baste the chicken with the pan juices, then continue roasting until the juices run clear and the chicken is no longer pink when the thigh is pierced with a paring knife near the joint, or the internal temperature is 160°F (insert a meat thermometer between the thickest part of the leg and the thigh), 5 to 10 minutes more.

Let the bird rest for 10 minutes before carving. Serve the chicken with or without skin.

SKINNY SCOOP It's best to use an organic air-chilled chicken, which is fed a better diet and also tastes better. Nutritional values will vary depending on which part of the chicken you eat, and if you serve it with or without the skin.

> ***Big Batch:*** Make two chickens and carve and refrigerate the second one to use for planned-over recipes on pages 252, 255, and 256.

Per Serving (¼ skinless chicken) ● Calories 288 ● Fat 10.5 g ● Saturated Fat 3 g Cholesterol 127 mg ● Carbohydrate 4 g ● Fiber 1 g ● Protein 42 g Sugars 2 g ● Sodium 685 mg

Pollo Asado (Latin Rotisserie-Style Roasted Chicken)

SERVES 4

1 (3½- to 4-pound) whole chicken, giblets removed, patted dry with paper towels

4 tablespoons white or apple cider vinegar

1 tablespoon mild cayenne pepper hot sauce, such as Frank's RedHot

2 teaspoons kosher salt

½ tablespoon ground oregano

1 teaspoon ground annatto or achiote (or sweet paprika)

1 teaspoon garlic powder

½ teaspoon ground cumin

FRIDGE: UP TO 4 DAYS

If you've been a Skinnytaste fan for a while, then you know how much my family loves our Latin food! On nights when there's no time to cook, we often find ourselves picking up roasted Peruvian or Colombian *pollo a la brasa*, complete with an avocado salad and rice and beans on the side. Since it's so much better making it from scratch, I came up with my own that my family loves! Achiote is the turmeric of Latin American cuisine and it will dye almost anything it comes across a vibrant red-orange. It's worth it, though! But if you can't find it, you can use sweet paprika in its place.

Place the chicken in a large container and rub the vinegar and hot sauce all over it, inside and out. In a small bowl, combine the salt, oregano, annatto, garlic powder, and cumin, and season the chicken inside and out with the mixture to evenly coat (it's best to wear gloves so you don't stain your hands). Refrigerate for 8 to 24 hours.

When ready to roast the chicken, preheat the oven to 450°F.

Transfer the chicken, breast side up, to a roasting pan with a rack, or to a large, rimmed sheet pan.

Roast the chicken with the legs toward the back of the oven until it starts to brown, about 20 minutes. Reduce the oven temperature to 350°F and continue cooking until the juices run clear when the thigh is pierced with a knife, or when the internal temperature between the thickest part of the leg and the thigh is 165°F, 45 to 55 minutes more.

Let the chicken stand uncovered for 10 minutes before carving. Serve with or without the skin.

> **Big Batch:** Make two chickens and carve and refrigerate the second one to use for planned-over recipes on pages 252, 255, and 256.

Per Serving (¼ skinless chicken) • Calories 278 • Fat 10.5 g
Saturated Fat 3 g • Cholesterol 127 mg • Carbohydrate 1 g • Fiber 0.5 g
Protein 41 g • Sugars 0 g • Sodium 826 mg

Chicken and Broccoli Rabe Wraps

SERVES 2

½ bunch (5 to 6 ounces) broccoli rabe, washed, 2 inches trimmed off stems

Kosher salt

1 tablespoon extra-virgin olive oil

2 garlic cloves, thinly sliced

Freshly ground black pepper

2 large (9- to 10-inch) whole wheat tortillas (I use Toufayan)

⅔ cup (about 5 ounces) jarred roasted red peppers, drained, patted dry, and sliced

6 ounces grilled boneless chicken breast or rotisserie chicken, thinly sliced, or leftover breast meat from Paprika Roasted Whole Chicken (page 248) or Pollo Asado (page 251)

PLANNED-OVER

I can't think of a more perfect, portable lunch than a wrap: it doesn't require heating, you don't need utensils, and the filling combos are endless. My favorite combination is this Italian chicken wrap filled with garlicky broccoli rabe and roasted peppers—it's delish and a great way to repurpose chicken from Paprika Roasted Whole Chicken (page 248) or Pollo Asado (page 251). You can also use the breast meat from a rotisserie chicken. That's a wrap!

Cut the broccoli rabe lengthwise into 1-inch pieces. Bring a large pot of salted water to a boil. Add the broccoli rabe and blanch for about 2 minutes. Drain and set aside in a colander.

Heat a medium skillet over medium heat. Add the olive oil, and when it is hot, add the garlic and cook until golden, 30 to 60 seconds. Add the broccoli rabe and season with ¼ teaspoon salt and pepper to taste. Cook until fragrant, stirring frequently, 1 to 2 minutes.

Working one at a time, place a tortilla on a work surface. Add half of the red peppers to the bottom third of the tortilla. Place half of the chicken on top, slightly overlapping the peppers, then top with half of the broccoli rabe.

Lift the edge nearest you and wrap it around the filling. Fold the left and right sides in toward the center and continue to roll into a tight cylinder. Slice in half and wrap the halves tightly in plastic wrap until ready to eat. Repeat with the remaining tortilla and filling.

SKINNY SCOOP You can double the ingredients to make 4 wraps, but it's best to assemble this the morning you plan on eating it so the wrap doesn't get soggy.

Per Serving (1 wrap) • Calories 405 • Fat 14 g • Saturated Fat 2 g
Cholesterol 72 mg • Carbohydrate 35 g • Fiber 4.5 g • Protein 33 g
Sugars 4 g • Sodium 975 mg

Rotisserie Summer Chicken Bowls with Smoked Paprika Aioli

(Q) (GF) (DF)

SERVES 4

SMOKED PAPRIKA AIOLI

½ cup light mayonnaise

Juice of 1 large lime

1 teaspoon smoked paprika

1 tablespoon finely minced fresh cilantro

SALAD

6 cup mixed baby greens

1 pound leftover Paprika Roasted Whole Chicken (page 248) or rotisserie chicken, skin and bones removed, torn into bite-size pieces (half white, half dark; about 3 cups)

1⅓ cups halved grape tomatoes

1⅓ cups steamed corn, from 2 fresh (or frozen) ears

½ small red onion, slivered

1 small (4-ounce) Hass avocado, sliced

Chopped fresh cilantro, for garnish

The base of this bowl is mixed greens topped with leftover rotisserie or roasted chicken, summer corn, tomatoes, and avocado, drizzled with a quick smoked paprika aioli. Since it takes the same amount of time to roast two chickens as it does one, I usually double up (see Paprika Roasted Whole Chicken on page 248 or Pollo Asado on page 251) and turn the leftovers into new dishes throughout the week. Or to save time, I pick up an already cooked rotisserie chicken from the store instead. This summer salad is quite substantial, making it an easy weeknight dinner for four (or cut the recipe in half and pack it for lunch).

Make the aioli: In a small bowl, combine the mayonnaise, lime juice, paprika, and cilantro and blend until smooth. If it's too thick, you can add a little water to loosen.

Make the salad: Divide the baby greens, chicken, tomatoes, corn, red onion, and avocado among 4 plates. Drizzle each with 2½ tablespoons aioli, garnish with cilantro, and serve.

Per Serving (1 bowl) ● Calories 511 ● Fat 35 g ● Saturated Fat 6 g
Cholesterol 96 mg ● Carbohydrate 20 g ● Fiber 6 g ● Protein 33 g
Sugars 5 g ● Sodium 280 mg

Chicken Souvlaki Pitas

Q

SERVES 4

TZATZIKI

¾ cup whole-milk Greek yogurt

½ small cucumber, peeled, grated, and squeezed dry

1 garlic clove, minced

½ teaspoon fresh lemon juice

½ teaspoon kosher salt

Freshly ground black pepper

SALAD

1 small cucumber, peeled, seeded, and chopped

½ cup diced tomato

2 tablespoons chopped fresh dill

2 tablespoons chopped red onion

½ teaspoon kosher salt

Freshly ground black pepper

Juice of ½ lemon

GYRO

4 (7-inch) pre-oiled gyro breads (such as Kontos) or naan breads

Olive oil spray

10 ounces cooked skinless rotisserie chicken breast, shredded, or leftover Paprika Roasted Whole Chicken (page 248)

These chicken souvlaki transform leftovers into a Greek delight in under 20 minutes—start to finish! Rotisserie chicken (or leftovers from a homemade roasted chicken on page 251) can be pretty awesome, particularly on busy weeknights when you don't want to cook a whole dinner from scratch but you still want a tasty home-cooked meal. Serve the chicken on warmed pita or gyro bread with a quick cucumber-tomato-dill salad and some homemade tzatziki. To make it gluten-free, skip the pita and serve over brown rice to make it a bowl.

Make the tzatziki: In a medium bowl, combine the yogurt, cucumber, garlic, lemon juice, salt, and pepper to taste. Mix well to combine.

Make the salad: In another medium bowl, combine the cucumber, tomato, dill, red onion, salt, pepper to taste, and the lemon juice. Toss well to combine.

Adjust an oven rack 4 to 6 inches from the heating element and preheat the broiler to high. Spritz the bread on both sides with olive oil, then transfer to a baking sheet and broil until golden and warmed and pliable, 1 to 2 minutes on each side.

Drain the salad, then put it back in the bowl.

To assemble: Spread some tzatziki on the warmed pita and top with the chicken and salad, with the remaining tzatziki on the side.

Per Serving (1 sandwich) ● Calories 396 ● Fat 8.5 g ● Saturated Fat 2.5 g
Cholesterol 69 mg ● Carbohydrate 48 g ● Fiber 2 g ● Protein 34 g
Sugars 7 g ● Sodium 912 mg

Herb Turkey Breast with Gravy

SERVES 10

1 tablespoon unsalted butter, at room temperature

2 garlic cloves, minced

2 teaspoon chopped fresh sage

1 teaspoon chopped fresh thyme

1 teaspoon Bell's Seasoning

1½ teaspoons kosher salt

1 (3-pound) boneless skin-on turkey breast

GRAVY

3 cups turkey or chicken broth*

2 fresh sage leaves

1 sprig of fresh thyme

½ teaspoon Bell's Seasoning

⅓ cup all-purpose flour or gluten-free flour mix

¼ teaspoon kosher salt

Freshly ground black pepper

*Read the label to be sure this product is gluten-free.

FRIDGE: UP TO 4 DAYS

FREEZER: UP TO 3 MONTHS

Everyone needs a basic turkey breast and gravy recipe to keep in their back pocket! This recipe is also great for intimate Thanksgiving or Friendsgiving dinners when you don't want to cook a whole turkey. Of course, the best part is always the leftovers. Slice this up and make a killer, warm open-faced turkey sandwich with gravy or a chilled Turkey Cranberry Salad (page 263) or Personal Turkey Pot Pies (page 260).

Preheat the oven to 350°F.

Prepare the turkey: In a small bowl, combine the butter, garlic, sage, thyme, and Bell's Seasoning with the salt to make a paste. Using your fingers, carefully loosen the skin from the breast meat and spread the butter mixture under the skin and all over the turkey breast.

In a shallow roasting pan, place the turkey skin side up and roast until the turkey is completely cooked through, basting once halfway through, until the thickest part of the breast reaches an internal temperature of 160°F, 40 to 45 minutes.

Adjust an oven rack 4 to 6 inches from the heating element and preheat the broiler to high. Brown the turkey under the broiler for 2 to 3 minutes, watching closely to make sure the skin does not burn. Transfer the turkey breast to a cutting board and loosely tent with foil. Let it rest for 15 minutes, reserving the pan juices for the gravy.

Prepare the gravy: While the turkey is resting, place 2 cups of the broth, the sage, thyme, and Bell's Seasoning in a medium pot and bring to a boil over medium-high heat. Cover and reduce the heat to low, simmering for about 10 minutes to let the flavors meld.

Place the remaining 1 cup room-temperature broth and the flour into a small blender and puree. When the turkey is done resting, add the pan juices and the flour mixture to the pot of simmering broth and cook over medium heat, stirring occasionally, until thickened, about 5 minutes. Stir in ¼ teaspoon salt and black pepper to taste, and discard the sage and thyme.

SERVE NOW: Thinly slice the turkey breast and serve with the gravy.

> **Big Batch:** Thinly slice the leftovers and store in the refrigerator or freezer for planned-over recipes on pages 260 and 263.

Per Serving (4 ounces + generous ¼ cup gravy) ● Calories 243
Fat 11 g ● Saturated Fat 3.5 g ● Cholesterol 92 mg ● Carbohydrate 4 g
Fiber 0 g ● Protein 31 g ● Sugars 0.5 g ● Sodium 535 mg

Personal Turkey Pot Pies

(DF) (FF)

PLANNED-OVER

SERVES 4

½ tablespoon olive oil

1 large shallot, chopped

3 tablespoons chopped fresh parsley

1 tablespoon chopped fresh thyme

1 tablespoon chopped fresh sage

2 small celery stalks, chopped

5 ounces frozen mixed vegetables

2¼ cups turkey or chicken broth

½ teaspoon chicken or turkey bouillon (I like Better Than Bouillon)

½ teaspoon kosher salt

⅛ teaspoon freshly ground black pepper

3 cups small-diced leftover cooked turkey breast, skin removed (see Herb Turkey Breast, page 259)

2½ tablespoons cornstarch

½ package (about 7 ounces) refrigerated pie crust (I like Pillsbury)

1 large egg, beaten

FRIDGE: UP TO 4 DAYS

FREEZER: UP TO 3 MONTHS

When I was a teenager I always came home from school ravenous. My mom worked full-time cooking in her luncheonette, and one of the few frozen foods my mom kept stocked at home were personal turkey pot pies. I just loved them! Making these pot pies from scratch is an easy way to use up leftover turkey (see Herb Turkey Breast on page 259)—they're slimmed down since the only crust is on the top. If you don't have leftover turkey, chicken also works.

In a large, deep nonstick skillet, heat the oil over medium heat. When the pan is hot, add the shallot, parsley, thyme, and sage and cook until almost soft and fragrant, 2 to 3 minutes. Add the celery and cook until the vegetables are soft, 3 to 5 minutes. Add the frozen mixed vegetables, 2 cups broth, the bouillon, salt, and black pepper, and bring to a boil. Simmer for about 5 minutes, stirring frequently, until the flavors meld. Add the turkey.

Meanwhile, combine the remaining ¼ cup broth with the cornstarch in a bowl and mix well to dissolve. Add to the skillet and cook over medium-low heat, stirring until thickened, 4 to 6 minutes. Remove from the heat and transfer to 4 oven-to-freezer-safe mini metal or foil pie plates. Let the filling cool completely in the pie plates on a sheet pan.

Preheat the oven to 400°F.

When ready to bake, roll out the pie crust and cut out 4 rounds slightly larger than the pie plates and place each piece over the turkey filling. Crimp the edges or fold over the edge of the pie plate and poke holes in the top of the dough with a knife. Brush with the egg and immediately bake on the sheet pan for about 35 minutes, or until the crust is golden.

FREEZE AND SERVE LATER: Freeze the pot pies without the egg wash: flash freeze for 1 to 2 hours, then cover each tightly with plastic wrap or transfer carefully to zip-top plastic bags. To cook, remove from the freezer, brush the pie crusts with egg wash, and place on a baking sheet. Bake at 400°F for 50 to 55 minutes, or until golden and heated through in the center.

Per Serving (1 pie) ● Calories 449 ● Fat 17 g ● Saturated Fat 5.5 g
Cholesterol 131 mg ● Carbohydrate 38 g ● Fiber 3 g ● Protein 36 g
Sugars 2 g ● Sodium 1,011 mg

Turkey Cranberry Salad

Q GF DF

PLANNED-OVER

SERVES 4

12 ounces leftover cooked turkey breast (see Herb Turkey Breast, page 259), diced

1/3 cup sliced celery

1/4 cup light mayonnaise

3 tablespoons dried cranberries

1 1/2 tablespoons chopped red onion

FRIDGE: UP TO 4 DAYS

This is my go-to turkey salad when I have Thanksgiving leftovers. It's similar to a Waldorf salad, and you can even add apples, walnuts, or pecans—delish! I usually eat it with a spoon right out of the refrigerator, but it's also great served in a wrap, as a sandwich, or over a bed of greens.

In a medium bowl combine the turkey with the celery, mayonnaise, cranberries, and red onion, and stir until combined.

Per Serving (generous 1/2 cup) • Calories 182 • Fat 5.5 g • Saturated Fat 1 g Cholesterol 76 mg • Carbohydrate 6 g • Fiber 0.5 g • Protein 26 g Sugars 4 g • Sodium 152 mg

Sheet Pan Herb Salmon with Broccolini and Tomatoes

SERVES 4 FOR 2 MEALS

Olive oil spray

2 lemons

10 sprigs of fresh parsley

2 tablespoons plus 2 teaspoons
   extra-virgin olive oil

2 (1½-pound) fillets wild salmon,
   skin on (1 to 1½ inches thick)

1 teaspoon kosher salt

Freshly ground black pepper

12 spears (12 ounces) broccolini,
   ends trimmed (from
   2 to 3 bunches)

1½ cups grape tomatoes, halved

2 tablespoons chopped fresh dill

1 tablespoon chopped fresh chives

1 tablespoon chopped fresh parsley

> FRIDGE: UP TO 2 DAYS

This easy sheet pan dinner takes the guesswork out of cooking fish. The salmon is cooked on a bed of lemons and herbs, and then it's finished with fresh lemon juice and herbs while the veggies cook on a second sheet pan. The fish is so juicy and flavorful, and the best part is it makes enough for two or three meals. Serve half for dinner tonight with the roasted broccolini and tomatoes, and save the second piece to transform into planned-overs you'll be excited about! Try the Spicy Salmon Poke Bowls (page 268), Salmon Fried Rice (page 267), or Salmon Niçoise Salad (page 271). The key to using salmon the next day is to not overcook it, or it will get too dry.

Position two oven racks in the center and top third of the oven. Preheat the oven to 350°F. Spray 2 large sheet pans with olive oil.

Slice one lemon into thin rounds and cut the second lemon into wedges for serving later. Place the lemon slices on one of the large sheet pans arranged in two areas where you will place the fish on top. Top the lemon slices with parsley and drizzle with 1 teaspoon olive oil. Transfer the salmon to the pan over the lemon slices, skin side down. Drizzle 1 teaspoon olive oil over the flesh side of the fish and rub all over, and season with ½ teaspoon salt and pepper to taste.

On the second sheet pan, place the broccolini and tomatoes and toss with 2 tablespoons olive oil, ½ teaspoon salt, and pepper to taste. Spread out in an even layer.

Roast the salmon on the center rack and the vegetables on the upper rack, cooking until the salmon is just barely opaque in the middle, about 20 minutes depending on the thickness of the fish. If you like the fish more well done, cook for about 5 minutes more. Toss the vegetables halfway through.

When the salmon is cooked, remove from the oven, top each piece with the fresh herbs, and serve with broccolini, tomatoes, and lemon wedges.

> ***Big Batch:*** Let the second piece cool, then cover and refrigerate for up to 2 days. Use it as planned-overs in Spicy Salmon Poke Bowls (page 268), Salmon Fried Rice (page 267), or Salmon Niçoise Salad (page 271), or in any salad or grain bowl.

Per Serving (6 ounces salmon + 3 spears broccolini + ¼ cup tomatoes)
Calories 370 ● Fat 19.5 g
Saturated Fat 3 g ● Cholesterol 94 mg
Carbohydrate 11 g ● Fiber 6 g
Protein 38 g ● Sugars 4 g
Sodium 371 mg

Salmon Fried Rice with Asparagus

Q GF DF FF

SERVES 4

1½ pounds leftover Sheet Pan Herb Salmon, skin removed (page 264)

2½ teaspoons vegetable or canola oil

1 tablespoon chopped fresh ginger

2 garlic cloves, chopped

4 medium scallions, thinly sliced, white and green parts separated

1 bunch thin asparagus (about 1 pound), ends trimmed, cut into 1-inch pieces

3 cups cold leftover cooked brown rice (preferably short-grain)

2 large eggs, beaten

1 cup shredded red cabbage

2 tablespoons soy sauce* or gluten-free tamari

1 tablespoon unseasoned rice vinegar

1½ teaspoons toasted sesame oil

Sriracha or chile-garlic sauce, for serving (optional)

*Read the label to be sure this product is gluten-free.

FRIDGE: REFRIGERATE WITHIN 2 HOURS OF COOKING FOR UP TO 3 DAYS

FREEZER: UP TO 3 MONTHS

Fried rice is the ultimate planned-over food because it requires day-old cooked rice (or you can use frozen cooked rice), otherwise it won't be dry enough to fry. Here I used leftover salmon from the Sheet Pan Herb Salmon (page 264). You can also swap the asparagus for bok choy or snow peas or even use up any leftover broccolini. The salmon can also be swapped for shrimp or chicken, or leftover Five-Spice Glazed Pork Tenderloin (page 280), if you prefer.

Flake the salmon into small chunks with a fork or knife. Set aside.

Heat 1 teaspoon oil in a large nonstick wok or deep skillet over medium-high heat.

Add the ginger, garlic, and scallion whites and cook, stirring, until fragrant, about 1 minute. Add the asparagus and 2 tablespoons water and cook, stirring occasionally, until crisp-tender, 3 to 4 minutes. Transfer to a plate.

Add the remaining 1½ teaspoons oil and swirl around in the skillet to evenly coat. Then add the cooked rice in an even layer. Cook, without stirring, for 2 to 3 minutes, or until the bottom of the rice becomes slightly crispy. Continue to cook, stirring occasionally, for 1 to 2 minutes, or until combined. With a spoon or spatula, push the rice to one side of the wok or skillet. Crack the eggs onto the other side. Cook, constantly stirring the egg, for 30 to 60 seconds, or until cooked through. Mix the rice and egg to thoroughly combine.

Return the asparagus, along with the cabbage and scallion greens, to the skillet and toss until warmed. Stir in the soy sauce, rice vinegar, and sesame oil. Gently fold in the salmon and toss, and serve immediately. Serve with Sriracha or chile-garlic sauce (if using).

Per Serving (scant 2 cups) ● Calories 518 ● Fat 19.5 g ● Saturated Fat 3 g Cholesterol 184 mg ● Carbohydrate 43 g ● Fiber 6 g ● Protein 43 g Sugars 3 g ● Sodium 639 mg

Spicy Salmon Poke Bowls

SERVES 4

SPICY MAYO

¼ cup light mayonnaise

1½ tablespoons Sriracha sauce

SALMON

1½ pounds leftover Sheet Pan
   Herb Salmon (page 264), cold

4 tablespoons reduced-sodium soy
   sauce* or gluten-free tamari

2 teaspoons toasted sesame oil

1 teaspoon Sriracha sauce

BOWLS

2 cups cooked rice (short-grain
   brown, sushi white, or black
   forbidden rice)

4 Persian cucumbers, diced
   into ½-inch cubes

1 medium (5-ounce) Hass avocado,
   sliced

½ cup shredded red cabbage

Jarred pickled ginger (optional)

2 scallions, green parts only, sliced
   for garnish

1 tablespoon furikake or black
   sesame seeds

Reduced-sodium soy sauce* or
   gluten-free tamari, for serving
   (optional)

Sriracha sauce, for serving (optional)

*Read the label to be sure this
   product is gluten-free.

FRIDGE: UP TO 2 DAYS

PLANNED-OVER

I usually make my poke bowls with raw tuna, especially when my friend Paulie goes tuna fishing and shares his catch! But I know that a lot of people don't have access to fresh tuna, or they get nervous about buying it, so these salmon poke bowls are an easy substitute. And now that I've tried these bowls with salmon, I may never go back to tuna! The key is to not overcook your salmon, so it's on the medium-rare side.

In a small bowl, combine the mayonnaise and Sriracha and thin with 1 tablespoon water to drizzle.

Flake or cut the cold salmon into large chunks. Drizzle with the soy sauce, sesame oil, and Sriracha and gently toss to combine. Set aside while you prepare the bowls.

Place ½ cup rice in each of 4 shallow bowls. In each bowl, arrange 6 ounces salmon, one-fourth of the diced cucumber and avocado, 2 tablespoons of the red cabbage, some pickled ginger (if using), and one-fourth of the scallion greens.

Drizzle with the spicy mayo, then top with the furikake and serve with extra soy sauce and Sriracha on the side (if using).

Per Serving (1 bowl) • Calories 513 • Fat 25 g • Saturated Fat 3.5 g
Cholesterol 96 mg • Carbohydrate 34 g • Fiber 5 g • Protein 37 g
Sugars 5 g • Sodium 939 mg

Salmon Niçoise Salad

SERVES 4

1½ pounds leftover Sheet Pan Herb Salmon (page 264)

POTATOES

1 pound baby red or Yukon Gold potatoes, quartered

1 tablespoon olive oil

½ teaspoon garlic powder

Kosher salt

Freshly ground black pepper

2 teaspoons whole-grain mustard

Grated lemon zest from ½ lemon

½ tablespoon finely chopped fresh flat-leaf parsley

SALAD

Kosher salt

4 large eggs

12 ounces green beans or haricots verts, ends trimmed

2 heads Bibb or Gem lettuce, roughly chopped (about 6 cups)

½ cup mixed or Niçoise olives, pitted

4 radishes, quartered

2 tablespoons capers, drained

Freshly ground black pepper

4 teaspoons extra-virgin olive oil

Juice of 1 lemon

¼ cup chopped fresh dill

There are a few things that any reputable Niçoise salad must have . . . potatoes, briny olives, and green beans. But instead of using the usual tuna, I used leftover salmon instead as a riff on this French classic. I'm not a fan of boiled potatoes, so here I roasted them and then tossed them with whole-grain mustard, which really elevates the entire salad. And since I'm not big on salad dressing, I simply finished this with a drizzle of olive oil and some lemon juice.

Remove the salmon from the refrigerator and break it up into bite-size chunks. Set aside.

Make the potatoes: Preheat the oven to 400°F. Add the potatoes to a 9 x 9-inch baking dish and toss with the olive oil, garlic powder, ½ teaspoon salt, and black pepper to taste, until evenly coated.

Bake for 30 to 35 minutes, tossing halfway through, until tender when a knife is inserted in the center. Transfer to a bowl and toss with the mustard, then season with ⅛ teaspoon salt, the lemon zest, and the parsley.

Make the salad: Set a large bowl of ice water by the stove. Bring a large, wide pot of water to a boil and season generously with salt. Gently add the eggs to avoid cracking, and cook for exactly 7 minutes for slightly runny yolks or 12 minutes for just-set yolks. Transfer the eggs to the ice bath and let cool completely, then peel. Add the green beans to the pot of boiling water and cook for 45 seconds. Immediately transfer to the ice bath and let cool completely, then dry. When the potatoes are done, assemble the salad.

On each plate, arrange one-fourth of the lettuce, salmon, potatoes, olives, green beans, radishes, and capers next to one another (or assemble on a large platter). Cut the eggs in half carefully, then place 2 halves on each plate, cut side up. Season the eggs with salt and pepper to taste, and finish everything else with the olive oil, lemon juice, and dill.

Per Serving (1 salad) ● Calories 530 ● Fat 26.5 g ● Saturated Fat 4.5 g Cholesterol 277 mg ● Carbohydrate 30 g ● Fiber 6.5 g ● Protein 44 g Sugars 4 g ● Sodium 867 mg

Slow Cooker Italian Pulled Pork

GF DF FF SC

SERVES 12

2 teaspoons olive oil

1 medium onion, chopped

1 carrot, chopped

1 celery stalk, chopped

¼ cup chopped fresh parsley

Kosher salt

3 garlic cloves, smashed with the side of a knife and chopped

¼ cup dry white wine

1 (28-ounce) can crushed tomatoes (I like Tuttorosso)

4 pounds boneless pork butt or shoulder roast, trimmed of fat cap and excess fat (about 3¾ pounds trimmed)

2 bay leaves

3 sprigs of fresh thyme

FRIDGE: UP TO 4 DAYS

FREEZER: UP TO 6 MONTHS

Testing new recipes in the slow cooker is challenging because you have to wait all day (without tasting!) before you know if it's a hit. Trust me, I've had many fails! My husband, Tommy, is always a little skeptical when I am testing something new for dinner in the slow cooker, and he's ready to order takeout . . . just in case! But this pork dish was so good the first time I made it, he even went back for seconds. Dinner win! It's sort of like a pork ragu and it's yummy on sliders, Parmesan-style, or over whole wheat pasta, mashed potatoes, or spaghetti squash. The possibilities are endless! Browning the pork and sautéing the onions are a must for me when slow-cooking for developing flavor in the final dish, so don't skip that step!

In a large skillet over medium-low heat, add the oil, onion, carrot, celery, parsley, and ½ teaspoon salt. Cook for about 8 minutes, stirring until soft. Add the garlic and cook for about 2 minutes more, until fragrant. Add the wine and cook to reduce, about 2 minutes more, then transfer to the slow cooker. Add the crushed tomatoes and stir. Depending on the brand of tomatoes you use, you may have to adjust the amount of salt that you add.

Season the pork all over with 1½ teaspoons salt. Brown the pork in the skillet over medium-high heat for about 4 minutes on each side. Transfer to the slow cooker, add the bay leaves and thyme, then cover and cook on high for about 5 hours or on low for 9 to 10 hours, until the meat is tender and easily pulls apart with two forks.

Remove the pork to a cutting board, discard the herbs, and use two forks to pull the pork apart, leaving some large chunks, then mix it back in with the sauce.

For an Instant Pot: Cut the pork into 4 pieces and season. Press sauté, spray the pot with oil, and sauté the meat in batches for 5 minutes on each side; set aside. Add the oil and vegetables and cook for 5 minutes. Add the wine and cook for 2 more minutes; press cancel to stop. Stir the pot well to prevent burning, then add the pork and remaining ingredients. Cook on high pressure for 50 minutes, natural release. Shred the meat with two forks.

> ***Big Batch:*** Store leftovers in airtight containers to use for Pork Shoulder Ragu with Cauliflower Polenta (page 275).

Per Serving (generous ¾ cup) ● Calories 228 ● Fat 7 g ● Saturated Fat 1.5 g Cholesterol 100 mg ● Carbohydrate 6 g ● Fiber 1.5 g ● Protein 34 g Sugars 3 g ● Sodium 411 mg

Pork Shoulder Ragu with Cauliflower Polenta

SERVES 4

1 medium head (about 1½ pounds) cauliflower, cut into florets

3 garlic cloves

1 tablespoon unsalted butter

¼ cup 2% milk

⅓ cup freshly grated Parmesan cheese, plus more for serving

2 ounces light cream cheese

½ teaspoon kosher salt

Freshly ground black pepper

3 cups leftover Italian Pulled Pork (page 272), reheated

Chopped fresh basil, for garnish

FRIDGE: UP TO 4 DAYS

Yesterday's Slow Cooker Italian Pulled Pork (page 272) gets turned into tonight's cauliflower "faux-lenta" (grain-free polenta)—a perfect pairing! Cauliflower is such a versatile vegetable; this creamy cauliflower puree has the buttery, comforting texture of a polenta without all the calories and carbs. Serve it with plenty of Parmesan on the side, for sharing.

Fill a large pot with water, bring to a boil, and add the cauliflower and garlic. Boil until the cauliflower is soft when pierced with a knife, 12 to 15 minutes. Drain well and return to the pot. Add the butter, milk, Parmesan, cream cheese, salt, and pepper to taste. Puree with an immersion blender until smooth. (A regular blender will work, but be sure to let the mixture cool before blending and fill only halfway in the blender so it doesn't explode on you.)

SERVE NOW: Add 1 cup cauliflower to each of 4 shallow serving bowls. Top each with ¾ cup pork, garnish with basil, and serve with more grated Parmesan.

MEAL PREP: Refrigerate the pork and the "polenta" in separate containers, then reheat in the microwave when ready to serve.

Per Serving (1 cup cauliflower polenta + ¾ cup ragu) • Calories 376
Fat 15 g • Saturated Fat 6.5 g • Cholesterol 124 mg • Carbohydrate 18 g
Fiber 6 g • Protein 43 g • Sugars 8 g • Sodium 778 mg

Instant Pot Colombian Beans

GF DF FF IP

BIG BATCH

SERVES 18

1 pound dried cranberry, pinto, or red beans

½ tablespoon olive oil

1 small onion, chopped

3 medium scallions, chopped

5 garlic cloves, crushed through a garlic press

2 teaspoons kosher salt

1 teaspoon ground cumin

½ teaspoon achiote or annatto powder (optional for color)

¼ teaspoon garlic powder

¼ teaspoon ground turmeric

2 medium tomatoes, chopped

¼ cup finely chopped fresh cilantro

1 smoked ham hock

1 bay leaf

1 sprig of fresh thyme

1 medium yellow plantain, cut into ¼-inch dice

> FRIDGE: UP TO 4 DAYS

> FREEZER: UP TO 6 MONTHS

Colombian-style beans is the meal I remember my mom cooking the most when I was a kid. I never really liked beans growing up, but that changed on one of my adult trips to Colombia. I was generously offered rice and beans with avocado on the side for lunch at every home I visited. Different regions of the country make the beans in unique ways. In Bogota, where my mom is from, they use ripe yellow plantains (which sweeten the beans) and serve it with chicharrón. When I make a big pot of beans in my Instant Pot, I like to use a smoked ham hock for a smoky flavor, but if you want to make your beans vegetarian you can just leave it out. To make this a meal, serve the beans over white or brown rice and with avocado on the side. Leftovers can be used in a filling for *pupusas* (see page 182) or Bean and Turkey Tostadas (page 279).

Rinse the beans and put them in a medium bowl. Cover with water by 2 inches and let soak for at least 8 hours or as long as overnight. Drain and discard the water.

Set your Instant Pot (or any electric pressure cooker) to the sauté setting. When hot, add the oil, onion, scallions, garlic, 1 teaspoon salt, cumin, achiote (if using), garlic powder, and turmeric and stir to combine. Cook for 2 to 3 minutes, until soft, then add the tomatoes and cilantro and cook for another 2 to 3 minutes, until soft. Press cancel, transfer to a bowl, and set aside.

Add the beans to the Instant Pot with 6 cups water, then add the ham hock, bay leaf, thyme, and remaining 1 teaspoon salt.

Cover and cook on high pressure for 40 minutes. Let the beans natural release, uncover, remove the ham hocks, and let cool. Remove the bay leaf and thyme and discard.

Set the Instant Pot to the sauté setting. Add the plantain and tomato-onion mixture to the beans and let it boil, stirring frequently to prevent burning, 20 to 25 minutes, until the plantains are tender and the beans are thickened to your liking.

Once the ham hocks have cooled, remove the meat from the bones and add it back to the beans. Discard the bones and skin.

SERVE NOW: Serve ½ cup beans with a side of white or brown rice, avocado, and hot sauce.

FREEZE AND SERVE LATER: Let the beans cool to room temperature, then transfer to freezer-safe containers. To reheat, microwave the beans from frozen or thaw overnight in the refrigerator before reheating.

No Instant Pot, No Problem! *Add ¼ cup more water and cook, covered, on low heat for about 2 hours, then uncover and cook as directed.*

Per Serving (½ cup) • Calories 119
Fat 1.5 g • Saturated Fat 0.5 g
Cholesterol 3 mg • Carbohydrate 20 g
Fiber 5 g • Protein 7 g
Sugars 3 g • Sodium 137 mg

Big Batch: Store leftover beans in airtight containers to use for *pupusas* (page 182) and tostadas (page 279).

Bean and Turkey Tostadas

Q GF

SERVES 4

QUICK SLAW

2 teaspoons olive oil

1 tablespoon fresh lime juice

2 cups shredded cabbage

2 scallions, chopped

⅓ cup chopped fresh cilantro

¼ teaspoon kosher salt

Cooking spray

½ pound 93% lean ground turkey

½ tablespoon ground cumin

½ teaspoon smoked paprika

½ teaspoon garlic powder

¼ teaspoon chili powder*

½ teaspoon kosher salt

1 cup leftover Instant Pot Colombian Beans (page 276)

4 tostada shells (I like Charras Original)

1 cup shredded reduced-fat cheddar or Mexican cheese blend*

1 lime, cut into wedges for serving

*Read the label to be sure this product is gluten-free.

We always have tostada shells on hand in the pantry (Charras brand are the best!) because my daughter Karina loves cleaning out my leftovers to make tostadas, which inspired these planned-overs. They are perfect for lunch, and you can double the portion for a hearty dinner. Leftover beans can easily be transformed into refried beans, although here I simply mashed them with a fork since they're soupy enough. If you have some *pupusas* (page 182) in your freezer, you can use them in place of tostada shells for an epic tostada!

Preheat the oven to 425°F. Line a large baking sheet with foil.

Make the slaw: In a medium bowl, mix the olive oil and lime juice. Add the cabbage, scallions, cilantro, and salt and toss to coat. Set aside.

Heat a large skillet over medium-high heat and spray with oil. Add the ground turkey, cumin, paprika, garlic powder, chili powder, and salt. Brown the meat, using a wooden spoon to break it into small pieces, until cooked through, 7 to 9 minutes.

Mash the leftover beans with a fork.

Assemble the tostadas: Spread ¼ cup mashed beans on the bottom of each tostada shell, then spoon one-fourth of the turkey into each tostada. Place in the preheated oven and bake for about 5 minutes, until heated through. Top with the cheese and place back into the oven to melt, 2 to 3 minutes more. Remove from the oven, top with the slaw, and serve with the lime wedges.

Per Serving (1 tostada) • Calories 323 • Fat 17 g • Saturated Fat 6 g
Cholesterol 59 mg • Carbohydrate 24 g • Fiber 4.5 g • Protein 24 g
Sugars 3 g • Sodium 601 mg

Five-Spice Glazed Pork Tenderloin

GF DF FF

BIG BATCH

SERVES 8

1/3 cup reduced-sodium soy sauce*
   or gluten-free tamari

4 tablespoons honey

4 garlic cloves, minced

1 tablespoon hoisin sauce*

2 tablespoons packed brown sugar

1 tablespoon rice wine (mirin)

1/2 teaspoon toasted sesame oil

1/2 teaspoon ground Chinese
   five-spice powder

1/4 teaspoon ground white pepper

2 pork tenderloins, about
   1 pound each

*Read the label to be sure this
 product is gluten-free.

FRIDGE: UP TO 3 DAYS

FREEZER: UP TO 3 MONTHS

Five-spice powder is a seasoning mix used widely in Chinese cooking. Combined with honey, hoisin, garlic, soy sauce, sesame oil, and brown sugar, this marinade lends an irresistible flavor to pork tenderloin, reminiscent of *char siu* (Chinese BBQ pork). We love this served with rice and steamed greens such as bok choy, kale, or broccolini. Make use of the leftover pork for Quick Five-Spice Pork Ramen (page 283).

Combine the soy sauce, 2 tablespoons of the honey, garlic, hoisin sauce, brown sugar, rice wine, sesame oil, five-spice powder, and white pepper in a bowl to make the marinade.

Reserve 2 tablespoons of the marinade and set it aside. In a large bowl or baking dish, rub the pork loin with the rest of the marinade. Cover and refrigerate for at least 8 hours or up to overnight. Cover and refrigerate the reserved marinade.

Position a rack in the upper third of the oven and preheat to 425°F.

Line a roasting pan with foil and place a wire rack on top. Place the pork (discarding the marinade it was in) on the rack, then pour 1 1/2 cups water on the bottom of the pan (to prevent the oven from smoking).

Transfer the pork to your preheated oven and roast for about 25 minutes.

Meanwhile, in a small bowl combine the reserved marinade with the remaining 2 tablespoons honey and 1/2 tablespoon hot water. This is the sauce you will use to baste the pork. After about 25 minutes, baste the pork with two-thirds of the baste, flip it, and baste the other side as well. Roast for 10 to 12 minutes more, or until a meat thermometer reads 160°F.

Adjust an oven rack 4 to 6 inches from the heating element and turn the broiler to high. Broil the pork for about 2 minutes to crisp the outside, keeping an eye on it so it doesn't burn.

Remove from the oven and let the pork rest for 10 minutes before slicing. Slice each tenderloin into 8 pieces and baste with the last bit of reserved BBQ sauce.

SERVE NOW: Serve with rice and steamed greens such as bok choy or broccoli.

> **Big Batch:** If you plan on making the Quick Five-Spice Pork Ramen (page 283), refrigerate or freeze any leftovers. Thaw in the refrigerator overnight before reheating.

Per Serving (2 slices) ● Calories 153
Fat 2.5 g ● Saturated Fat 1 g
Cholesterol 74 mg ● Carbohydrate 7 g
Fiber 0 g ● Protein 24 g
Sugars 6 g ● Sodium 213 mg

Quick Five-Spice Pork Ramen

PLANNED-OVER

SERVES 4

4 large eggs

6 cups low-sodium beef or chicken broth

2 medium scallions, white and green parts separated, sliced

4 thin slices fresh ginger, cut into matchsticks

2 garlic cloves, minced

¼ teaspoon freshly ground black pepper

1 tablespoon reduced-sodium soy sauce

4 baby bok choy, halved lengthwise and crosswise

2 (3-ounce) packages instant ramen noodles, seasoning discarded

½ cup sliced shiitake mushrooms

6 ounces leftover Five-Spice Glazed Pork Tenderloin (page 280), thinly sliced (if frozen, thawed)

1 teaspoon sesame seeds, for garnish

Sriracha sauce, for serving (optional)

Instant ramen noodles are synonymous with quick, easy meals, but this is not like the ramen you had in your college days, void of protein and veggies. Each bowl is filled with crisp baby bok choy, shiitake mushrooms, thinly sliced pork tenderloin, ramen noodles, and an egg with a gloriously runny yolk, all floating in a gingery broth (throw away those seasoning packets!). The only thing that makes it better is a drizzle of Sriracha at the end. And because we're making it a planned-over dish using leftover Five-Spice Glazed Pork Tenderloin (page 280), it's still a quick dish! The leftover pork freezes well, so you can have this whenever a ramen craving strikes. And of course, this can be made with chicken or tofu instead if you're not a fan of pork.

Bring a small pot of water to a boil over high heat. Add the eggs to the water and cook for about 6 minutes for a perfectly runny yolk, or a few minutes longer for a firm yolk. Run under cold water or transfer to an ice bath right away to stop the cooking, then peel.

Bring the broth to a boil in a large pot with the scallion whites, ginger, garlic, pepper, and soy sauce. Cover and cook for about 5 minutes, until fragrant.

Add the bok choy and partially cook for about 5 minutes, then add the ramen noodles and mushrooms. Simmer for 3 to 4 minutes, until the bok choy is tender and wilted and the noodles are cooked. Add the sliced pork tenderloin and heat in the broth for the last minute.

Divide the soup among 4 bowls (1½ cups soup with 1½ ounces pork slices), and add 1 soft-boiled egg, cut in half, along with the scallion greens and sesame seeds. Serve the Sriracha alongside (if using). This is best when eaten right away.

Per Serving (1½ cups + egg + pork) ● Calories 295 ● Fat 10 g
Saturated Fat 4 g ● Cholesterol 223 mg ● Carbohydrate 23 g
Fiber 1.5 g ● Protein 28 g ● Sugars 7 g ● Sodium 744 mg

Homemade Wontons, Three Ways

FF

SERVES 5

50 store-bought wonton wrappers

FREEZER: UP TO 6 MONTHS

Let's just say we LOVE dumplings and wontons in my house. We travel long and far to find the best wonton spots in Flushing and Chinatown in NYC, but they're also fun to make at home from scratch . . . and easy thanks to packaged wonton wrappers. Wontons keep in the freezer for months; this means that with a little prep you're less than 10 minutes away from a home-cooked Chinese meal! You can serve them steamed with Soy Dipping Sauce (facing page), or you can use them to make your own homemade Wonton Soup (page 289). Here I've created three versions—a spicy vegetarian wonton, a shrimp and celery wonton, and a chicken chive wonton. It's hard for me to pick a favorite, they are all so good!

Spicy Veggie Wontons: In a food processor, combine the mushrooms, onion, bok choy, scallions, coleslaw mix, basil, ginger, and garlic and process until smooth. Transfer to a large bowl and add the soy sauce, *sambal oelek*, and sesame oil and mix well.

Shrimp and Celery Wontons: Combine all the ingredients in a medium bowl.

Chicken Chive Wontons: Combine all the ingredients in a medium bowl.

Place one wonton wrapper in the center of a cutting board, keeping the rest covered in plastic wrap. Place ½ tablespoon of the filling in the center of the wonton wrapper. Using your finger, brush the perimeter of the wrapper with a little water. Fold the wonton wrapper in half, forming a triangle, squeezing out as much air as possible, and seal. Fold the corner ends up and press the ends together. Repeat until all the wontons are filled.

SERVE NOW: Fill a large pot with 2 inches of water. If using a bamboo steamer, cook in batches of five, 1 inch apart. If using a steamer basket, cook in batches of five. Place the steamer in the pot, cover, and steam for about 7 minutes, until the dumpling wrappers are slightly translucent.

Serve with Soy Dipping Sauce (recipe follows) or add them to your homemade Wonton Soup on page 289.

FREEZE AND SERVE LATER: Place the wontons on a parchment-lined plate, cover them loosely with plastic wrap, then place them in the freezer until completely frozen, about 1 hour. Transfer them to a plastic bag. Cook directly from frozen, adding 1 to 2 minutes to the cooking time.

SKINNY SCOOP Cabbage leaves work great as a liner in the steamer basket to keep the dumplings from sticking to the bottom.

Spicy Veggie

1 cup minced portobello mushrooms

½ small onion, diced

1 cup chopped bok choy leaf, white and leafy part

2 medium scallions, diced

2½ cups packaged coleslaw mix (green cabbage, carrots, red cabbage mix)

1½ tablespoons chopped fresh basil

1 tablespoon grated fresh ginger

1 garlic clove, minced

1 tablespoon reduced-sodium soy sauce

1 tablespoon *sambal oelek* (Sambal chile paste)

1 tablespoon toasted sesame oil

Per Serving (10 wontons) • Calories 277
Fat 4 g • Saturated Fat 0.5 g • Cholesterol 7 mg
Carbohydrate 51 g • Fiber 3 g • Protein 9 g
Sugars 2 g • Sodium 642 mg

Shrimp and Celery

1½ pounds peeled and deveined raw large shrimp, finely chopped

1 medium celery stalk, finely chopped

3 medium scallions, finely chopped

2 tablespoons sherry cooking wine

1 tablespoon reduced-sodium soy sauce

2 teaspoons sesame oil

½ tablespoon grated fresh ginger

1 garlic clove, minced

Per Serving (10 wontons) • Calories 381
Fat 3.5 g • Saturated Fat 0.5 g • Cholesterol 170 mg
Carbohydrate 49 g • Fiber 2 g • Protein 32 g
Sugars 0.5 g • Sodium 910 mg

Chicken Chive

1¼ pounds ground chicken

½ cup minced fresh chives

2 tablespoons sherry cooking wine

1 tablespoon reduced-sodium soy sauce

1 tablespoon grated fresh ginger

2 teaspoons toasted sesame oil

1 garlic clove, minced

Per Serving (10 wontons) • Calories 421
Fat 12 g • Saturated Fat 3 g • Cholesterol 105 mg
Carbohydrate 47 g • Fiber 1.5 g • Protein 28 g
Sugars 0 g • Sodium 633 mg

SOY DIPPING SAUCE

SERVES 4

This basic soy dipping sauce is perfect for serving with wontons. A little goes a long way, and the leftovers are also great over steamed rice or greens.

3 tablespoons reduced-sodium soy sauce* or gluten-free tamari

1 teaspoon sugar

2 tablespoons seasoned rice vinegar

1 tablespoon sesame oil

1 garlic clove, crushed

1 scallion, diced

*Read the label to be sure this product is gluten-free.

Mix the ingredients in a small bowl and serve with steamed wontons. To store, transfer to a small glass jar with a fitted lid and refrigerate.

Per Serving (1½ tablespoons) • Calories 50
Fat 3.5 g • Saturated Fat 0.5 g • Cholesterol 0 mg
Carbohydrate 5 g • Fiber 0 g • Protein 1 g
Sugars 4 g • Sodium 521 mg

FRIDGE: UP TO 7 DAYS

Wonton Soup

Q

SERVES 4

6 cups low-sodium chicken or vegetable broth

1-inch piece fresh ginger, thinly sliced

1 garlic clove, minced

4 baby bok choy, halved lengthwise

20 frozen wontons, Chicken, Veggie, or Shrimp (page 284)

1½ cups sliced shiitake mushrooms

1 tablespoon reduced-sodium soy sauce

1 teaspoon toasted sesame oil

Scallions, green parts only, sliced, for garnish

FRIDGE: UP TO 4 DAYS

FREEZER: UP TO 6 MONTHS

This quick and easy wonton soup is loaded with veggies, and thanks to the frozen wontons, it takes under 15 minutes to make. Any of the wontons on page 284 work in this soup . . . and I've even made it with a mix of all three flavors when that's all I had left in my freezer. I've also made this soup with store-bought wontons from Trader Joe's or Costco! You can use whatever veggies you have on hand—sub baby bok choy with spinach or kale, and if you don't like mushrooms, just leave them out or add some bean sprouts. For added protein you can add shrimp, leftover sliced roast pork (see page 280), cooked chicken, or tofu. Like it spicy? Top your bowl with red chili oil or *sambal oelek*.

Bring the broth to a boil in a large pot. Smash the sliced ginger with the side of a knife to bring out the flavor and add to the pot with the garlic. Cover and cook over medium heat for about 5 minutes.

Add the bok choy and partially cook for about 5 minutes, then add the frozen wontons and mushrooms and simmer for 3 to 4 minutes, until the wontons are heated through and the bok choy is tender and wilted. Remove and discard ginger. Stir in the soy sauce and sesame oil. Divide the soup among 4 bowls. Garnish with scallions.

SERVE LATER: Refrigerate or freeze broth without wontons. Reheat on the stove, adding the wontons and cooking for about 3 minutes, or until heated through.

Per Serving (1½ cups) ● Calories 273 ● Fat 8 g ● Saturated Fat 1.5 g
Cholesterol 53 mg ● Carbohydrate 30 g ● Fiber 2 g ● Protein 18 g
Sugars 2 g ● Sodium 772 mg

Gyro Loaf

GF DF FF

**SERVES 8
(MAKES 2 LOAVES)**

1 large red onion, roughly chopped

8 garlic cloves

1 tablespoon salt

1 tablespoon ground oregano

1 tablespoon dried rosemary

1 tablespoon ground marjoram

1 tablespoon ground cumin

1 teaspoon freshly ground black pepper

1 pound ground lamb

1 pound 93% lean ground turkey

Juice of ½ lemon

FRIDGE: UP TO 4 DAYS

FREEZER: UP TO 6 MONTHS

Gyro sandwiches are characterized by their meat filling—usually a combo of lamb and beef roasted on a vertical spit. Unless you live next door to a Greek restaurant or you have a vertical spit lying around at home (I don't!), this is a great homemade version I often make at Tommy's request. Rather than making it on a spit, I form the meat (I use half ground lamb, half ground turkey) into a flat loaf and bake it like a meatloaf. Once it cools, I slice the loaf into thin strips and pan-fry them to get that signature crispy texture. Lamb is a must here—using half turkey doesn't change the flavor much but it certainly cuts back on the fat. To make this a Greek-style meal, we like to turn it into a gyro platter and serve the meat over crisp greens with cucumbers, tomatoes, olives, and tzatziki (see the recipe for Greek Gyro Salad, page 293).

Adjust an oven rack to the center of the oven. Preheat the oven to 350°F. Line a sheet pan with foil.

Place the onion, garlic, salt, and spices into a food processor and process until finely minced. Transfer to a stand mixer fitted with a paddle and add the meats and lemon juice. Process on medium-high speed until the meat becomes very smooth, sticky, and pasty, 3 to 5 minutes. It should not resemble meatloaf. Using a spatula, scrape all the meat from the edges of the bowl and transfer to the prepared sheet pan.

Divide the meat and form two 4 × 10-inch loaves, about 1½ inches thick, smoothing down the top and edges (the loaves should be flat on the top and sides, like a rectangle).

Bake for 45 to 55 minutes, until cooked through in the center with an internal temperature of 155°F. Remove from the oven, let it cool for 10 minutes, then transfer to a cutting board. Slice one loaf into sixteen ¼-inch-thick slices and refrigerate or freeze the second loaf for another night.

SERVE NOW: Heat a nonstick skillet over medium-high heat and brown the meat for 1 to 2 minutes on each side. Serve over salad (Greek Gyro Salad on page 293), with rice pilaf, or in a pita with tomatoes, tzatziki, and red onion to make a sandwich.

> **Big Batch:** Use leftovers for the Greek Gyro Salad (page 293) or freeze to serve later. Let the loaves cool without slicing and wrap them in plastic, then transfer to freezer bags. Thaw overnight, slice, and pan-fry until crispy, about 2 minutes on each side.

Per Serving (4 slices) ● Calories 264
Fat 18.5 g ● Saturated Fat 7 g
Cholesterol 83 mg ● Carbohydrate 4 g
Fiber 1 g ● Protein 21 g
Sugars 1 g ● Sodium 496 mg

Greek Gyro Salad

GF

SERVES 4

1 cooked Gyro Loaf (page 290), sliced into 16 slices

6 cups chopped romaine or iceberg lettuce

4 Persian cucumbers, diced

⅛ small red onion, sliced lengthwise

3 Campari tomatoes, quartered

¼ cup pitted Kalamata olives

2 ounces crumbled feta cheese

1 cup Tzatziki sauce (page 256)

FRIDGE: UP TO 4 DAYS

I'm usually a big fan of gyro sandwiches, but whenever we go for Greek food, I skip the pita and get the delicious strips of lamb over a big salad. Once I started making my own gyro meat (using half turkey and half lamb; see page 290), this became our go-to way to eat it at home! Tommy likes his over iceberg, but I always serve mine over romaine—feel free to use whatever lettuce you prefer. Homemade yogurt Tzatziki sauce (see page 256) as a dressing is a must; if you're meal prepping, just pack it on the side.

Heat a skillet over medium-high heat and brown the meat for 1 to 2 minutes on each side, until heated through and slightly crisped.

SERVE NOW: In a large bowl, combine the lettuce, cucumbers, and onion. Divide among 4 plates (1½ cups each) and top with the tomato wedges, olives, feta, and meat. Drizzle with the tzatziki sauce.

MEAL PREP: Divide the salad in 4 meal prep containers, top each with 4 slices of meat, and pack the tzatziki on the side. Eat cold or heat the meat if desired.

Per Serving (1 salad) • Calories 404 • Fat 24 g • Saturated Fat 10.5 g Cholesterol 102 mg • Carbohydrate 19 g • Fiber 6 g • Protein 29 g Sugars 7 g • Sodium 902 mg

Basil Pomodoro Sauce

GF DF FF

BIG BATCH

Everyone needs a basic tomato sauce to keep frozen for those nights you want to whip up a quick pasta dinner, or to use in Eggplant Parmesan (page 174), Roasted Vegetable Lasagna (page 181), Zucchini Rollatini (page 177), etc. This simple Pomodoro sauce is made with just a few ingredients: extra-virgin olive oil, crushed tomatoes, garlic, onions, and carrots to slightly sweeten the sauce ... and of course lots of fresh basil. I don't add salt because the canned tomatoes I love, Tuttorosso New World Style, already have salt. If you use a different brand, you may have to adjust the salt to your taste. Pasta sauce is one of the easiest things to make as well as a great starter recipe for freezer cooking.

MAKES 7 CUPS

6 garlic cloves

1 tablespoon extra-virgin olive oil

½ large onion, finely chopped

1 cup finely chopped carrots

Kosher salt

2 (28-ounce) cans crushed tomatoes (I like Tuttoroso)

⅓ cup chicken or vegetable broth*

16 large fresh basil leaves, torn with your hands

*Read the label to be sure this product is gluten-free.

FRIDGE: UP TO 4 DAYS

FREEZER: UP TO 6 MONTHS

Smash the garlic with the side of a large knife by using the palm of your hand over the knife to apply pressure.

Heat a medium to large saucepan over medium heat. When it's hot, add the oil and garlic and sauté until golden and fragrant, 1½ to 2 minutes. (Tip: Because I don't use a lot of oil, I tilt my pan to one side, so the garlic is submerged in the oil and cooks evenly.) Remove the garlic and set it aside.

Add the onion and carrots to the pot with a pinch of salt and sauté, stirring on medium-low heat until soft, 5 to 6 minutes. Add the crushed tomatoes, broth, and garlic, cover, and simmer on medium-low for about 20 minutes, until the vegetables are soft. Remove from the heat, stir in the basil, and adjust the salt to taste if needed.

Big Batch: Let the sauce cool, then divide it into 1- or 2-cup freezer-safe containers. Label the containers with the name, portion size, and date. To thaw, transfer to the refrigerator 1 to 2 days before using, or you can heat the frozen sauce over low heat on the stovetop.

Per Serving (½ cup) ● Calories 45 ● Fat 1 g ● Saturated Fat 0 g ● Cholesterol 0 mg Carbohydrate 9 g ● Fiber 2 g ● Protein 2 g ● Sugars 4 g ● Sodium 274 mg

ACKNOWLEDGMENTS

Writing a book takes a village. From concept to recipe development and testing, to everything that goes along with photography and design, and I am so grateful for my whole team, and for my friends and family.

To the Skinnytaste readers and dedicated fans—this book is for you. Seeing my recipes in your kitchens and following along on your health journeys brings me so much joy! This meal prep book, after all, was your idea, and I am so happy to make it happen!

To my husband and kids, thanks for always being so supportive and gladly willing to act as my taste testers.

And, of course, I'm so grateful to work with my friend Heather K. Jones, RD, on this fifth cookbook—who would have thought that meeting at a food blogging event so many years ago would lead us here!? Your energy, spirit, and positive vibes make this whole process so much easier. And a big thank-you to Heather's amazing team, Danielle Hazard, Donna Fennessy, and Jackie Price, for paying attention to all the details.

To my aunt Ligia Caldas, who has been by my side with all my books, I don't know how I would do it all without you.

To the most epic agent of all time, Janis Donnaud, I am so glad to always have you in my corner!

To the stellar team at Clarkson Potter: Doris Cooper, Jenn Sit, Erica Gelbard, Stephanie Davis, Ian Dingman, Stephanie Huntwork, Patricia Shaw, and Kim Tyner, I love working with you all.

To my talented photographer, Aubrie Pick, and her team, thank you for making such gorgeous photos, even with all the bumps in the road.

Mom, Ivan, and family, thanks for the constant love and for being my cheerleaders since day one.

And last but not least, to all my girlfriends, both near and far, thank you for always supporting me on this fun and crazy ride!

Published in the United States by Clarkson Potter/
Publishers, an imprint of Random House, a division
of Penguin Random House LLC, New York.
clarksonpotter.com

CLARKSON POTTER is a trademark and POTTER
with colophon is a registered trademark of Penguin
Random House LLC.

Library of Congress Cataloging-in-Publication Data
is available upon request.

ISBN 978-0-593-13731-4
Ebook ISBN 978-0-593-13732-1
Target edition ISBN 978-0-593-23249-1

Printed in Germany

Book and cover design by Ian Dingman
Photographs by Aubrie Pick

10 9 8 7 6 5 4 3 2 1

First Edition